"KING OR NOT . . . I MUST HAVE YOU!"

David of Windsor, recently crowned King Edward VII, receives a confidential ultimatum from the British Parliament. His lover, Mrs. Wallis Simpson, must be sent away from him "without further delay" for the good of the country. His angry and defiant response will change the course of history. . . .

David asked Wallis to come with him to his study. He was white-faced. She began reading the letter, at first very slowly and then more rapidly. . . .

When she finished, she said, "I must leave immediately."

"Leave?" His voice was shaking. "You'll do no such thing. If I cannot marry the woman I love as King, then I'll marry her as an ex-King . . ."

RICHARD HOUGH

Born Royal

The Lives and Loves of the Young Windsors

BANTAM BOOKS

NEW YORK · TORONTO · LONDON · SYDNEY · AUCKLAND

BORN ROYAL
A Bantam Book
Bantam hardcover edition / December 1988
Bantam paperback edition / February 1990

Library of Congress Cataloging-in-Publication Data

Hough, Richard Alexander, 1922–
  Born royal : the lives and loves of the young Windsors
/Richard Hough.
    p.   cm.
  Bibliography: p. 310
  Includes index.
  ISBN 0-553-28227-1
  1. George V. King of Great Britain, 1865–1936—Family.
2. Windsor, House of.   3. Great Britain—Kings and rulers—
Biography.   4. Great Britain—Princes and princesses—Biography.
5. Windsor, Edward, Duke of, 1894–1972—Childhood and youth.
6. George VI, King of Great Britain, 1895–1952—Childhood and youth.
I. Title.
DA573.H58   1988
941.083'092'2—dc19
[B]   88-22236
                                                          CIP

Published simultaneously in the United States and Canada

Bantam Books are published by Bantam Books, a division of Bantam
Doubleday Dell Publishing Group, Inc. Its trademark, consisting of the
words "Bantam Books" and the portrayal of a rooster, is Registered
in U.S. Patent and Trademark Office and in other countries. Marca
Registrada. Bantam Books, 666 Fifth Avenue, New York, New York 10103.

PRINTED IN THE UNITED STATES OF AMERICA

OPM   0 9 8 7 6 5 4 3 2 1

CONTENTS

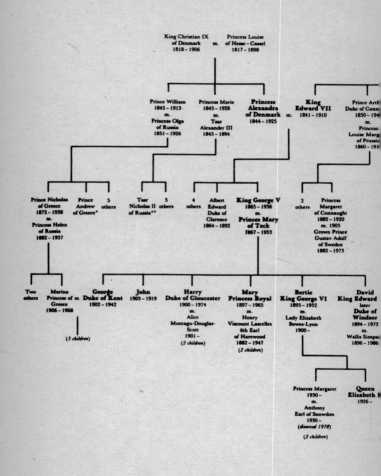

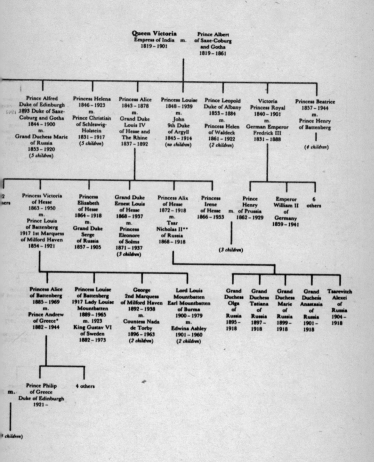

Queen Victoria
Empress of India m. **Prince Albert**
1819 – 1901 of Saxe-Coburg
and Gotha
1819 – 1861

Prince Alfred
Duke of Edinburgh
1893 Duke of Saxe-
Coburg and Gotha
1844 – 1900
m.
Grand Duchess Marie
of Russia
1853 – 1920
(5 children)

Princess Helena
1846 – 1923
m.
Prince Christian
of Schleswig-
Holstein
1831 – 1917
(5 children)

Princess Alice
1843 – 1878
m.
**Grand Duke
Louis IV**
of Hesse and
The Rhine
1837 – 1892

Princess Louise
1848 – 1939
m.
John
9th Duke
of Argyll
1845 – 1914
(no children)

Prince Leopold
Duke of Albany
1853 – 1884
m.
Princess Helen
of Waldeck
1861 – 1922
(2 children)

**Victoria
Princess Royal**
1840 – 1901
m.
**German Emperor
Fredrick III**
1831 – 1888

Princess Beatrice
1857 – 1944
m.
**Prince Henry
of Battenberg**
(4 children)

**Princess Victoria
of Hesse**
1863 – 1950
m.
**Prince Louis
of Battenberg**
1917 1st Marquess
of Milford Haven
1854 – 1921

**Princess
Elizabeth
of Hesse**
1864 – 1918
m.
**Grand Duke
Serge
of Russia**
1857 – 1905

**Grand Duke
Ernest Louis
of Hesse**
1868 – 1937
m.
**Princess
Eleonore
of Solms**
1871 – 1937
(3 children)

**Princess Alix
of Hesse**
1872 – 1918
m.
**Tsar
Nicholas II**
of Russia
1868 – 1918

**Princess
Irene
of Hesse**
1866 – 1953
m.

**Prince
Henry
of Prussia**
1862 – 1929

**Emperor
William II
of
Germany**
1859 – 1941

6
others

(3 children)

**Princess Alice
of Battenberg**
1885 – 1969
m.
**Prince Andrew
of Greece***
1882 – 1944

**Princess Louise
of Battenberg**
1889 – 1965
m. 1923
**King Gustav VI
of Sweden**
1882 – 1973

**George
2nd Marquess
of Milford Haven**
1892 – 1938
m.
**Countess Nada
de Torby**
1896 – 1963
(2 children)

**Lord Louis
Mountbatten
Earl Mountbatten
of Burma**
1900 – 1979
m.
Edwina Ashley
1901 – 1960
(2 children)

**Grand
Duchess
Olga
of
Russia
1895 –
1918**

**Grand
Duchess
Tatiana
of
Russia
1897 –
1918**

**Grand
Duchess
Marie
of
Russia
1899 –
1918**

**Grand
Duchess
Anastasia
of
Russia
1901 –
1918**

**Tsarevitch
Alexei
of
Russia
1904 –
1918**

**Prince Philip
of Greece
Duke of Edinburgh**
1921 –

4 others

m.

(children)

PREFACE

In the course of the research and writing of my family history of the Mountbattens and my biography of Lord Mountbatten, it was impossible to ignore the lurking presence of the first Windsors, the six children of King George V and Queen Mary. Lord Mountbatten knew all these cousins well, except of course the last unfortunate son, and frequently talked about them, granting me a valuable insight into their lives and personalities.

Lord Mountbatten always claimed that David, future King and Duke of Windsor, was "my greatest friend," and he cherished warm memories of Bertie, before and after their time together at Cambridge. Their association became more important and more intimate after the abdication of Edward VIII and the Duke of York's accession as George VI.

My work on these earlier books also brought me into touch with other relations and acquaintances of the Windsors, who knew or worked or played with them as children and young people. This led me to look into their upbringing, in nursery and schoolroom, naval or military college; their relations with their parents and grandparents (very different these were, too), and their nursemaids, tutors and equerries.

As Prince Philip commented on a reference to him I had written in *Louis and Victoria,* "There's nothing remarkable

about me. It's only my position that's remarkable." Whether
or not that is to be believed, it was the remarkable position of
these children that governed their lives, granting them im-
munity from many everyday responsibilities, chores and duties, and piling on many more responsibilities and privileges
in their place—all designed to single them out for public
respect and attention.

As for their private lives, in their time there was much
less exposure than today, which makes what we now know
about them all the more fascinating.

In this book I have attempted to show what life was like,
from cradle to the marriage altar, for these young Princes
and one Princess, born around the turn of the century and
destined to grow up through great social change and conflict
to which they had to adapt themselves, their rank notwithstanding. Some of these "poor little privileged Princes" did
better, or were more colourful, than the others. But I found
them all singularly engaging.

It will at once become evident that in these informal
portraits I have allowed myself generous licence with the
dialogue, such as playwrights and scriptwriters permit themselves, within certain limits, when filling out the portraits of
their subjects. The subsidiary characters, and the equerries,
nursemaids, tutors and so on, are all authentic; but rather
than leave them as shadowy as their masters and mistresses
would have wished them to remain, I have given them the
means to record and comment on events and characters, as
they would no doubt have wished to do, and perhaps even did.

This, then, is a "dramatic biography"—or biographies—in
the mould and spirit of Laurence Housman's play *Happy and
Glorious*, later developed as *Victoria Regina*. Poor Housman
was refused a stage licence for all of them until 1935, when
the Lord Chamberlain showed a chink of enlightenment by
clearing several for public presentation. In this less censori-
ous age I need not (I hope!) fear a fate like Housman's, which
cost him so much anguish and money. Though this book is in
narrative rather than dramatic form, I would echo the words
of his defence, that it is "neither indecent, nor libellous, nor
blasphemous, nor liable to cause a breach of the public peace."

Richard Hough

CHIEF CHARACTERS
IN ORDER OF APPEARANCE

George, Duke of York. Later Prince of Wales and King George V; second son of Edward VII; married to . . .

May (Mary), Duchess of York. Later Princess of Wales and Queen Mary.

David (Edward). Eldest son of George and May; later Prince of Wales, King Edward VIII and Duke of Windsor.

Bertie (Albert). Second son of George and May; later Duke of York and King George VI.

Lala, Mrs Bill. Nursemaid to children of George and May.

Finch, Frederick. Manservant to George and May's sons; later valet to David.

Mary. Only daughter of George and May; later Princess Royal, Countess of Harewood.

Victoria, Queen Victoria. Mother of . . .

Bertie (Albert, not to be confused with his grandson above), Prince of Wales. Later King Edward VII.

Harry (Henry). Third son of George and May, later Duke of Gloucester.

Alix (Alexandra), Princess of Wales; later Queen Alexandra, wife of Edward VII.

Louis, Admiral Prince Louis of Battenberg. Later 1st Marquis of Milford Haven, father of . . .

Dickie, Prince Louis of Battenberg. Later Lord Louis Mountbatten; son of . . .

Victoria, Princess Louis of Battenberg. Later Marchioness of Milford Haven; grand-daughter of Queen Victoria.

Hansell, Henry ("Mider"). Tutor to children of George and May.

George (Little George). Fourth son of George and May; later Duke of Kent.

John. Fifth son of George and May.

Andrew, Prince Andrew of Greece. Father of Prince Philip, and husband of . . .

Alice, Princess Andrew of Greece. Elder daughter of Louis and Victoria.

Nicholas, Tsar Nicholas II, Emperor of all the Russias. Husband of . . .

Alicky (Alix), Empress of all the Russias. Youngest sister of Victoria, Princess Louis of Battenberg.

Greig, Louis. Equerry; later Comptroller of Household to Bertie.

Buccleuch, Duke of. Father of . . .

Alice Scott, Lady. Wife of Henry, Duke of Gloucester.

Cecilia, Countess of Strathmore. Mother of . . .

Elizabeth Bowes-Lyon. Wife of Bertie, Duke of York, and sister of . . .

David Bowes-Lyon.

Wallis Warfield, later Spencer, later Simpson, later Duchess of Windsor. Wife of David.

Cassel, Sir Ernest. Grandfather of . . .

Edwina Ashley. Later Mountbatten, wife of Dickie.

Marina, Princess of Greece. Wife of George, Duke of Kent.

Lascelles, Henry (Harry), Viscount. Later 6th Earl of Harewood, husband of Mary, only daughter of George and May.

Jamie, James Stuart. Later 1st Viscount Findhorn; friend of Elizabeth Bowes-Lyon.

PART ONE

CHILDHOOD

My soul, sit thou a patient looker-on,
Judge not the play before the play be done;
Her plot hath many changes; every day
Speaks a new scene; the last act crowns the play.

Francis Quarles

1

The evening visit by their infant son had become something of an ordeal, and the Duke and Duchess had come to dread it. George, Duke of York, was reading *The Times* newspaper; the Duchess was trying to compose herself for what lay ahead. She glanced at the clock and as she did so it chimed five times. "Please don't fret, Ma'am," her lady-in-waiting, Lady Mary Lygon, said. "Perhaps it will be all right tonight." —"Quite right, my dear. Quite right," declared the Duke from behind his newspaper; then to his wife: "He is no doubt over-tired, May."

The Duchess, Princess May of Teck before her marriage, picked up her embroidery and began working at it, but her mind was elsewhere. At her wedding on that beautiful July day three years earlier, she had no idea that the whole business of conceiving and bearing children would be quite so taxing and unpleasant. Recently she had begun to understand that the contact with her children, while still infants, was highly unsatisfactory, too, leading her to wonder in what way she was failing them.

In the homes of her relatives, the hour or so when the children were brought down from the nursery, tidy and washed, was a happy event, with perhaps a story or a game, and then a good-night kiss before Nanny took them to bed. Then why, May York asked herself yet again, did her first-born appear to find the proximity of his father and mother so distressing? Could it be that something in the room alarmed the boy and that it was nothing to do with dear Georgie and herself? She glanced round the drawing room. Could it be the swinging of the clock's pendulum? It was a pretty room, with her own choice of light grey striped wallpaper. There was a large religious painting of a child with arms raised to heaven on the wall by the door, and many heavily framed pictures on the inlaid table beside which she sat: mostly of her family and Georgie's relations, with Grandmama Queen Victoria dominating. It wouldn't be the tall standard lamp, heavily carved, with the shade of patterned material—and long tassels—again her own choice. Not the screen behind her chair, surely? That could frighten no one. It was patterned with flowers; and there were bowls of summer flowers everywhere about the room, too. How she loved flowers—had done since her early childhood. No child could be frightened of flowers!

The early evening summer sun was pouring in through the windows of York Cottage, making everything look so pretty. But then came the sound, distant but seemingly inevitable, of a crying child, approaching across the hall. May steeled herself for the onslaught. A piercing scream from just outside the door almost drowned the sound of Nanny's knock.

In a voice that she attempted to keep steady, May York called out, "Come in." The Duke put down his newspaper regretfully: he had been immersed in a long leading article about the crisis in Crete between those wretched Turks and equally wretched Greeks . . .

Mrs Green entered, her two-year-old charge in her arms. She was a tall, angular woman in her late thirties, her grey hair pulled tight back into a bun, with prominent cheekbones, a large, distinctive nose, and rather bad teeth revealed as she spoke soothingly to the pretty, fair-haired boy. But David was not at his best; in fact he was looking awful, his cheeks stained with tears, his mouth wide open. He was totally preoccupied with his own misery, eyes open only intermittently, then burying his head in the starched bosom of Nanny as if it were the only place where he could seek consolation.

Mrs Green said, "I am sorry, Your Royal Highness. I don't know what comes over him when he is downstairs."

In a state of anguish, May rose from her chair and began to walk towards the boy, arms outstretched. But this only led to the volume of sound rising higher and she stood still, the tears welling up in her own eyes. "My little boy . . ."

"Take him away, Mrs Green," ordered the Duke in the firm quarterdeck voice of a naval officer. "The boy's hysterical."

Mrs Green backed away, a distraught expression on her face, holding the child tightly. But once outside her face changed. She stopped pinching the little boy and put his wet cheek to her own, murmuring, "There my little boy, all over for tonight." And she stroked his thin, fair hair, dried his tears with a lace handkerchief, kissing him repeatedly. "Dear little David, dear little David!"

At the first landing up the stairs, the only sound her charge was uttering was deep, heaving sobs. Yes, all over for tonight. Now it would be smiles and more kisses, and the sound of a soothing voice before falling into a deep sleep.

Prince David, future Prince of Wales, future King Edward VIII, future Duke of Windsor, was to remember the regular evening ordeal in Mrs Green's arms all his life. "It was terrible!" he was to recall. "But why did she do it? I suppose it was to demonstrate, according to some perverse reasoning, that her power over me was greater than that of my parents."

But it was more, much more, than that. A member of the Duke and Duchess's household later explained the true reason for the nightly ordeal at York Cottage. "Mrs Green was not a mentally stable woman," she said. " She was unable to have children herself and her husband had left her. But before she was married she had completed a full training as a children's nursemaid, and had found employment in the Duke and Duchess of Newcastle's place. The Duchess had given her a good reference when she was no longer needed and that had been good enough for the Duchess of York, young, newly married and inexperienced."

Mrs Green had directed all her frustrated maternal feelings to the infant David. He was an easy baby to love. "He was a cuddlesome little thing," the young under-nurse, Mrs Bill or "Lala," declared. "Such a pretty little boy, just lay in his cot gurgling when he was not asleep"; then, significantly, she added, "I wasn't allowed to touch him."

Many months passed before anyone in the household knew what was going on: that Mrs Green, fearful of his mother attracting any of the boy's affection, was determined to turn him against her by associating mother with pain in his mind. When the first suspicions were aroused, the downstairs staff were fearful of mentioning it, afraid that this half-mad woman might attack them. It was Mrs Green's treatment of Bertie, David's younger brother, that at last brought affairs to a head.

Bertie, Prince Albert Frederick Arthur George, had been born on 14 December 1895 in the Duchess's bedroom at York Cottage. The date seemed to indicate an ill-omened start to the baby's life, for it was Queen Victoria's black day of mourning, the anniversary of the death of her *good* beloved, *noble* husband, Prince Albert. The fact that thirty-four years had now passed since the Prince Consort's untimely end, and the distinctly uneven course of their married relationship, did not diminish the Queen's annual orgy of grief. "Grandmama was rather distressed that this happy event should have taken place on a darkly sad anniversary," wrote the Queen's eldest son to his own son, George York. And he went on to suggest that the baby should be named Albert ("Bertie") to console her, and that she should be asked if she would act as the baby's godmother.

All this concern was quite unnecessary, as the aged Queen's diary reveals:

Found telegram from Georgie . . . saying that dear May had been safely delivered of a son at three this morning. Georgie's first feeling was regret that this dear child should be born on such a sad day. I have a feeling it may be a blessing for the dear little boy and may be looked upon as a gift from God!

2

York Cottage, where Prince David and Prince Albert, together with their younger sister and brothers, were brought up, had been built as an annexe to Sandringham House some years earlier to help meet the social appetite of their grandfather, Queen Victoria's eldest son. When George married and needed a home and was made Duke of York, his father presented him with the building.

"It was, and remains, a glum little villa," George York's biographer noted, "encompassed by thickets of laurel and rhododendron . . . The local brown stone in which the house was constructed is concealed by rough-cast which in its turn is enlivened by very imitation Tudor beams." Harold Nicolson wrote of the Duke's own sitting room, "Its north window, blocked by heavy shrubberies, was rendered even darker by the red cloth covering which saddened the walls." He did not point out how much more cheerful, and in much better taste, was the Duchess's sitting room, to which was brought the unfortunate Prince David every evening. For May York brought a refreshing good taste into a royal family "little given to intellectual pursuits, without much in the way of artistic tastes or taste."

May was the daughter of an impoverished German Duke

and Duchess, a pretty, lively creature who had a modest, but real, interest in the arts. When her name had come up as a candidate for the hand of Queen Victoria's eldest grandson, Prince Eddy (Albert Victor), Queen Victoria reacted very unfavourably. "May Teck will *never* do," she wrote to her youngest granddaughter when the German girl's name was put forward as a possible candidate for marriage and the role of future Queen-Empress. But Queen Victoria was at length persuaded to invite her to Balmoral, the Queen's enormous and hideous Scottish castle, and at once capitulated to her charm and pretty looks. Queen Victoria never minded changing her views on people when presented with the evidence of her own eyes. That was in August 1891, with the guns blasting away on the grouse moors. Prince Eddy was enchanted with May, proposed to her during a ball, and was accepted *very* promptly. The nation, always deeply interested in court goings-on, and especially courtships and marriages, rejoiced and the Court breathed a deep sigh of relief.

The dramatic events that followed this engagement turned out to be a blessing to the nation and the Empire. Prince Eddy had been a worry almost since birth. His health was never robust, his mental resources were limited, his self-discipline was negligible, his appetites were unrestrained although the general public, in that more discreet age, knew nothing of what today would be a national scandal. His tutor did what he could with the boy, and he was sent away to prepare for a naval career. His younger brother went with him. George was Eddy's only real friend, and George's patience with him astonished and delighted his parents. In September 1880 the two Princes were sent round the world in a naval vessel. The government was aghast, fearing for the safety of the heir to the throne. This infuriated the Queen who thought it an excellent idea. In the event the boys came close to drowning in a storm off Australia. The good the two-year voyage did to Prince Eddy's health and development was soon dissipated and the problems began again, culminating in his association with a scandal in a homosexual brothel in Soho, London. The royal ranks closed to shield the general public from knowledge of this and other unseemly goings-on. His father's "greatest wish" had been to keep his eldest son "simple, pure and childlike as long as possible." This was not to be. In fact there was good reason to believe that Eddy had succumbed to syphilis by his mid-twenties, when the Queen and his own mother and father were fretting because he would not get married.

He was twenty-seven when Princess May suddenly came into his life. Five weeks later, with the nation already preparing for the romance and glitter of a Royal Wedding, Prince Eddy contracted flu. Natural poor health and the effects of over-indulgence helped to develop it into pneumonia, from which he died on 14 January 1892. Queen Victoria wrote of "the terrible calamity which has befallen us as well as the Country. The feeling of grief & sympathy is universal & great. Was there," she asked, "anything so sad, so tragic?"

Then like the unexpected happy ending to a fairy tale, the pretty Princess overcame her grief and in a trice was engaged instead to the very much brighter, more responsible and personable younger brother, George. Pressure from Queen Victoria and from all members of the court hierarchy would certainly have been applied. Thankfully, it was not required, and the nation and Empire soon enjoyed their Royal Wedding after all.

David was born to George and May York on 23 June 1894, at a time when the European powers were busy carving up Africa for themselves, and Japan had decided to go to war with China. The birth took place at White Lodge in Richmond Park, the home of May's parents, and he was christened Edward Albert Christian George Andrew Patrick David, the last four names for the patron saints of England, Scotland, Ireland and Wales. He stuck to David all his life.

May's third child, born on 25 April 1897, was a girl—"my dear little Diamond Jubilee baby" as Queen Victoria loved to call her. Her grandfather actually wanted her to be called "Diamond," but that was abandoned when it was pointed out that she would then carry with her for life the year of her birth. She was finally christened, in Sandringham Parish Church, Victoria Alexandra Alice Mary—and was known always as Mary to distinguish her from her mother, May.

A more lovely baby was hard to find [wrote her
biographer], with her blue eyes, golden curls, and
rosy cheeks—"La belle rose anglaise!" as Madame
Poincaré was led to exclaim involuntarily the first
time she saw her. And it is interesting to notice
that, even from those days of earliest babyhood, the
words seem to have always been the ones which
best describe the Princess.

Mercifully, Princess Mary was post-Mrs Green. What a thing
child would have done to the nurse's crazed mind does no
bear thinking about. As it was, contentment reigned in the
nurseries at York Cottage. David at six years was an angelic
little child. Bertie was happier, although he remained rather
"peakish" and was less robust than his older brother. The
appalling diet, and periods of actual starvation, he had suf
fered in his infancy had weakened him permanently and
ruined his digestion for life.

These three children, all born within a period of less
than three years, formed a tight-knit group, for May York was
now granted a much-needed if brief period of relief from
childbirth. David, as the eldest, was the natural leader in all
games and activities, worshipped by Bertie, while Mary
early a tomboy, was more independent. They adored Lala
who gave them all her love and attention. David later told
how she provided love with firmness and how Finch was the
sergeant-major when necessary. He did not often have to
apply punishment, but when he did, they remembered it for
a long time.

When Mary was still a baby, David once insisted on
charging in and out of the night nursery when Lala was trying
to get her to sleep. She protested, but the boy was in a wilful
mood and continued to make a row. At length, Lala marched
into Finch's room and said, "That boy is impossible. If you
don't give him a thrashing, I will." Finch went into action at
once, seized hold of the boy and took him into his bedroom,
kicking and yelling, and gave him a thoroughly good beating
on the bottom.

"I yelled more out of hurt pride than pain," David
recalled; "and, as Finch was leaving the room with the air of a

man who had performed a distasteful but inescapable duty, I shouted after his receding back that I would get even with him. 'You just wait!' I cried. 'I will tell Papa what you have done.' "

Instead, the furious, frustrated boy was summoned to his mother's bedroom. May had heard about the affair, and instead of comforting David, which would not have come naturally to her anyway, she rebuked him thoroughly and ordered him to apologize for being such a nuisance.

Mary was always known informally as Goldilocks. She was a pretty little girl who turned out to be the best behaved of this first trio of children. This exemplary record began with her birth, which gave her mother very little trouble and was soon over. "What a *dear* little thing!" Lala commented on first seeing her wrapped in the beautiful embroidered shawl, earlier used to wrap up the baby boys. Most nannies make some such comment, but Lala extended her exclamation into prediction. "She is going to have Your Royal Highness's hair and beautiful skin. A thing of beauty is a joy for ever, that's what they say, Ma'am."

And Lala was proved right, as she was in most things. Princess Mary "grew into a peach," and at three years even her father, not given to emotion and favourable expressions of opinion about his children, was heard to speak well and affectionately of her. Her hair was the same tight curly russet as her mother's, though lighter (hence her nickname) her blue-grey eyes were wide apart like her brother David's and her smile was warmly confiding.

3

In the middle of July 1900 the three children came to stay on the Isle of Wight with the Queen at Osborne House—"for the sea and the brisk healthy weather." David later wrote of Osborne as "that utterly un-English house in imitation of an Italian villa, near Cowes . . . Even as a child I was struck by the ugliness of the house, which was described as "a family necropolis." The floors of the corridors and passages were inlaid with mosaic; let into the walls were numerous alcoves each displaying in life size a white marble statue of a dead or living member of Gangan's family."

There is a photograph of the children taken on the lawn on 8 August with Queen Victoria. Queen Victoria is in her invariable black, wearing a broad-brimmed black hat topped with black ostrich feathers spread out like the *fleur de lys*. The baby on her lap is May's youngest son, Harry, four months old. David stands by his great-grandmother looking severely and responsibly at the camera, while Bertie appears anxious. Mary, between them, is looking into the distance as if expecting a friend. She is three years and three months old. She is sitting on a wickerwork chair, David is in long trousers, standing, while his younger brother sits on a cushion,

bare knees thrust out before him—knees which, as we sha
see, are almost as great a source of concern as his digestion

All the children—six, four and three—are in identic
sailor suits; Mary wears a hat, a round one carefully contrive
to look like Jack Tar's. Only the stoniest heart could fail to b
moved by this pretty trio, beginning their lives at almost th
beginning of a new century, which for the boys especially wi
hold so much unhappiness.

The old Queen, in the sixty-fourth year of her reign an
looking down at the baby on her lap with almost sightles
eyes, has only six months to live. As the slow exposure of th
lens is concluded and the gentleman in the black suit emerge
from beneath his black cloth cover, the scene depicted in h
photograph bursts into life for the three children, less anima
edly for the old lady and not at all for the infant, who
gently lifted from the sovereign's lap by Lala, after a dee
curtsey. "Go off and play now, children," David, Bertie an
Mary are told by the Queen in a voice that is still precise bu
as faded as her eyes, and they are soon far away, their crie
echoing across the gardens of Osborne. Here, on the Isle
Wight, the sea is the first attraction, and under the super
vision of Finch there will be throwing of pebbles, and late
before lunch, a paddle in the warm sea, with much health
screaming and splashing.

At lunch on that day of the photograph, while the thre
children ate thinly sliced mutton with carrots and butter
mashed potatoes, Lala said, "Your mother and father wi
arrive this afternoon from London with Grandpapa.* Mr Finc
will take you to the jetty at Cowes and he will take you o
board to greet them. The Princess of Wales will be wit
you."

This was welcome news, less because they would se
Mama and Papa than because it meant an outing, and tha
meant seeing what Papa called "the ordinary people," wh
always formed a cheering crowd, waving Union Jacks. It als
meant the chance—and Mary was as keen as the boys o
this—of one of the officers taking them down to the engin
room of the yacht, with its exciting, heavy smell of hot oil an

*The Prince of Wales, soon to be King Edward VII.

sight of glistening brass and thrusting pistons and whirling shafts . . .

"Why are they visiting Osborne, Lala?" David asked. "Papa will soon be busy shooting grouse."

"They have come to talk to the Queen, and to talk to you."

"What about—what do they want to tell us?"

Lala rose from her seat to ring the bell for the pudding. "That is not my business, Mary. Nor is it your business until you are told. Come along, Bertie, you are holding us all up again." Bertie's plate was still half full: eating held small pleasure for the boy and he was accustomed to Lala's impatience.

There was storytime before the expedition to Cowes. Lala read to them, under the big cedar tree. There were distant glimpses of the sea, with a big liner heading east, its white wake like a chalk line, and a fully-rigged three-master moving with stately grace towards the Channel, no doubt making for some Continental or Baltic port. Lala was reading *The Would-Be-Goods* by E. Nesbit from the *Illustrated London News:* ". . .When we were sent down to the country to learn to be better children, we felt it was rather good business . . ." It was very hot, even in the shade, and Bertie and Mary dozed off to the soporific sound of insects, seagulls and Lala's voice—". . . The Moat House was the place we went to stay at." But not David, he lay on the scarlet rug, eyes wide open, relishing the music of the words, his imagination at work, surmising what was to come of these children in their adventures and already relating them to his own life.

Finch appeared at three o'clock precisely. Considering how much they saw of one another, and how frequently their duties overlapped, his relationship with Lala was a good one, mainly because they could both laugh and make light of happenings that might have been taken over-seriously. Lala had heard the sound of his boots on the gravel as he left the house, and she stopped reading before he arrived. She smiled up at him from her wickerwork chair. He was "on parade," as he called it when he was to be in the presence of his master and mistress, his boots shining like the glittering sea behind him, serge suit with jacket and waistcoat buttoned as tight and straight as the creased trousers. His neatly trimmed beard was beginning to grey, like his master's. In this informal company he was carrying his hat, a trim brown bowler.

"It's time we were on our way, Mrs Bill." In the early days he might have added, "You'll see that they are clean and tidy." But a long time ago he had learned that she was faultless in this service. "I'll have the landau sent round in five minutes."

"We'll be ready, Mr Finch." They both had a muted but still distinct north country accent, which added a note of steadiness as well as unity to their talk.

The open landau was drawn up at the porticoed front door of Osborne House, James the elderly coachman and Egerton the footman in their bottle-green uniforms in correct positions awaiting their passengers. Finch lined up the three children alongside the landau to await their grandmother, who (as usual) turned up late and laughing.

Princess Alexandra—"Alix"—fifty-five years old, was dearly loved by what she called her "Georgie pets," the children of her second son, now lined up in their engaging sailor suits in the sunshine. As she emerged through the front doors of Osborne House, in a long white dress and huge white hat, accompanied by her lady-in-waiting, the two boys bowed and Mary gave a deep curtsey. "My darling Georgie pets," she greeted them. "Oh how lovely, lovely!" and embraced them each in turn. "We are going on a lovely little voyage together. Perhaps we can play some games on the way—some exciting deck quoits? Would you like that?"

Alix would have continued to chat to them but Finch, advancing discreetly from his customary background position, indicated to the lady-in-waiting that they might be late for the carefully timed departure of the royal yacht. Assisted by Egerton, Alix ascended the steps into the landau and sat down in the forward-facing seat, patting it on either side as an invitation to the two boys to sit next to her, while Lady Treadgold and Mary sat opposite.

Never once during all this arranging or while the horses drew the landau down the drive to the lodge where the lodge-keeper and his wife came out to bow and curtsey, on to the East Cowes road and to the town itself—never once, all this way, did the chatter of grandmother and children cease. Alix listened to every word as if each were the most important she had ever heard.

The townspeople were out on the side of the road into East Cowes, some of them with flags and giving a cheer as the landau passed. Not only was the Princess of Wales loved by the people as she was by her young family, but patriotism was very strong in 1900, with the war in South Africa going better now after the early setbacks. "Soldiers of the Queen . . ." Alix smiled from beneath her parasol, and the children gave little waves with their hands as they had long ago been instructed to do on these occasions.

"There she is—isn't she beautiful?" David exclaimed as the *Osborne* came into view, anchored some distance out in the roads—a pretty yacht indeed, white painted with a blue line running from the graceful bow to the stern. She had a single tall raked funnel, from which black smoke emerged to be gently carried away on the south-west breeze. There were yachts of many shapes and sizes taking advantage of this perfect afternoon to sail in Spithead, but all kept a discreet distance from the *Osborne*, which soon would have the Standard fluttering from her mainmast.

Then came the ritual, the magic of which never failed for Bertie and was always enjoyed by his elder brother and his sister. The royal barge was alongside the jetty, gleaming like a table set for dinner, ratings holding her with hooks, a lieutenant standing at attention by the gangplank. The barge was like a miniature of the *Osborne*, even to the black smoke drifting from the single funnel. Then they were all on board, seated beneath the awning, while the launch gathered speed to the sound of increasing revolutions of the little reciprocal steam engine astern.

"Hooray! We're going," Bertie could not resist exclaiming, and was kicked by David. "Don't be common," he rebuked him. "Anyway it's 'Cast off!' and 'Full ahead!,' you ought to know that."

Alix made no comment. She had, for a few moments, stopped talking, but was singing softly from *HMS Pinafore* instead:

We sail the ocean blue,
And our saucy ship's a beauty;
We're sober men and true,
And attentive to our duty.

Captain Charles Windham RN, the *Osborne's* Captain, was at the head of the gangway when the launch came alongside: bosun's pipe playing, Windham and his second-in-command both standing stiffly at the salute; and most impressive of all, the yacht manned and dressed by the yachtsmen in summer white. The Captain gave no hint of the anxiety that was pressing upon him, and answered the Princess of Wales's enquiry as if there was all the time in the world. Vice-Admiral Sir John Fullerton had warned him when he had first taken up the appointment that the Princess had no idea of time, to the continuous exasperation of the Prince of Wales, and he had allowed a margin of ten minutes. Not enough, and the simple business of transporting this small but precious party across to Portsmouth to synchronize with the arrival of the royal party from London was at risk of getting out of hand.

HMS *Osborne* cast off from her buoy and at exciting and unusual speed steamed north-east across Spithead, paddles tearing into the water. Behind the multitude of masts and yards of a hundred or more men o'war, behind the soaring cranes and the buildings making up the Royal Dockyard, behind the church spires and tall buildings of Portsmouth, the Downs were just visible in the heat haze. Invisible were the great forts built into the sides of these hills to guard this vital dockyard from Napoleon Bonaparte a hundred years ago; invisible, too, from the *Osborne* was the massive bulk of HMS *Victory's* hull, still afloat in the inner harbour. But David and Bertie had both been taken round Nelson's old flagship and knew well, from their sailor father's lips, the story of Nelson's great fight at Trafalgar to save England from invasion and conquest by the French. Indeed, above Bertie's bed at York Cottage there was a painting of the one-armed, one-eyed hero descending the quayside steps which they were now approaching at quarter speed. Nelson was going aboard the *Victory* for his last great triumphant battle, and his death—and how the crowds were waving and cheering in that painting.

The family party stood on the quay. May York was there, in a long dark coat, fur at the collar, and a matching hat of vast dimensions, decorated with much fruit and many flowers. "How can she bear the heat?" Alix remarked, quite loudly, to Lady Treadgold. There were several ladies-in-waiting in the party, too, all in hats to emulate the Duchess of York's, and no fewer than three equerries.

But doininating them all simply by his presence stood Bertie, the Prince of Wales, who would be King Edward VII when his ancient mother died. He was in the uniform of Admiral of the Fleet, a black band round his arm. He was fifty-eight. Unlike his son, he was chatting to those about him, and as soon as the *Osborne* came alongside the quay, he raised his tricorne and waved it towards his wife and grandchildren. "Hoor-ray!" he called out, his guttural accent evident even from that single word. "Welcome to Portsmouth, even if you are very late." And he blew a kiss in the direction of his grandchildren before clamping back into his mouth the cigar which was almost as big as the capstan beside him.

A few minutes later, George York was shaking the hands of his two boys. "I hope you have been behaving yourselves," he remarked in a voice that did not conceal his doubts. Then he kissed his daughter, Mary, a smile at last breaking out on his face. By contrast, the grandfather pretended to try to pick up David, grunting and exclaiming, "Too big!" Bertie got the same treatment; then when he saw Mary he handed his cigar to one of his equerries, bent down and lifted her off her feet. She squeaked with delight at the delicious tickle of his beard and placed her arms round his neck. "Darling Grandpapa!"

Mary received a kiss of a more perfunctory nature from her mother, who shook the hands of her boys, that curious little shy sideways smile on her lips. Today was the 8th of August; on the 17th she would be making the return journey across Spithead; then to Lord and Lady Barnard at Raby Castle—and that would be a relief! Such rest! Oh, she was so tired. And these children were so wearisome.

4

So May, Duchess of York, was tired! Yes, the half-blind
Queen observed this at dinner at Osborne House that evening. And what reason did she have to be tired? The shrewd
old lady looked down the table and thought about this with a
touch of resentment, recalling her first reaction to the proposal that this young woman would make her grandson a
good wife. "May of Teck—oh May of Teck would never do!"
Well, perhaps her first instinctive reaction was right. She was
not showing the same tough resilience as Alix. Just consider
what a dance her eldest son had led dear Alix, who had never
once complained—one woman after another, Lady Warwick
until a couple of years ago, and now the Hon. Mrs George
Keppel! "I do not understand," the Queen had once exclaimed to one of her ladies-in-waiting "why dear, good Alix
puts up with it." But it was May, whose Georgie had never
looked at another woman, who complained so much about
her lot in life—May with those darling sweet little children,
who had sat beside her on the lawn that very morning in
their dear sailor suits, being photographed.

The Queen, who could scarcely see the bowl from which
she spooned up a little soup, had not failed to observe May's
apparent lack of affection for her children, the way she almost

shrank from them, touching them only as a point of duty—or so it seemed. To the discreet background sound of the Royal Marines' band behind the screen, and of silver against Meissen china as the diners spooned up their turtle soup, Queen Victoria silently considered in turn those about her at the table who would take over the reins of monarchy when she died.

She knew that her own death was not far distant. Her heart was behaving with singular irregularity and she felt pains in her chest sometimes even from turning over in her bed. Before long she must join beloved Albert. And what would she have to tell him when they met again after all these years, in that mysterious world to which all were destined, Queen-Empress and boot boy alike?

Queen Victoria glanced towards her major-domo, Patel, and the Indian at once passed the message by a raised hand to the house footmen for the soup bowls to be removed. Then she turned, oh so slowly, towards her eldest son on her right and asked him, "Where will you be shooting grouse next week?"

With those few words, conversatio⁻ at the dinner table was authorized and the murmur of voices could be heard from all parts. The Prince of Wales told his mother on which estate in north Yorkshire he would be shooting grouse on "the glorious twelfth" and chatted about domestic and social matters, eschewing as always any state affairs. Then, when he asked the Queen with great concern in his deep guttural voice, "How are you, dear Mama?" she knew what he was referring to. For scarcely a week had passed since his younger brother, Affie, had died in Germany, and he had returned from the funeral the previous day. With awful irony, while there he had learned from his sister, to whom he was devoted, that she was suffering from terminal cancer, too. Thank goodness, he was pledged to secrecy, and he had cried last night as he prayed that his beloved mother might be taken before her eldest daughter.

Yes, death was in the air, the Queen's eldest son recognized, for on the day before Affie had died, the King of Italy had been horribly assassinated. Now, at this dinner table in

Osborne House, the Prince of Wales's train of thought turned from that dreadful event to a failed attempt on the life of Affie in 1870. In an attempt to lift the spirits of the Queen, he remarked, "Do be consoled, dearest Mama, that we might have lost Affie when he was in Australia and that Irishman nearly shot him. So we can say that the good Lord granted him an extra thirty years of precious life."

"Yes, you are quite right. And, so far, four months of your life." And she briefly smiled at her son as she reminded him of his visit to Belgium in April, when an anarchist student had fired at him through the open window of his railway carriage. The Queen's smile was treasured for its rarity, and for its natural radiance which contrasted so strongly with the expression of her mouth—almost an inverted "U"—when in repose.

The warmth and cheer this brought to the Queen's eldest son faded before the salmon had been removed and the massive sirloin of beef was carved by Ranger. With the departure of the Queen and the other ladies at the end of the meal, the Prince fell into one of his black depressions. The other men talked men's talk among themselves for a while, until his son called across the table, "Dear Papa, you are very silent tonight. Is there anything wrong?"

"Yes, dear boy," he answered, putting down a cigarette and lighting a cigar instead. "I am preoccupied with the subject of death."

Captain Windham, at the far end of the table and rather drunk, took the liberty of intervening. "Sir, may we beg you instead to think of life? And youth rather than age?"

The Prince looked at him in some surprise but decided not to take offence at the naval officer's forwardness, chiefly because the suggestion was a rather sound one. "Yes, Captain Windham, I will do as you say." The presence of Georgie reminded him of his three little grandchildren, whom he loved dearly. Tomorrow, he determined, he would invite them for a romp on the lawn before he left for London in the afternoon. They always enjoyed that, and so did he.

Sadly, Queen Victoria did learn of her eldest daughter's fatal illness and it added to the mounting depression which

seized her in the closing months of 1900. "Very seedy,"
George wrote to May of his grandmother's health. Although
the military news from South Africa was much better, men
were still dying out there on the veldt, and the Queen
learned in October of the death from enteric fever of her
grandson Prince Albert Victor, yet another blow. "Did not
feel well," she dictated to her youngest daughter for her
journal on 9 December, "though they say I am getting better."

She was not. On Christmas Day her oldest and closest
friend, and lady-in-waiting, Jane Churchill, died. "All fall
around me, and I have become more and more lonely."
Amidst almost unprecedented winter storms at the turn of
the year, she sank lower in mind and body. "Another year
begun & I am feeling so weak and unwell that I enter upon it
sadly." She did not linger long into the twentieth century.

On 20 January all the children were in quarantine at
York Cottage as David had had German measles, and even
their parents were not allowed to visit the nurseries where
they were confined, except for a vigorous walk once a day.
Then one morning Finch came into the schoolroom and said
very solemnly, "Your mother and father have been called to
the Isle of Wight. Your great-grandmother is not at all well."

The children heard the sound of the carriage coming
round, and watched out of the window as their mother and
father hurried out of the front door and climbed in. The
children waved but George and May did not look up. Then
they were off down the drive to the station, the horses going
very fast. David experienced a chill of apprehension and a
suspicion that they were at the beginning of a new age as well
as a new century.

The following evening, 21 January 1901, the old lady
passed quietly away, surrounded by as many of her huge and
scattered family as could get there in time. Lala, who still
slept with the three eldest children in their night nursery,
awakened them at seven o'clock the next morning with the
words, "The Queen died last night. The nation mourns." It
sounded rather formal put like that, but it was the most
important and solemn event for the royal family since the
monarchy had been reinstated in 1660. As Lala told the
children, the Queen had reigned for twenty years before Lala

had even been born, and to the children Lala seemed quite old.

When they went out later in the day with Finch for a walk through the woods, he suddenly stopped them and said, "Listen!" They did so for almost half a minute until Mary asked, "Listen to what?"—"Listen to the silence," he replied. And it was true. No sound of guns, no sound of birds, no sound of trains. Even the wind, like the Queen, had died. A great hush seemed to hang over the whole country. Then a cock pheasant—suddenly startled—flew over their heads, wings batting the air urgently and screaming protest; and they walked on.

"What do you think it will be like, David?" Bertie asked as they dressed for the journey to Windsor and the funeral. David would know. He knew everything.

"Oh, there'll be a lot of people and a coffin with Gangan's body in it."

"Shall we see her dead?" Bertie wondered if he would burst into tears at the sight of her dead body as he used to do sometimes (to the old Queen's dismay) when he was with her alive.

"No, silly, the lid will be nailed down."

Mary, listening to this conversation with some horror, wondered what it would be like to be in a nailed-down box. She thought she might cry. Then Finch came in, dressed in a black suit and black tie, looking solemn but steady, as always.

They did not travel in the royal train; instead a special carriage had been added to the 12.55 to London. Lala had remained behind to look after Harry, and the children were accompanied by an under-nurse, Miss Waverley (or "Bun"), Finch, and a boy of sixteen who had recently been employed to help him.

As they sped across the flat East Anglian countryside, the shadow of the engine's smoke racing over the fields, the reason for their journey was soon forgotten and they began to behave normally—that is to say they began to giggle and wriggle, pushing each other about and breaking briefly into games. Finch did not protest. Sensible fellow that he was, he

recognized that it was not natural for young children to
sustain funereal solemnity all day long.

But shortly before they arrived in London, as he tidied
them up, he gave them a homily about their responsibilities.
"It's very unusual for children as young as you are to attend
funerals," he said. "As you know, your father is too ill to
attend, and your mother is nursing him down at Osborne, so
you will be representing the new King's eldest son and heir
to the throne. And you will be judged on your behaviour at
Windsor." He smiled. "So no pinching and punching!"

Poor Papa had succumbed to the German measles in
spite of all the precautions. He lay in bed upstairs at Osborne
while his dead grandmother, in white dress with her lace
wedding veil and white widow's cap, her silver crucifix lying
in her hands, lay in state downstairs. But tomorrow she
would leave Osborne for the last time, and with great pomp
and demonstrations of grief be carried across Spithead to
Portsmouth. The next day her coffin would be placed on a
train destined for London. And many thousands of her subjects would kneel down and pray as the train sped through
the countryside.

But the streets of London, at the special request of the
Queen, were not draped in black, and as the three York
children, cheered by all who recognized them, proceeded in
a royal carriage through the streets, only the people were in
mourning while hangings of purple cashmere with white satin
bows appeared to celebrate the new reign rather than grieve
for the old one.

It had been a spring day in winter for the children's
journey to London, but the weather changed in the night and
Finch felt obliged to rise from his bed and bank up the fire
twice in the children's room in Windsor Castle. He got very
little sleep himself as a consequence. Accustomed as he was
to responsibility, it was a taxing time for him, his special
concern being for Bertie, who had so far escaped the measles
but was nearly always the first to go down with some illness.

A bitterly cold east wind was whistling about the castle
ramparts, and Finch kept the children indoors for as long as
possible before the ceremony. Then he led them along the

stone corridors of the visitors' apartments where they had been sleeping, down grim, chill, stone steps to the quadrangle, where they felt the full impact of the swirling east wind. Here there were many ladies and gentlemen dressed all in black, moving in pairs or groups towards St George's Gateway and thence in slow, informal procession past the round tower and down the lower ward to the entrance to St George's Chapel. In this exalted crowd the three children were conspicuous and attracted much curious and mainly approving attention. There were several other children, but none as young as the Yorks. The boys were in black velvet suits with white wing collars and knee breeches, and carried top hats, while Mary, in a long black velvet dress under her fur-trimmed dark coat, attracted many smiles. "Goldilocks!" And she did look tenderly fetching with her curly russet hair peeping out from beneath the simple wide-brimmed black velvet hat.

Within the noble interior of the chapel, decorated to the late Queen's instructions with masses of hot-house flowers, an usher guided Finch and the three children down the side aisle to their seats alongside an ancient tomb with a recumbent carved statue of a duke. Poor Mary, not yet four years old and bewildered and fearful of this whole experience, gazed with terror at the stretched-out stone figure, imagining it to be, if not Gangan's corpse, then certainly someone else's dead body. She uttered not a word, but held Finch's hand very tightly as she sat down next to him.

While Mary lapsed into the frozen detachment from the world in which only the very young can find relief, Bertie continued to look about him in wonder and anxiety. It was all so vast by contrast with the little Sandringham church with just his family about him, and behind, the familiar and comforting faces of the indoor and outdoor staff.

David, on the other hand, felt a growing sense of restlessness and increasing crossness. Such a waste of time! He wrote later, "The occasion was mournful beyond description, and no doubt the elderly and the sage who witnessed it must have shared a sense of the passing of a great era of peace and security, and a foreboding of the inevitable changes that would profoundly affect their own lives while altering Britain's destiny. But at seven [actually at six] one's sense of destiny is limited, and one's appetite for historical pathos even more so. I remember now only the piercing cold, the interminable waits . . ."

The longest wait on that momentous, freezing day was for the old Queen herself. A great stickler for promptness all her life, she would *not* have been amused at the broken timetable for her last public appearance. The reason for the delay in the arrival of the gun carriage with her coffin was the weather and its effect on the horses of the Royal Horse Artillery, due to draw it from the railway station to the entrance to the chapel.

The horses had been waiting for an hour and a half and were thoroughly cold, impatient and nervy when the coffin was carried from the train outside to the gun carriage, upon which it was placed. One of them, fed up with the whole business, reared and broke its trace. The other five, emulating it, broke their traces too, leading to chaos and pandemonium and to the coffin's almost being thrown on to the station forecourt.

While Royal Horse Artillery officers and troopers struggled to regain some sort of order, a quick-witted naval captain took the initiative. "I distinctly saw Prince Louis go up to King Edward," reported a fellow naval officer who was in charge of the naval contingent, "and whisper something in his ear, at which the King nodded an assent. Prince Louis then came over to me and said, 'Ground arms and stand by to drag the gun carriage.' "

A third naval officer, on instructions from Prince Louis, darted back to the train and emerged less than a minute later with a length of emergency communication cord. This was then secured to the gun carriage and at Prince Louis's orders the sailors began to drag it away on its journey. The RHA officers were furious, but the King interceded on behalf of the Navy, which was proving more effectual than the Army on this occasion. "Let him manage everything," the King ordered, referring to Prince Louis.

It seemed appropriate at the time for Captain Prince Louis of Battenberg to settle the crisis, for he was married to the late Queen's youngest, and favourite, grand-daughter, another Victoria. Their infant son was called Dickie.*

*Became Earl Mountbatten of Burma, who was to encourage actively the marriage in 1947 between his nephew Philip and George and May's first grand-daughter, Princess Elizabeth: now Queen Elizabeth II.

5

What with German measles and quarantine, the terrible weather and the ordeal of Queen Victoria's funeral, and its aftermath, the early weeks of 1901 were not much fun for David, Bertie and Mary. On top of this, there was "The Voyage." Long before the Queen's death, it had been decided that their parents should go on an imperial voyage—and what a voyage it was to be! Gibraltar, Malta, Port Said, Colombo, Singapore, Australia, New Zealand, South Africa, Canada . . . The Empire George York would one day rule, the Empire that deserved the thanks of the Mother Country for the aid it had given during the South African War.

May hated the sea and dreaded the whole thing. Tempers were short at York Cottage after the funeral, and, as always under these circumstances, the servants were affected by the atmosphere, and even Lala's sunny disposition clouded over.

Yet another cause of friction and short temper was the new King's failure to create the children's parents Prince and Princess of Wales, as was customary. He only added the title "Cornwall" before their ducal title, York. For the present, at least, they were to retain their old rank, although this omission was later corrected by the father. But as Queen Victoria once wrote, "Anyone can be a duke, but only members of the royal family may call themselves prince." And now they were to do this long and exhausting tour of the Empire, meeting thousands of people, as a mere duke and duchess. All those connected with George and May—secretaries, valets, equerries, ladies-in-waiting, servants—were outraged at this break with tradition. And what about May's family? They, too, were outraged. In answer to May's letter with the news, her aunt wrote, "My ire is up & hot that the legitimate historical Title is not to be continued nor borne by you & George! Oh! what a terrible mistake so to upset old traditions! and why? because *he* [King Edward] will not be superseded? What else can it be?"

Suddenly, with the spring, the children's lives were transformed. On 16 March 1901 they once more travelled down to Portsmouth, this time in the royal train, with the new King and Queen (Grandpa and Grandma Alix), Papa and Mama and many members of the royal families of Germany and Britain. The train slowed down at many of the stations where the platforms were lined with cheering crowds, in contrast with the weeping citizens who had watched the passage of the late Queen the previous month.

In the afternoon the children were taken to see their parents' ship. "Pretty!" exclaimed Mary when she first set eyes on the liner *Ophir*. And no one could disagree with this judgement. The liner was painted all white with a single black line running from stem to stern at main deck level. She had two sturdy but gracefully proportioned funnels from which whiffs of smoke drifted up into the blue sky, and she had a marked cut-away amidships which gave her a special touch of character. Her Captain was Commodore Arthur Winsloe RN, who was supported by twenty-seven more naval officers and 125 ratings, and a company of 525 in all for the royal couple.

Commodore Winsloe took them below decks to the living quarters—a large cabin and a drawing room for each, panelled in rosewood and satinwood, with inlay, and on the floor (hardly a deck) a deep-pile Saxony carpet of a delicate fawn colour specially chosen by May. Then they were taken to inspect the smoking rooms and writing rooms, with seats upholstered in blue leather, and the spectacular dining cabin with oak-panelled walls and a long table to seat fifty-six.

The time had come to say goodbye. Mary's fifth birthday was still four weeks away, and she could not comprehend the idea of not seeing her parents again until November. She could not understand why her mother was crying and why her cheek was wet when she was kissed goodbye; it had never happened before. But as everyone seemed to be crying—even Papa—she did what seemed to be expected of her and burst into tears, too. Even her brothers were kissed by their father, something else she had never witnessed before. What a peculiar day it was! Then Finch took her by the hand and led her and the boys away.

But that was not the end of it by any means. David and Bertie especially were thrilled to be taken on board the royal yacht *Alberta,* smelling of fresh paint and hot grease. Grandpapa and Grandmama Alix were already on board, the King wearing his yachting cap and monkey jacket with the collar turned up against the wind, while Alix was muffled up in a silver fox coat, a thick veil concealing her face and securing her hat.

Everyone had cried at the departure luncheon (which the children had not attended, luckily for them), including the King himself. He was still looking quite miserable, until he caught sight of them on deck. At once he crouched down, rather painfully, smiled and greeted them, embracing them in turn.

"My Georgie pets!" Alix, Lady Treadgold at her side, limped across the deck to join them. The yacht was already under way, out of the harbour towards Spithead and the Channel as she, too, kissed them in turn. "Grandpapa and I are looking after you now, just as if Grandpapa was your father and I was your mother." She tried to scowl but really she was smiling and soon laughing. "So you must be very very good little Georgie pets."

All three children remembered vividly the day of the departure of the *Ophir* with their parents on board. The yacht steamed out for two miles ahead of the liner, which "looked

like a white fairy-tale vessel" as she cut her way through the
white horses of the Solent. Then the yacht turned through
sixteen points and headed back towards Portsmouth, and the
Ophir slipped past, little more than a cable-length away.

George and May were standing on the bridge wing waving. Then the liner gave three long hoots on her siren, which
was answered by the yacht, Mary putting her fur-gloved
hands over her ears and grimacing. In a minute or two the
figures of their parents were hardly visible. Then they disappeared into shelter. At the same time, Alix decided that it
was time to go in. "Let's go where it's *warm!*" she exclaimed
with a shivering laugh, putting her arms round Mary and
Bertie—for love first, and support for her bad leg, too.

Mary was the only one of the children who felt a serious
sense of loss with the departure of her parents. The boys in
later years, if asked, would have replied truthfully that they
were overwhelmed with a sense of relief from strain. Mary
was at Sandringham for her fifth birthday, missing her
mother and father still, but feeling much more cheerful. For
a present she was given a tricycle, which she learned to ride
with remarkable speed and fearlessness. There *were* lessons,
but . . .

Mademoiselle Hélène Bricka was supposed to give the
two boys and Mary their first lessons. "Brickie" was an elderly,
stout, round-faced lady from Alsace who had taught Princess
May when she was a young girl. She had a marked French
accent, her heart was of pure gold, and her ability to cope
with unruly boys and tomboys was negligible. The children
were, in fact, very fond of her, but she was ripe game for
teasing, which brought out the worst in them. With the
departure of the parents, Brickie's task became even more
difficult. "Queen Alexandra always believed that having fun
was more important than having education," one of her ladies-
in-waiting wrote in her memoirs. "And King Edward having
had so much trouble with his own education did not believe
in it, especially for children he knew and loved."

David recalled a typical scene shortly after the *Ophir*
had sailed away and they were staying at Marlborough House.
"When Grandpapa and Grandmama had no one to lunch, we

would often go down to their dining room after our lunch and romp about and chat to them while they had theirs.

"In this congenial atmosphere it was easy to forget that Mademoiselle Bricka was waiting for us upstairs with her French and German primers. If we were too long in going, she would enter the dining room timidly to warn us that we were already late for our lesson. Usually my grandmother would wave her away, and my grandfather, puffing at his cigar, might add reassuringly to the governess, 'It's all right. Let the children stay with us a little longer. We shall send them upstairs presently.' "

David then recounted how, when they left London for Sandringham, the King and Queen saw to it that they left Mademoiselle Bricka behind.

Sandringham meant more than freedom from Mademoiselle Bricka; it meant freedom to do almost whatever they liked for day after day during that particularly beautiful spring when the daffodils and then the bluebells seemed to bloom with special profusion in the woods. They spent most of their time on two wheels—three in the case of Mary—racing along the gravel drives, David challenging Bertie to races which he always won, while Mary insisted on joining in, too. There were frequent falls, Mary in her rashness once falling off at great speed and cutting her knee badly. She was alone at the time, held her tears in check and made her way home with blood pouring down her bare leg.

"Oh no, it hardly hurts at all," she declared stubbornly to Lala as the wound was cleaned and bandaged. She was on her tricycle the next day, slackening her bandage which impeded her knee movement.

On fine afternoons, Finch took them down to the sea where they played ducks and drakes and many other games. It was too cold even to paddle, but they contrived to get wet all the same.

6

In November 1901 the parents returned from their imperial tour. While they could now enjoy their new if delayed title Prince and Princess of Wales, the children's freedom ceased abruptly, never in all their lives to be regained in such carefree innocence. David was to remember a morning at York House, St James's Palace, where they now lived when in London.

"Bertie and I heard my father stamping up the stairs. He had a noticeably heavy footfall, but on that particular morning it sounded more ominous than ever. Besides, it was not his habit to come often to our room. In some apprehension we watched the door. When it opened, it revealed next to my father a tall, gaunt, solemn stranger with a large moustache.

" 'This is Mr Hansell,' my father said coldly, 'your new tutor,' and with that he walked out of the room, leaving us alone with Mr Hansell . . ."

This meeting—or confrontation—between tutor and pupils had been arranged some time ago, but neither of the boys' parents had thought it necessary to inform their sons. In fact Hansell was present only to size up his future charges, and left soon after informing them, without much joy or eagerness, that lessons would start at the end of April.

Henry Peter Hansell, then thirty-nine years of age, was an archetypal Victorian public school master, unmarried, tweedy, pipe-smoking, athletic, practical, brisk, lacking an exceptional academic record and a sense of fun, but as solid and trustworthy as the limb of an English oak. "We viewed him not exactly suspiciously but with a cautious, even apprehensive, eye," said David. Bertie, always quicker to show admiration, was paradoxically also more nervous about the future than his older brother. But in the event, their tutor's impact was softened by the nature of his first duty when he arrived at York House on the last day of April 1902. For a very great royal event was now imminent: nothing less than the first coronation for sixty-four years.

Hansell had sensibly decided that his two charges needed some groundwork in history, of which they were more ignorant even than mathematics, geography, and the sciences. Besides, he had read history at Magdalen College, Oxford, and naturally derived more satisfaction from teaching it than any other subject. So, on many days during May, he asked Finch to see that they were well wrapped up and arranged for a carriage to come round to York House and collect himself and the boys.

It was what Hansell called "living history," and David and Bertie were much impressed by it. "It was all very exciting," David wrote of this time. No one had ever thought of taking them to the historic sites and buildings of London and explaining their place in the nation's history. "This is where your grandfather will stand as the Archbishop of Canterbury places the crown upon his head. It will be no different from when King John was crowned on the same spot on another twenty-fifth of May in 1189, seven hundred and thirteen years ago." Then, turning his severe gaze on David, he added, "And it is the same spot where one day you will be crowned."

David turned away to conceal his fury and embarrassment. He *hated* anyone referring to his being King at some future time. Once, when Bertie had pointed at a drawing of Edward II in a history book and said, "That'll be you when Grandpapa and Papa are dead," he had kicked him hard and then left the room. All his life David hated formality and the trappings of royalty, and from childhood dreaded what was in store for him.

But David and Bertie learned a lot from these outings, which took them by boat down the Thames to Greenwich, and in the other direction to as far distant a palace as Hampton Court.

"In one week's time your grandfather will be crowned and I trust you will be advantageously placed to watch every moment of the ceremony," said Hansell one morning.

"Yes, Mider*," said Bertie, "We know." Indeed, who did not? The stands in the Mall had been erected, already most of the decorations were complete: thousands of Union Jacks, the flags of many nations, and miles of ribbon, adorning every lamp-post and draped from almost every window. The capital was full of foreigners, from curious French and German citizens to the crowned heads of Europe.

But for once, Hansell was wrong. How could he know that in three days' time, the King would be struck down and that it would suddenly be feared that he would not survive to be crowned in Westminster Abbey?

"If Grandpapa dies will father be crowned King instead?" Bertie asked Lala as he was being put to bed. "Then David will be Prince of Wales."

Lala handed him a cup of warm milk. Well trained to suppress any signs of self-importance in her charges, Lala answered perfunctorily, "Yes, of course," and at once began to read *The Tailor of Gloucester* by Miss Beatrix Potter—"In the time of swords and periwigs and full-skirted coats . . ."

Downstairs May York** wrote to a friend in Scotland that it was just horrible in London, that the King would be operated upon tomorrow and the removal of the appendix was a very dangerous operation, and that many sufferers died un-

---

*The two boys were formally supposed to address him as "Mister" but Bertie mispronounced this as "Mider," and so it remained, to their tutor's chagrin.

**Although she was now Princess of Wales, this informal name is retained for clarity until she becomes Queen.

der the chloroform. Moreover, the King was old and not very
fit. The city, she told her, was full of relations and foreign
royalties who did not know what to do as everything was in
confusion and they did not know whether to return home or
wait until the King died or survived.

The King survived the long operation, and survived it
well. When he emerged from the effect of the chloroform,
typically his first words enquired for his son: "Where's George?"
Then he asked, "Will my people ever forgive me?" And
finally he asked for his dog and went back to sleep. Not only
did his people forgive him, but a wave of relief and adulation
swept the nation and Empire. After a brief convalescence on
board the new royal yacht *Victoria and Albert* the King was
belatedly crowned in Westminster Abbey on 9 August 1902.

The scene, as always, was one of great splendour. "Bertie
and I, dressed, I remember, in kilts, and I believe Mary, too,
watched the service from a box reserved for the Princes of
the Blood Royal . . . " Even though so many years had
passed since the last coronation, the long ceremony was
performed without a hitch, until the octogenarian Archbishop
of Canterbury, Dr Frederick Temple, stumbled as he mounted
the steps of the throne, crown in his hands. He was, however, caught by the stout figure he was about to crown, and
recovered himself.

The day of the coronation was grey and overcast, typical
of that awful summer of 1902. Worse was to follow. While
George went yachting at Cowes with the King, May took the
children up to Scotland. Besides Marlborough House in London and Frogmore in Windsor Park the following year, the
King gave his eldest son a castle on Deeside in Scotland
called Abergeldie, "I trust you will be pleased with Abergeldie,"
George wrote to May from the relatively warm south of
England. May was *not* pleased with it, not at first anyway. It
was cold and primitive, and the weather was terrible.

"Really, this weather is too depressing," May replied to
Georgie. "I feel quite in the blues & wretched . . . The
garden here is not bright & pretty yet." (This was mid-August!)

Bertie remembered the rain, too, and the cold; and his
digestion was going through one of its frequent bad phases.
He wasn't very well that summer and was often in bed, and

that always made him cross and short-tempered. But there were compensations. The castle was full of ghosts and dark passages, dungeons and deep cellars, where the children frightened one another with ghostly games. Abergeldie has a tall stone tower surmounted by a cupola infested with bats. They were told it was haunted by the ghost of Kittie Rankie, who was accused of being a witch and was burned at the stake at the top of the hill overlooking the castle.

Another, and different, excitement was going out on windy days to a foot suspension bridge that spanned the Dee. They used to race over it, making it swing even more, challenging one another and then carrying boulders to the middle and dropping them into the water . . .

Then, with the end of that summer, the family returned to York Cottage, where the flatness of East Anglia replaced the rugged, mountainous scenery of Scotland. And life became earnest again for all three older children. A room on the second floor became the schoolroom where Hansell reigned supreme and the two boys, aged eight and six, began serious lessons.

Mary's life now took a more serious turn, too. Lala was left to look after Harry alone, while a female "Finch" was appointed to take care of Mary. Else Korsukawitz was a German "plump as a sausage," good-tempered and cheerful, not at all like Mademoiselle José Dussau, her first tutor, who was a Protestant Frenchwoman.

"Mademoiselle Dussau," wrote David, "had a sharp and agile tongue, and Bertie and I were soon to suspect that she had but little use for small boys. Minor misdemeanours became crimes in her steely eyes, and all were passed on in detail to our parents. Those dreaded visits to the Library became ever more frequent."

Mary, however, grew quickly to like this new style in her own schoolroom, relishing discipline and conformity. "She began, to our surprise," David recalled, "to fall in with this prudish attitude; her threat 'I'll tell Mama,' although seldom carried out, had a powerfully subduing effect upon us."

"The Princess's life was a full one," wrote one of Mary's biographers. "She used to get up at seven o'clock, and ride either in Hyde Park when in town, or in Windsor Great Park when the Court was in residence at the Castle."

But Sandringham was her favourite for riding—there it was wonderfully free and open and you could canter for miles, sometimes breaking into a full gallop. Best of all was riding down to the sea and along the sands.

Then it was breakfast at 8.30 with Mama unlss she was away, and 9.30 to the schoolroom. French, German, geography, history. And then, at York Cottage, a break for a more unusual subject—deportment. An ex-Cameronian Highlander, Mr McCoy ("Jock" of course), came to give David, Bertie and Mary drill, marching up and down, left-right-left-right, a-bout turn. "Head back, chin in, come along now, straight as a ramrod!"

At one o'clock it would be lunch with Lala and Finch and one or two of the teachers. Sewing and painting for an hour after lunch. Then she would be free and would either ride again or go out bicycling with David and Bertie, and perhaps some cricket with Mr Hansell.

Bertie practised golf at every opportunity, *determined* to be good, and almost more important, to show Mr Hansell he was good.

> One day [one of Mary's biographers recounted] the Prince begged his sister to come and watch him make a wonderful drive, for this time he had really "got it." So off they went, and the small Prince teed up his ball with the most precise care, and settled himself down for his stroke. Three times his club hit the earth with a resounding smack, sending up the turf in every direction, but at last the ball trickled forward about a foot. The Princess, watching his tragic performance with gleeful eyes, could contain herself no longer, and cried, "Oh, Bertie *dear,* don't be so violent. You'll lose the ball if you're not careful!"

To add further weight and confirmation of the seriousness with which their father was taking the boys' education, another appointment was made to the second-floor schoolroom

—"A venerable Anglicized Frenchman," as David recalled him, "with a black beard, a bald head, and the improbable name of Gabriel Hua." Monsieur Hua was nominally appointed as Official Librarian to the Household of Their Royal Highnesses the Prince and Princess of Wales; but his first duty was to teach the boys French; just as, later, a Professor Eugen Oswald came in daily when they were in London to drum some German into their heads.

All these changes and upheavals, which left David unperturbed, had an unsettling effect on the more sensitive and insecure Bertie. And there was another reason for the unfortunate reaction of this second son to the different and more earnest life that he was now obliged to face; and it was not as funny as it may sound: it was knock-knees. This minor imperfection he had inherited from his father (his mother's legs were famed for their perfection, though not many people saw them). Along with all the other blessings of his early childhood, David had escaped knock-knees.

Sir Francis Laking, Physician-in-Ordinary and Surgeon-Apothecary to the Prince of Wales, who had saved the King's life and was regarded with awed respect for that reason alone, recommended splints to straighten Bertie's legs. "Oh, those terrible lengths of wood!" Bertie would exclaim in later life. Laking first fitted the splints in early February 1904, demonstrating to Finch at the same time, as it would be he who would be solely responsible for these correctives. A few days later, on 17 February, as Bertie got out of his bath and Finch appeared with the dreaded appliances with their leather straps that might have been made for a naval flogging frame, Bertie burst into tears and began kicking him on the shins.

Finch recognized the familiar signs of an imminent tantrum and seized him firmly and sat him on a chair. He hated the splints, too, and hated this morning and evening ritual of strapping them on. "Now, Bertie, this is not going to be forever—not like those poor boys we saw at Dr Barnado's Home for the Disabled, the ones with only one leg, walking on crutches for all their life."

"But they hurt so," Bertie complained through his tears.

"Yes, I know, and I am very sorry. But you'll get used to them after a while and then when your legs are as straight as the splints, we'll have a great bonfire up at Sandringham and *burn* them."

That prospect cheered up the boy a little, and he allowed Finch to strap them on before carrying him to his bed. The splints would remain on all night, causing discomfort rather than pain but waking him up several times, and then it was difficult to get to sleep again. During the day he had to wear them for not less than six hours.

On 26 February Bertie wrote to his mother: "This is an experiment! I am sitting in an armchair with my legs in the new splints and on a chair. I have got an invalid table, which is splendid for reading but rather awkward for writing at present." Then, with characteristic stoicism, "I expect I shall get used to it."

Alas, he did not! One evening, after Bertie had pleaded with Finch while he had his bath, and there were more tears, Finch relented. Of course, the word got back to Laking, who told Bertie's father, and Finch was ordered to the Library, just as if he had been one of the boys after a misdemeanour. When George York had listened to Finch's explanation, he stood up and drew his trousers tight against his legs, revealing his own knock-knees. "Just look at me, Mr Finch," he ordered. "If that boy grows up to look like this, it will be your fault."

But another price had to be paid for the splints. Although Hansell did not have to listen to Bertie's pleadings, he suffered the worry of seeing the boy's work deteriorate. Bertie was never at his best in the schoolroom anyway. He lacked self-confidence, becoming unnecessarily wrought up if he made a mistake or did not understand a point during a lesson. He was by no means a stupid boy but he was slow to learn to control his emotions and suffered as severely from a sense of inferiority to his brother as he did with his digestion— and the two were probably related.

"Prince Albert's early morning work is rendered almost useless by the splints," Hansell reported to the boy's father. "Practically all Prince Albert's work with me has been combined with the splints. It is now quite certain that *such a combination* is impossible . . ."

Sir Francis Laking, pleased with the results so far, relented and limited the wearing of the splints to bed at night.

The year of the splints, as it came to be known, coincided with another ordeal for Bertie. Hansell, in conformity with current thinking, decided the left-handed boy should write with his right hand. We can, then, imagine him writing to his mother awkwardly not only because of the posture forced on him by the splints, but also because, having just learned to write with his left hand, he is forcing himself to convert to right-handed writing.

1904 was also the year of the stutter. Now, whether it was caused by the strain of the splints, his poor state of health in general, or being forced to use his right hand against his natural inclination, who is to tell? It came quite suddenly and it was a very bad stutter, at once increasing his isolation and adding further weight to the burden of being different from and *inferior* to his fellows.

At the age of seven, in the robust atmosphere of York Cottage, with a father who was impatient with any defect and parsimonious with words of sympathy, a mother who was congenitally awkward with her children anyway, and a brother and sister who enjoyed a good tease and had endless fun imitating Bertie's speech, it was very hard to bear. Only Finch with unchanged expression heard him out as he laboured through what he wanted to say. And then there was Lala.

Lala saw little of her old charges now. Another boy had been born to the Yorks, on 20 December 1902—George, after his father—to join Harry in the nurseries. But she still kept track of what was going on with the older children, as her diary reveals:

> October 14th 1904. Caught sight of Bertie today & called him to me. Poor little fellow, he has developed a bad stutter to add to his burdens. But he lifted his kilt. "L-L-look at my kn-kn-knees, Lala" he said, proudly. And I clapped my hands & said, "They're lovely and straight, Bertie."

Hansell was never unkind about the boy's stammer but only just kept his exasperation in check. His reports on Bertie's work led to many confrontations with his father in the dreaded Library. Hansell's insensitivity is shown in a surviving letter to his sister at this time.

> York Cottage
> Sandringham
> Norfolk

> 15 December 1904

> My dear Gladys,

> Pheasant shooting four days a week here, and very good bags, I understand. The weather remains inclement with driving rain from the north-east. I trust that you are well and that the children flourish. Prince David makes fair progress but I am at my wits' end to know what to do about his brother. M. Hua and Dr Oswald are making no progress with French and German conversation, they tell me, and I shall have to report this to their father this week. I shall also, once again, press him to send these two older boys to a preparatory school, where they will benefit from mixing with other boys and the competition in the class and on the playing field. But previously the Prince of Wales has been adamant that they should have exactly the same upbringing as he had—"Nothing wrong with my education under Dr Dalton," he will say.

> Your affectionate brother,
> (signed) Henry

French and German conversation indeed! It was hard enough for Bertie to speak in his mother tongue . . .

Bertie's temperament, setbacks and misfortunes made him difficult to educate. In the singular and testing environment of a royal household with only the family and staff for company, conversation and example, the odds were even more heavily loaded against a boy of unusual sensitivity who *rarely felt completely well*. "Driven in upon himself," wrote one of his biographers, "he alternated between periods of dreamy abstraction, during which it seemed impossible to command his concentration, and outbursts of emotional excitement, sometimes of high spirits and exuberance, sometimes of passionate weeping and depression."

Two of Bertie's characteristics saved him during this very difficult childhood—his courage and his essential niceness. Of all George and May's children, Bertie was blessed with the sweetest temperament: perhaps in that extraordinary household only Lala had the perception to recognize Bertie's qualities, by contrast with the charm and good looks which clothed the more feckless and less steady elder brother.

7

Their biographers have tended to deny that George and May were cold and distant with their children. Certainly their intentions were of the best, but . . . George, soon to become George V, is not a difficult character to sum up; a pure Victorian, unimaginative, inflexible in his views, a good-natured soul, "without too much up top" as the contemporary phrase had it. George did not understand, any more than he approved, much that went on about him, and he certainly no more understood young children than the movement of a ballet, if he ever saw one; and his children feared him, as he intended, especially when he fell into one of his irrational rages.

It is more difficult to understand May York: fastidious, shy and unconfident, blessed with an artistic eye, which led to the cheering-up of all her homes and gardens, and as inhibited as her husband, who loved her and totally relied upon her. Queen Victoria's eldest daughter, the Empress Frederick, wrote of May that she "does not seem to have the passionate tenderness for her little ones wh. seems so natural to me. She has something very cold and stiff—& distant in her manner—each time one sees her again one has to break the ice afresh . . ."

For all their good intentions, and by contrast with George's mother and father, George and May were not good parents and in their relationship with their children they were as distant as the moon from the attitudes taught by Dr Spock after the Second World War. "There is no doubt," wrote one of David's biographers, "that King George and Queen Mary failed in their relationships with their children and were for different reasons temperamentally unsuited to parenthood." It was not that they did not *like* children, for they played naturally and uninhibitedly with other people's children. They just never got the hang of parenthood; probably the father failed to recognize this unhappy truth but it is, sadly, true that their mother did, and felt her failure badly.

The greatest sufferer from this state of affairs was not the family's first victim of misfortune, Bertie, but David. Bertie exasperated his father, who was often highly critical of him; but in David his father experienced a growing failure of trust, and that was much worse.

While their grandfather was alive, he continued to play the vital patriarchal role in the lives of George and May's children. "In my gallery of childhood memories, the portrait of my grandfather seems bathed in perpetual sunlight," David wrote. "He was in his sixties, in the twilight of his life, when his personality began to mean something to me," he recalled of these years of Edward VII's reign. "Few men could match his vitality, his sheer *joie de vivre* . . . And while I can remember him, of course, as the regal figure of solemn ceremonies, I like best to recall him presiding over a well-laden table or making gallant gestures towards beautiful women."

Even under the heavy pressures of his office, the King could always spare time for his grandchildren, whom he adored indiscriminately, accepting Bertie's stutter and Mary's self-righteousness with seeming indifference. There was nothing these three eldest children enjoyed more when staying at York Cottage, than receiving a message that they would be welcome at the Big House up the drive. There they would be hugged in turn by Alix—all softness and sweet scent—and by the King—aroma of cigars and brandy and a beard softer and fuller than their father's. Then chatter and laughter and games.

The burdens of a monarch are infinitely greater than those of a Prince of Wales—especially one who had for so many years been excluded from state business (and almost all other business) by his mother; but whenever the King and Queen were at Sandringham (every arrival shortly followed by the rattle of gunfire as the master of the house and his numerous guests set about shooting pheasant, woodcock and other game) the children's hearts lifted. At least once a day and often twice, they would be called to the Big House, and Hansell and the other tutors knew that there would be no more work that day.

In retrospect, childhood tends to form into neat sections like the chapters of an autobiography. For David and Bertie, the first weeks of the year 1906 marked the opening of a new and memorable chapter. It was one in which, for the first time, they became more fully aware of a world outside their own—a world beyond the sea of faces, the waving crowds, the flags and bunting which was all that they had known up to that time.

Once, a year or two earlier, Hansell had organized football games with the boys from local villages, but these boys were so much in awe of the two young Princes, and so fearful of kicking them, that the games were a terrible, even ridiculous, failure. After that, the gulf between palace and people seemed wider than ever, and David and Bertie felt more rather than less isolated. If ever proof were needed of their specialness and the destiny that faced them, these games provided it, and they were never to forget them.

But now, suddenly, the world of politics, of conflict over national issues, could no longer be excluded from the schoolroom at York Cottage, Sandringham, Norfolk. And, coincidentally, David was to make his first tentative steps from that schoolroom towards the hurly-burly, the discomforts and pleasures of life outside the walls of Sandringham and Marlborough House, Abergeldie and Frogmore.

The first reason for all this was the General Election of 1906, the most important and far-reaching in its consequences for many years, making it a memorable one for the two elder Princes.

It all began on a wet Monday in November 1905, with their parents six thousand miles away under the burning sun of "the jewel in the crown"—India. Hansell entered the schoolroom, promptly at nine o'clock as always, with a newspaper under his arm, pipe clenched between his teeth, and for the first time began his first lesson with current affairs as the subject. He had obviously prepared his words carefully.

"Today England is on the brink of a most important election to decide which party shall govern our country," he said. "There is a great restlessness amongst the people. Our early defeats in the Boer War when you were both very young left a lot of our people dissatisfied with the running of the Army, and more recently certain sections of the people have become dissatisfied with the continuing gulf that separates the rich and the poor. They think that more should be done to relieve the lot of those who are very poor or sick or cannot find work.

"It is not my business to give you my personal opinion about all this. But you are now old enough to be taught to understand how our democracy works."

Mr Hansell placed his pipe on his desk and made his way to the boys' desks, unfolding the newspaper on the way. "Now I want you to look at this carefully." He then opened the paper to show them a page depicting the leaders of the two main political parties in an attitude of climbing a ladder, neither the Conservative Party leader, Mr Balfour, nor the Liberal Party leader, Mr Campbell-Bannerman, looking very dignified.

"What you must do is to cut out these two ladders and these two men, as instructed, and pin them to the back of the door. When the results from each constituency are known, you must move the winning party's leader up his ladder. The first to reach the top will be invited to Buckingham Palace and asked to form the next government."

He turned to David. "You, as the elder boy, have first choice." (It was always the same—David first as the elder.) He chose the more cheerful-looking figure, which happened to be Campbell-Bannerman, while Bertie automatically backed the Conservative Balfour—a coincidental presage of their adult political prejudices.

When the first results were announced, David, in the shape of Campbell-Bannerman, at once went into the lead. With a weary feeling of inevitability, Bertie watched day by day as the gap widened, and the landslide Liberal victory left Mr Balfour only halfway up the ladder. Always second, *always* second! Sometimes he felt like kicking his brother; sometimes he did so!

Hansell tried to cheer Bertie up as he surveyed the final result, with Mr Campbell-Bannerman, covered in pin holes, peering down from the top of the ladder. "As he removed the dirty, torn pieces of paper from the schoolroom door," David the winner wrote, "he remarked philosophically that, while some people would no doubt regard the results as disastrous, he was confident that the good sense of the British nation would in the end prevail against the wild policies of such extremists as Mr Lloyd George."

Bertie was not too sure about that. He had overheard many hostile remarks about that extreme radical, the Welshman Lloyd George. But worse still, he had been told, was Winston Churchill, "turncoat and traitor to his class", who had crossed the floor of the House of Commons to join the Liberals.

The defeat of Bertie's Mr Balfour was offset to some extent by a great naval occasion the following month. In Bertie's eyes, the Royal Navy was goodness, strength and patriotism, far from the petty bickering of party politics. There were no turncoats or traitors in the Navy.

Both Hansell and Finch had told the boys about the greatest battleship in the world being built at Portsmouth: more than twice as many big guns as any other, the fastest in the world, too. It was as well that both David and Bertie were keen on the Navy, because, with the inevitability of the tide, they were both going into it, just like their father, and his dead elder brother, and Great-uncle Alfred, who became an admiral before he died. And it was appropriate that the first whiff of salt air entered their schoolroom in the year of the *Dreadnought*'s launch, and completion.

David and Bertie confessed to one another that they dreaded the return from India of their parents. One reason was the inevitable tightening of the screw of their schoolroom discipline. Mr Hansell had warned them that their father would enquire especially closely into their mathematics. "You need good mathematics, algebra and geometry to get through your naval examinations," he told them. Unfortunately, Mr Hansell was not a natural teacher of mathematics, and in the parents' absence there was a grave loss of schoolroom hours anyway—for the usual reason: too much time spent at the Big House. And poor Mr Hansell was not in a position to remonstrate with the King-Emperor on that subject.

8

The homecoming of George and May was all pleasure for Mary and Harry. For Bertie there was also a good deal of apprehension. Before leaving York Cottage, Lala had offered him a word of warning, with the best intentions in the world for the boy she loved. "You must be prepared for your Mama and Papa to be very dark when you first meet them," she had said. "They have been in the tropics such a long time."

This had set Bertie's mind racing anxiously. "Very dark," Lala had said; and Bertie, when alone, searched the school-room shelves for Helen Bannerman's story *Little Black Sambo*. Was that really how Mama and Papa were going to look? Bertie, then, was especially quiet as he stood on the Hard at Portsmouth in his sailor suit with his sister and brothers, and Finch and Hansell and Lala, and a score or more of close relations.

It was, however, a perfect May day, and Bertie's heart lifted as the great white battleship *Renown* came into sight. (That would be the next model he would make after the *Dreadnought*— HMS *Renown*.) All the men o'war in sight were manned and dressed, and as their party descended to the shining teak and brass barge, the guns of the forts boomed out their salute. Ten minutes later they were alongside the hove-to battleship, the barge scarcely moving against the ship's gangway as they disembarked and made their way up the ladder.

Bertie felt sick with anxiety. Then he saw his mother in a long white fur-trimmed coat, wide white hat and veil, standing beside his father. His father looked no more than a little sun-tanned, his mother as pale as her coat and hat. What had Lala meant? No embracing welcome, of course; Bertie had not expected that, and he gave a little bow as he took first his mother's gloved hand and then his father's. "Well, you have grown!"—"How are you, little Harry?"—"What a lovely day to meet you all again!"—"How are Grandpapa and Grandmama?"

The greetings were scarcely over when their father took David and Bertie aside and, in a severe voice, said "And how are the lessons going? I hope that Hansell has been keeping you up to the mark and that you have been diligent." They paced along the scrubbed white deck, ratings standing to attention as they passed. Bertie felt the slight vibration as the engines' revolutions were increased and the battleship gathered speed for the last two miles of its long journey. The ladies, talking a little way away, held their hats against the breeze of motion.

"It is only a year before I hope you, David, will be going to Osborne Naval College," continued their father relentlessly. "As you know, mathematics is the most important subject in the Royal Navy. They do not care a fig for Latin or Greek or any of those ridiculous dead languages. So I have prepared some written questions which I will give you in the train to London, and I would like you both to answer them by the end of the week-end. Is that clear?"

"Yes, Papa."
"Yes, Papa."

Although he had recently joined his brothers in the schoolroom, Harry, at six years, was not subject to the severe questioning and testing by his father after the family reunion. At this time—summer 1906—"little Harry" was undersized, although he was later to grow to be the tallest in the family. The fact that he had two younger brothers is a sad contradiction of his

mother's intentions. On 11 April 1900 May had written to her
Aunt Augusta eleven days after Harry's birth: "I think I have
done my duty & may now *stop*, as having babies is highly
distasteful to me tho' when once they are there they are very
nice! The children are so pleased with the baby who they
think flew in at my window & had to have his wings cut off!"

The next month, on 17 May 1900, the old Queen again
stood as godmother to the latest Georgie-May child, record-
ing in her journal that "he is a very pretty little boy." She
also recorded his somewhat doom-laden names of Henry,
after her recently deceased son-in-law Prince Henry of
Battenberg; William to honour her grandson, the Kaiser, who
was to set Europe ablaze in fourteen years' time; Frederick
after the Field-Marshal Lord Roberts, hero of recent wars;
and Albert, her late husband, whose very name was synonymous with dark tragedy.

Harry, however, appeared not to be overcome with misery over this and grew up a cheerful boy, "high-spirited and
vigorous," wrote his biographer; but, like Bertie, he "showed
serious signs of nervous tension." In these early years he also
showed signs of precarious health and remained undersized
until puberty, although—unlike Bertie—he was given all the
necessary nourishment, care and attention in his nursery
years.

Harry, like Bertie before him, attracted the special concern of Lala, still in command of nursery matters. But Lala
also noted an inexplicable degree of concern for Harry by his
father, by contrast with his seeming indifference to the well-
being of his older boys. Shortly before the parents went off
on their second long tour, Lala noted in her journal.

October 12th 1905

It is so good to see how much interest in the health
of little Harry HRH shows. He comes quite frequently to my nursery to enquire how he is &
whether I am giving him the right food. I do not
take offence at these enquiries, although others might
under similar circumstances, because it is so heart-
ening to have his support and interest in the care I

endeavour to lavish on the little palefaced fellow. If
only he had shown the same interest in the care of
Bertie during those dreadful early months in his
life! Still, better later than never.

Later, and some time after the conclusion of the visit to
India, there is proof of George York's continuing concern for
the welfare and health of his third son. After learning that
Hansell had taken Harry out, in spite of the very cold Norfolk
weather, which had led to a touch of flu, he wrote to him (5
February 1909): "You must remember that he is rather fragile
& must be treated differently to his two elder brothers who
are more robust."

All this reflects the influence of George's naval upbringing and experience, which taught that a severe and inflexible
discipline must be applied to a young sailor's training, matched
by an equally deep concern for the disadvantaged and disabled.

David, separated by almost six years from Harry, saw
little of him. " I was fond of him," he wrote later, "but was
naturally much closer to Bertie at that time. If there were any
rough games, Harry kept well out of the way, naturally
enough. I was distantly aware that he was often ill, but then
so was Bertie—Mary and I were the fit ones—and it did not
seem to bother him very much. It was not that Bertie was
braver than Harry—I don't think either of them knew the
meaning of fear—but Harry became used to being cosseted
because of his delicacy, and no one ever cosseted Bertie."

Harry's father knew all too well how much stamina was
needed to survive training for the Royal Navy. A severe
attack of flu, with its after-effects on one of Harry's lungs,
decided George York that his third son should not have to
suffer the ordeal of naval training—May seems to have had
little or no say in the fate of any of her children. Another
letter from Hansell to his sister records the royal decision on
the future of Harry, and his own reaction to it:

Marlborough House
London S. W.

18 April 1910

My dear Gladys,

You will recall that in my last letter I told you that
Prince Harry has been at Broadstairs convalescing
from influenza at the country residence of Sir Francis Laking, who saved the life of our beloved King.
He is being looked after by Sister Edith Ward, and
the Prince tells me that he is not behaving very
well and that he needs the discipline of a *school!*

You know how earnestly I have endeavoured
to persuade HRH of the benefit a preparatory school
life could offer the Princes, and though I failed in
the cases of Princes David and Albert, it is possible
that my earlier efforts may have helped to persuade
HRH that this would be the best arrangement for
his less sturdy third son.

Sir Francis Laking certainly believes that a
preparatory school is preferable to a rough naval
training. So Prince Harry is to attend St Peter's
Court School in Broadstairs, the headmaster being
my old friend Mr Alan Richardson. Is that not
splendid? Now I can give all my time to Prince
George and Prince John—though there is little I
can do with the latter, alas!

Your affectionate brother,
(signed) Henry

9

Prince George and Prince John were two more of George and May's "mistakes," born long after May had declared she would have *no more* and George had declared that he was "raising not a family but a regiment." Prince John, the younger of this pair, was born on 12 July 1905, three months before his mother and father departed on their tour to India and Burma. Early press pictures show a fine, lusty infant lying upon a cushion, and Lala especially was proud of him, declaring him to be the most beautiful of all the children.

By the time his mother and father returned from the East, John was showing worrying signs of abnormality. He was a most engaging boy, but somewhere in his genes was concealed the mental instability of the Hanovers, which had previously affected, to a greater or lesser degree, several of Queen Victoria and Prince Albert's children and grandchildren, most notably Prince Albert Victor. Traces of it were to be found in both Bertie and Harry, manifested in outbursts of temper or despair, with weeping or hysterical laughter. In adult life, these sons succeeded in controlling the worst extremes, but, like their father, they were always liable to lose their tempers too readily.

Bertie's official biographer, John Wheeler-Bennett, has

written of how easily rebuffed he was and "prone to take his
weaknesses and mistakes too seriously," which found expression in "acute depression or in outbreaks of anger." His
failure to master the simplest mathematics would lead to his
being seized with despair. When "problem after problem
resisted his efforts to solve them, he would ultimately dissolve into angry tears." A few years later we find references
to the "squalls of temper which . . . left him exhausted in
both mind and body."

Prince John grew to be a beautiful little boy, whose
mental disability, related to epilepsy, only made him more
loved and cherished by those about him, including his older
brothers and sister. Hansell did what he could with the boy
in the schoolroom but eventually it was recognized that he
was seriously holding back his brother. Moreover, like his
distant forebear, King John, he suffered from epilepsy, and
the fits became more alarming as he grew older.

By contrast, Prince George caused his mother and father
the fewest anxieties of all their children: as good-looking as
David, brighter and much more robust than Bertie or Harry,
George was as near a complete success from the start as any
boy can reasonably expect to be. Laziness was his one failing,
but he was sensible enough to recognize this weakness and
pull himself up by his bootstraps when necessary.

David wrote of this time when his lifelong friendship
with George was already maturing, "I found in his character
qualities that were akin to my own; we laughed at the same
things. That winter we became more than brothers—we became close friends."

Of Mary, at the time of her tenth birthday on 25 April 1907,
we catch glimpses from her own accounts in later life, in her
father's journal and in letters, diaries and reminiscences of
her contemporaries. She is clearly still a tomboy, and glorying in it, though shy in adult company outside her immediate
family. She loves every activity that tests her eye and her
strength, and is already a fair tennis player and an accomplished swimmer.

Above all, Mary loved riding—"her chief open-air delight." She had been given a donkey called Ben when she was six and she doted on him. Molly followed, then others, and her father at once recognized that she would make a first-rate horsewoman, better than her elder brothers, as they were the first to agree. "Loving horses, she rode better than Bertie or I; her yellow curls concealed a fearlessness that commanded our respect."

Some time before the special bond was struck between David and George, "the three musketeers," as they called themselves, formed a very close relationship. "In the country, and especially at Sandringham, Mary, Bertie and I were never at a loss for something to do," David recalled. "The happiest hours were those in which we three were left to our own resources. Mary was our close companion in many of our activities . . . Mary could at times be quite a 'Tomboy'; but at others, supported by her formidable 'Mademoiselle,' she wielded a sweet tyranny over our lives."

At ten Mary grew her russet-gold hair to shoulder length. Never was the "crowning glory" cliché truer; for the prettiness of infancy had not lasted and her face though "amiable and pleasing" (as a contemporary noted), had become less good-looking than her brothers'. As one newspaper referred to her, "She was the woman with the plain face and warm heart."

Herbert Asquith (shortly to become Prime Minister) wrote of Mary at this time, "She has that shy, girlish charm which leaves one with an impression of nervous pleasure and fatherly respect." She did, indeed, respect her father, but Mary did not go in daily fear of him as David and Bertie did. Their father did not believe that girls needed the same firm hand as boys, and besides he doted on his only daughter and loved her company. What Mary really lacked was the company of girls of her own age. Days, sometimes weeks, would pass when she saw no girls at all and the only women she saw were her tutors and the female members of the staff. She was probably closest to her personal maid, Else, in whom she confided her most secret thoughts.

Many years later, Else was quoted as saying: "When there was no one else present we would talk to one another as sisters. She told me everything—people she liked and disliked and why, all about her brothers, even about her father and mother—how she loved them and how she thought it a shame that Prince David and Prince Albert did not seem to love them as much as she did, in fact did not seem to love them at all. And I would tell her, when asked, what it was like to be sixteen, what happened to your body, and all that. But she never asked me what went on downstairs or anything about the other servants."

Mary, when grown-up and a married woman, spoke fondly of Else. "She was an unusually intelligent and perceptive girl, absolutely discreet, so that I felt I could tell her my most important thoughts. It was a great relief to have her. I could talk to her about things I could never say to Mlle Bricka or Mlle Dussau."

One of Mary's biographers draws attention to an unexpected talent: "Mary grew up very like her mother, whose rather low-pitched voice she inherited: Dame Nellie Melba thought the Princess might have developed as a concert mezzo-soprano but for the restraints imposed by the blood royal. Edward and Albert had different views on the subject, and when Mary took singing lessons from a Mr Hutchinson they lurked beneath the music-room window at Frogmore giving 'quite a passing imitation of the midnight serenades of a tom-cat.' "

Mary was educated entirely at home, in spite of the many arguments put to her mother and father in favour of her going away to school. The first of the children to face the outside world, three years before Harry was sent to St Peter's Court, was David. The results of their father's tests of David and Bertie's mathematics were all that the two boys feared. "One of the questions was the average weight of the stags Papa had killed at Balmoral during the previous stalking season," Bertie recalled. "These were recorded carefully in his game book, and David and I had to look up this total, which was not small, and was recorded in pounds, stones and hundredweight, add them up and divide by the total number."

David, recalling this minor nightmare in his memoirs, wrote, "The problem was more complicated than it sounds but my father maintained that *anybody* over ten years old should be able to solve so simple a problem; but on returning to the schoolroom Bertie and I found that we had been given a task of brain-racking complexity."

The boys never found the answer, but their father's answer to this failure was to engage a special mathematics master, Mr Martin S. David of Tonbridge School, who worked quite compatibly with Hansell. He went right back to the basics of figure work and soon brought them up to a reasonable level, though not yet high enough to pass the naval examination.

There are two unexplained mysteries about the future George V's attitude to his elder boys' education. The first is why he did not discover earlier the inadequacy of Hansell's powers as a teacher—and not just in mathematics. "I do not wish to be critical of Mr Hansell," David noted, "but on looking back over those five curiously ineffectual years under him, I am appalled to discover how little I really learned . . . Although I was in his care on and off for more than twelve years, I am today unable to recall anything brilliant or original that he ever said."

The second mystery is why he held so stubbornly to his decision that they should share his own sailor's education, because he began to see, when he became Prince of Wales, how hopelessly inadequate it was for a future monarch.

As his official biographer wrote:

He was well aware that his education as a sailor had ill fitted him for many of his new responsibilities. It had been only during his father's reign, nine swiftly moving years, that . . . he had done something to repair the gaps in his knowledge of English and Constitutional History and to attain the normal educational standards of the average public school boy at the leaving age. These gaps had not yet been repaired, that standard not reached when he came to the Throne . . . He was still methodically plodding on with his education when his reign was half over.

So it seems inexplicable that just at this time, when he was
becoming aware of his sons' poverty of knowledge and at-
tempting belatedly to correct his own, he should launch them
both into the same narrow seas of a naval education which he
had navigated so fruitlessly himself. Nevertheless, he stuck to
the bigoted view: "My brother and I never went to a preparatory school; the Navy will teach David all that he needs to
know."

Fortunately their new teacher was brilliant and introduced enough mathematics into David's mind to ensure that
(helped a little by his rank?) he passed his preliminary examinations well enough, with the consequences that his father
wrote exultantly in his diary (18 February 1907): "David went
up before a Committee and was examined to see if the
Admiralty would give him a nomination for the Navy. I am
glad to say that he did remarkably well, they said he is the
best boy they had examined, which is very gratifying."

Picture, then, this thirteen-year-old, in blue round jacket
with brass buttons and cadet's white collar tab and naval cap,
climbing into the black royal Daimler outside Marlborough
House on a sunny May day, with his father. He has said
goodbye to Bertie, who is suitably impressed with the uniform, and to his mother, who goes so far as to take him in her
arms and wish him success and happiness. The Daimler
moves out into the Mall, heading for Waterloo Station, while
in the dark privacy of the motor, the cadet—to his shame and
chagrin—bursts into tears.

"In the train," David recalled, "my father calmed me
with stories of his early naval life. Steaming down Spithead to
Cowes he fell silent. Then, just before the Admiralty yacht
touched the dock, he said, 'Now that you are leaving home,
David, and going out into the world, always remember that I
am your best friend.' "

David had none of the advantages of an accompanying tutor
and brother, which his father had enjoyed: he was alone, he
was "a pampered royal," he was small, pretty and vulnerable.
A contemporary who rose high in the service recalled David's
arrival, escorted by the Prince of Wales.

"When we arrived back from leave, the new termers were already there—they were always given two days start 'to find their sea legs'—although the sea was no more than a splash of grey-blue in the distance. Just as soon as we found out who this new termer was, we seniors ensured that he had a bad time.

"Looking back on it now, I do see that we were nothing better than a pack of hounds. But it had long been a tradition to give all new termers a miserable time to show them their place—and also, incidentally, prepare them for the gunroom where they would later find themselves, under a regime that made Osborne seem like a tea party."

Osborne Naval College was a collection of tatty buildings run up around the stable blocks of the house, which had been neglected since the death of the old Queen. The living quarters and lecture halls alike were cold and austere, and set about the main hall. This was called "Nelson" and carried his motto "There is nothing the Navy cannot do" in gigantic brass letters on its main oak cross-beam.

The first taste for David of what he was in for was to have his fair hair forcibly dyed. "I was cornered by my betters," David wrote, "and made to stand at attention while one of them poured a bottle of red ink over my head. The ink dropped down my neck, ruining one of the few white shirts I possessed; a moment later the bugle sounded for quarters, and the sixth termers dashed away to fall in their ranks." Having read of the dire consequences of "sneaking," David took the full consequences without making excuses.

The hardening process was difficult to bear, and it was greatly to his credit that David, without any knowledge of what was likely to happen to him, bore the ordeal very well. "I watched him at this time," wrote a future friend, "and I could see what he was going through even if I could only imagine what the contrast must have been with his previous life."

David himself wrote in general terms of this time:

At first it seemed especially hard, because I was caught up, without the previous experience of school, in the unfamiliar community life of small boys, with

all its fierce and subtle relationships. Formerly I
had had Finch to take care of my clothes and pick
up after me; I now had to look out for myself. And
from the comfortable rooms of our different homes
I found myself thrust, in company with some thirty
other boys, into a long, bare dormitory. The orbit
of my living shrank to a hard, iron bed and a
black-and-white sea chest with three compartments
in which to keep my clothes, a tray, and a private
till.

Another future admiral, who knew even at the time that his
own mind was being narrowed, his sensitivity and physical
endurance hardened, while his instinct to question was being
stunted, recalled those days in 1907:

> We were taught that there were only two ways
> of doing anything: the Navy way, which was consis-
> tently right, and the non-Navy way, which was as
> invariably wrong. No deviation was countenanced.
> We were being made into stereotypes, just as our
> predecessors (who had in turn condemned the in-
> troduction of the steam engine, the high explosive
> shell, the breech-loader, the torpedo and of course
> the submarine) had been rigidly trained not to think.
> All experimentation was damned, and poor Ad-
> miral Tryon, who fourteen years earlier had lost his
> flagship and his life in a collision playing fancy
> tricks on manoeuvres, was cited as the victim of his
> own dangerous experimentation. Leaving subordin-
> ates to use their initiative indeed!
> Mathematics, science, navigation and engineer-
> ing—that was all. No Latin, no logic, no geography
> (though we were to cruise the world), and no his-
> tory not even naval history.
> And this was at a time when the Royal Navy
> was supposed to be experiencing the greatest re-
> forms of all time, under the firm and steady hand of
> "Jackie" Fisher, the great modernising admiral.

End of second term: faithful Finch was standing on the Hard
at Portsmouth. David caught a glimpse of him from the ferry
and waved. At once a cadet captain behind him spoke sharply:
"Cadets do not wave. Nor do gentlemen *wave*, you common
fellow." Finch did not wave back, not because he did not
wish to be thought "common" but because it was quite impossible to identify one uniformed cadet from another among
those massed at the prow of the paddle boat.

But the pleasure and excitement were only delayed by a
few minutes. Never mind cadet captains, never mind that in
three weeks David would be returning to the prison of Osborne, never mind that the mid-morning sky was dark grey
and an easterly sleet was driving across the harbour. He was
beside Finch, who had meant security and kindness and
understanding for as long as he could remember, wearing
the long beautifully cut tweed coat he had been given by the
family, which was reputed to have once belonged to the
unfortunate Duke of Clarence.

The handshake was formal: the eyes of man and boy said
all that there was to say, and they walked towards the railway
station, Finch's height causing David to appear even more
diminutive than his five feet three inches.* Still without more
than a formal word of greeting, Finch led the way to the
first-class compartment reserved exclusively for them, a sign
of the return to privilege and comfort.

The train moved off without delay, the sleet beating at
the windows, through the great naval city, pavements thronged
with sailors, some with a woman on an arm. The smoke blew
horizontally from factory chimneys and a thousand chimney
pots, the electric trams fought their way through the wet and
the horse traffic like tramp steamers through the crowded
Dover Straits.

"I know what you're looking forward to best, Master
David."

"And what's that, Finch? Food?"

They both laughed. This was just as it ought to be, and
as David had dreamed it would be. The steam heat in the
compartment was full on and David discarded his blue rain-

*He eventually grew to five feet seven inches.

coat, which Finch automatically took from him, folded, and placed on the rack above.

"What do you think it will be for dinner tonight?"

Finch had no idea but at once trotted out the menu, finger-against-finger enumerating the courses, each one a known David favourite: "Thick fish soup . . . roast woodcock with thick rich gravy . . . ," ending with, "and a full box of chocolates open in front of you."

David laughed and smacked his lips. "Do you know, Finch, the food is sometimes so terrible I can't eat it in case I'm sick. One day when I was nearly faint with hunger and had been playing rugby all afternoon, I remembered that I had had a perfectly splendid meal in the sick bay when a cut was being bandaged. So I pretended I was terribly ill and went to see Matron. She jolly soon saw through my wheeze and called me a 'malingerer.' "

"So she threw you out—quite right, too." But Finch was smiling.

"She was going to, but I started blubbing—wasn't that awful? And I think I said something like, 'All I want's some good food . . .' And, do you know, Finch, she was so grand that she cooked me a plate of buttered eggs, and I had fresh bread and jam, too."

Finch stood up and looked out of the window. They were speeding through the Sussex countryside and the sleet had turned to snow, which was already lying on the lines of the plough furrows. "All this talk about food makes me hungry. Perhaps I can persuade you to take luncheon," he suggested with a smile. "Who is to know, there might be woodcock on the dining-car menu."

10

Finch and his charge finally reached Wolferton as dusk was closing about the Sandringham estate. It was snowing heavily, covering the carriage wheel marks across the station yard before Ben pulled up the horses as Finch and David emerged. "Good evening, Sir. Good evening, Mr Finch." Then to David again, "Looks as if we might have a white Christmas, Sir."

"I hope so. Could you fetch out the toboggans first thing tomorrow, Ben?"

As he stepped into the hall of York Cottage, David felt like some returning naval hero hot from an engagement instead of a roughly handled second-term cadet. All those familiar smiling faces; all that chatter and laughter. He felt like crying but managed to restrain himself and "behave like a proper grown-up," as Finch had suggested. Mary, Harry, Bertie (not looking very well), George (five tomorrow and shouting loudest) and little John, two and a half but still in Lala's arms. Lala herself, plump darling face all smiles. And Mama, in long sky-blue silk dress, trimmed with white sequins, stepping forward to greet her eldest son, a brief cold touch of her cheek, but her expression and voice warmer: "Welcome home, David. And a happy Christmas."

And lastly, Papa, emerging from his study, a cigarette between his lips, the newspaper under his arm. "Ah, the prodigal son—back in his home port!" His family greeting invariably sounded a facetious note. David shook his hand and after answering a few routine questions about his journey by train and across London, carried out his dreaded duty of handing over the term's report. "As soon as the affectionate homecoming salutations were disposed of," David later wrote in his memoirs, "I handed the fateful envelope to my father, who, evincing no immediate interest in its contents, put it casually in his pocket."

David had calculated that, firstly, it might not be such a bad report after all; in fact he thought he had done rather well, and, secondly, if he was going to be summoned to the Study it would be after dinner. Dinner came and went, Mary was especially merry and had to be silenced; Bertie cheered up after eating his specially prepared mild meal that looked to David like bread and milk; Harry, allowed up for dinner for only the second time, ate in awed silence; the lady-in-waiting, Lady Airlie, told a long and, to David, completely unfunny story about a maiden aunt. And they all had just one Charbonnel & Walker chocolate. But still, not bad.

The summons never came. "What a relief!" he said to Finch when he came into the boys' room to say goodnight. Finch was looking relieved, too. But, as David described the following morning:

> Finch appeared with a long face and a chilling summons to the Library: and a minute later those red, cloth-covered walls witnessed a painful scene. My father looked me in the eye. "David," he said, "I am sorry to have to tell you that you have a bad report. Read it."
>
> It was a curt, cruel document that bore no relation whatever to my own appraisal of my efforts. The sad fact was that mathematics, that spectre of Mr David's tutoring, had in all its hideous aspects pursued me to Osborne. My father's remedy for this crisis was to engage a master from Osborne; and, as soon as the Christmas festivities were over,

I buckled down to work, forgoing in the interest of
my survival a great part of my leave.

In January 1909, a little more than a year from that unhappy
time when his elder brother spent the greater part of his
holiday time "swotting maths" instead of skating on the lake,
tobogganing and hurling snowballs, Bertie faced the same
ordeal David had endured as a first termer at Osborne.
Knowing that Bertie was destined for the college, too, David
had spared him some of the details of his own sufferings, but
Bertie had a pretty good idea that he faced a black future.

His mother, on the other hand, was less concerned
about Bertie's departure for the rough and tumble of the
outside world than she had been for David. "I am pleased
with Bertie," May mentioned to Lady Mary Coke on one
evening between Christmas and the New Year in 1908. They
were at Marlborough House in London for a state luncheon
at Buckingham Palace the next day. "I think he is showing
real promise."

"Why do you say that?" her lady-in-waiting asked. "You
have so often said that Bertie is handicapped by bad health
and a less bright mind than David."

May put aside her embroidery and poured out more
coffee. "My poor Bertie is tortured by indecision, self-doubt,
a temper, and his terrible stammer. He will grow out of them
all given time. And he knows how to *knuckle down* and fight
his deficiencies," she added with emphasis. "He does not
look it, but Bertie is a *fighter*, while dear David seeks the
easy way out. Just look at how Bertie has knuckled down and
fought to improve his mathematics . . ."

Bertie's standards of mathematics had been even lower
than his brother's, and in spite of Mr David's heroic efforts, it
had seemed, only six months ago, that even the most lenient
examining board must fail him for the Navy. This is how one
of Bertie's biographers described his mathematics in 1908:
"He seemed unable to master its fundamentals, and its intri-
cacies evaded his comprehension altogether. Moreover, he
loathed the subject, yet was keenly conscious and somewhat
ashamed of his weakness in it. Despair would seize hold of

him as problem after problem resisted his efforts to solve them and he would ultimately dissolve into angry tears."

Earlier, his father had taken him to task for not applying himself to his work. "You must really give up losing your temper when you make a mistake in a sum. We all make mistakes sometimes, remember now you are nearly twelve years old and ought no longer to behave like a little child of six."

But ominous though his prospects looked, it was in this twelfth year that Bertie for the first time showed his true colours, and those near to him recognized the development. Lala was the first to see the change; she, after all, was the closest to him.

> Poor Bertie got into a terrible pet this morning [she wrote in her journal for 20 April 1908]. David said he burst into tears, kicking his desk and crying out against the cruelty of life and how he hated everybody and couldn't understand a thing. He came to see me in the afternoon complaining that his stomach hurt and he felt as if he was going to be sick. I gave him some of the usual pink medicine and we had one of our little chats. I asked him about the scene in the schoolroom, which he shares with Harry now, and he burst into tears again. But it was shame now, not anger, this time. "Oh Lala, what shall I do?" And then before I could answer, he answered himself. "I've got to pull myself together," he said in a very grown-up way, not stuttering at all, the dear boy. "I'm going to get through that examination, Lala, you watch me." And then we laughed and I hugged him before he went off for his tea. All's well that ends well, I told him.

Bertie's biographer writes of his "developing pertinacity" at this same time; and Finch recognized a new Bertie emerging from the chrysalis of childhood. Somehow he drove himself to understand the fundamentals of arithmetic, even picked up the meaning of "x" in algebra and contrived to shape in his mind the isosceles triangle for his elementary geometry.

On 5 November 1908 this pale-faced little boy, who had so little presence and no knowledge or experience of the world outside, who could scarcely articulate to a stranger and carried for all to see the marks of undeveloped confidence and self-belief, dressed in the morning for the Royal Navy's Examining Board. It was Finch who gave his shoes a last polish, who straightened his broad white collar and with an affectionate smile handed him a clean handkerchief. "That's for blowing your nose not for blubbing into. Any of that nonsense before you go in, Master Bertie, and the admiral will know it at once."

Bertie smiled, rather stiffly, "I'll do my best, Finch."

"Of course you will. Like the music hall song, 'You'll knock 'em in the Old Kent Road.'" And Finch believed it, for he, above anyone, knew the strength that burned within the body of this boy.

At five minutes to eleven that morning, Bertie was waiting in an annexe to the office on the first floor of the Admiralty in Whitehall. There was the sharp smell of polish in the air, and the naval paintings of desperate engagements hung against shining oak-panelled walls. As the great clock struck eleven times, a naval lieutenant in dress uniform presented himself, bowed and said, "Perhaps you would come this way, Sir?"

There they were, sitting in red leather seats behind a long semicircular desk, each with a pad and a glass of water: a Royal Marines colonel, the Flag-Commander of Devonport Naval Base, the headmaster of a great public school, a member of parliament called Wedgwood-Benn; Lord O'Hagan; and in the centre the formidable figure of Admiral Sir Wilmot Fawkes. But the Admiral was smiling as he addressed Bertie— "Good morning, Your Royal Highness. I hope you will sit on the chair in front of you, and then we can have a little talk."

"Th-th-thank you, s-s-s-ir."

The members of the Board had been warned of the stutter, but none of them had believed it could be as bad as it was during those first minutes. "He could scarcely utter at all and I remember thinking, How can this boy ever give an order? What about an emergency? No, no, this is impossible," Lord O'Hagan recalled. "But Fawkes was wonderful with him, unpatronizing, but kind and practical. And as we all chipped in with a question or two, the stutter began to fade, and in perhaps ten minutes we were carrying on a normal conversation, and he was telling us with great enthusiasm about the model of the *Invincible* he was working on. I took to him greatly—he didn't look like one, but all the same I recognized a fighter."

When Bertie withdrew, there was not a dissenting voice. "Splendid fellow." "If he had been a costermonger's son there would not have been the slightest hesitation in passing him."

It had been a fine effort, but Bertie was only halfway there. In early December came the written examinations, which he faced with equal anxiety, but with an equally successful outcome. French oral: 100 per cent. Geography: 61 per cent. English: 82 per cent. Mathematics: 72 per cent. —"very fair indeed, except that in Geometry he seems to have done below the average."

"So the die is cast and little Bertie will be going to Osborne College in January," Lala noted in her journal. "He looks terribly young and fragile to be thrown out into the real world. But, funnily enough, I feel more confidence in Bertie overcoming his difficulties and handicaps than I did with his elder brother."

And so, at the end of his twelfth year [wrote his biographer], Prince Albert completed the second stage of his life. The first—the nursery—had been dominated by "Lala" Bill; the second, the schoolroom, by Finch and Mr Hansell . . . It was a very cloistered life that he had led. He had never been "on his own," never had contact with the world outside the routine of the royal peregrinations, never mixed with boys of his own age . . . He was now to be precipitated, tender and unprepared, into the hard world of competitive life, where standards of achievement were more than a little likely to be set by physical prowess, and where the fact that he was the son of the Prince of Wales would prove neither asset nor protection.

PART TWO

ROYAL EXPECTATIONS

We are the children of splendour and flame,
Of shuddering, also. and tears . . .

Sir William Watson, *Ode in May*

1

There is a photograph of "The boys' room, Marlborough House," showing David and Bertie's beds side by side. White counterpanes with a skirt of floral material cover the beds and at the base there are two chairs draped neatly (for the cameraman no doubt) with pleated folded dressing gowns, slippers beside them on the floor, while between the beds there is a wall shelf carrying a small clock.

On this shelf, too, there are standing pictures, and many more on the table at the end of the beds and on the walls, which are papered with a floral design, chosen, no doubt, like the other decorations, by the boys' mother. The pictures are of a religious nature, or of relatives and friends, "For dear Bertie—Toria"—"Sonny—with regards to David." Prince this, the Grand-Duchess that, King So-and-so, His Imperial Highness . . . In a four-door glass-fronted cupboard there are numerous objects close to a boy's heart—a sextant, a small globe, knick-knacks and, though not identifiable, certainly some of Bertie's carved model men o'war.

This Edwardian, masculine room is, one feels, more cheerful than the boys' father's, or grandfather's rooms when they were at this age. It has none of the mausoleum-like gloom of their great-grandmother's time, with death and mourning predominant.

It was from one of these beds that Bertie, wearing his pyjamas, sprang early on the morning of 7 May 1910, nine months after the Russian Imperial State visit. He ran to the window, drew aside the curtains and looked out. It was a still, clear, sunny dawn, the daffodils in bloom along the Mall and in St James's Park. But above Buckingham Palace, six hundred yards distant, the Royal Standard at half-mast told of death in the night.

Bertie had known that his grandfather's condition was serious. Three days earlier, when he was due back at Osborne, and David at Dartmouth, their father had told them, "I have wired your captains that I want you both to remain with me here. Your grandpapa is very ill, and the end may not be far off." The Queen had been summoned back from her holiday in Corfu, arriving by fast train two days earlier.

Bertie turned from the contrasting scene of spring delight, and death in his family, and called out, "Wake up, David. Grandpapa is dead. Come and see, the flag is at half-mast."

Finch arrived a few minutes later while the boys were dressing. "You have seen that your grandfather died in the night," he said in a solemn voice. He adjusted Bertie's tie and gave his shoes a brief shine with the soft cloth he always carried for this purpose. "It is going to be a difficult day for you both, but even more difficult for your father and mother."

Finch gave his attention to David, arranging the handkerchief in his top pocket neatly. "Have you brushed your teeth?" he asked. "I know you consider yourself almost grown-up at fifteen; I also know you still sometimes forget." Then he reverted to the subject of the day ahead. "Your mother and father have been up almost all the night, and now they face the duties and responsibilities of monarch and consort. You must be quiet and considerate when in their company. To begin with, your father wishes to see you both in his Study."

For once, this call did not ring with the too familiar dread, and they left their bedroom together, David restraining Bertie from running. There was not a sound in Marlborough House, and only a faint hum and clatter of hooves of early morning traffic in St James and Pall Mall.

Characteristically, David made much of the events of that early morning.

> My father's face was grey with fatigue, and he cried as he told us that Grandpapa was dead. I answered sadly that we had already seen the Royal Standard at half-mast. My father seemed not to hear as he went on to describe in exact detail the scene around the deathbed. Then he asked sharply, "What did you say about the Standard?"
>
> "It is flying at half-mast over the Palace," I answered.
>
> My father frowned and muttered, "But that's all wrong," and repeated as if to himself the old but pregnant saying, "The King is dead. Long live the King!" He sent for his equerry, and in a peremptory naval manner ordered that a mast be rigged at once on the roof of Marlborough House. An hour later the Royal Standard was broken and flying "close up" over the house, as it was to do wherever my father resided during the twenty-five years of his reign.

It was not until later, through the royal grapevine—servants, equerries, ladies-in-waiting—that the boys learned of the last days and hours of King Edward's life. It seemed that he had returned from his favourite hotel in Biarritz on the evening of 27 April. He appeared to be in good health, if tired from the long rail journey and Channel crossing, but insisted on keeping to his programme and attending the opera at Covent Garden. The next morning he faced the realities of a political crisis by giving an audience to Prime Minister Herbert Asquith, who was determined to trim the power of the House of Lords in spite of the reduced majority he now commanded as a result of the recent general election.

The King attended the opera on 29 April—*Siegfried* this timed—and went by royal train to Sandringham the next morning. A bitter east wind sprang up that night, but the

King insisted on going out to inspect his pedigree stock after his long absence abroad. If only he had been in Corfu with the Queen! Instead he caught a cold on his chest, which was highly vulnerable after fifty years of almost continuous cigar smoking. Ironically, his last dinner guest in London on his return was Sister Agnes Keyser, who had set up one of the King's favourite charities, the hospital named after him. He would have been wise to have put his frail health into her hands. As it was, the next night (5 May) there appeared this rare—and in the event final—entry in his diary: "Dined alone."

Although clearly very unwell and constantly wheezing, the King insisted on dressing the next morning in his formal frock coat to receive Lord Knollys. Appropriately, his last visitor was his dearest friend, Sir Ernest Cassel, the international banker. "I am very seedy but I wanted to see you," the King said indistinctly, while insisting on rising from his chair.

That evening Dr Laking signed a bulletin on the state of the King's health which, he said, was causing some anxiety—an understatement if ever there was one! Later, the Queen, in a characteristic act of generosity, invited the King's mistress and companion of so many years, Mrs George Keppel, to sit beside the dying King. It was also fitting that the last news from outside for this great sportsman was not of some national catastrophe or further political crisis, but of one of his race horses. "*Witch of the Air* won the Spring Two-Year-Old Plate at Kempton Park by half a length," his son George whispered in his father's ear. "I am very glad," murmured the King, and died soon after, at fifteen minutes before midnight.

When he returned at last to Marlborough House the new King George wrote, "I have lost my best friend and the best of fathers. I never had a cross word from him in my life. I am heartbroken and overwhelmed with grief but God will help me in my great responsibilities and darling May will be my comfort as she always has been."

2

For the four boys and for Mary, the accession to the throne of their father meant many changes in their lives. In place of Frogmore, the family moved into the chill grandeur of the royal apartments in Windsor Castle; in Scotland Balmoral Castle became their home in place of Abergeldie; in London they took up quarters in Buckingham Palace (always referred to as BP). It was the least loved of their homes. David especially hated the musty smell of this Palace and the enormous distances that had to be covered along the heavily carpeted corridors. "We used to say we had to make an appointment in order to see my mother," David wrote.

Of the old homes, only York Cottage at Sandringham remained theirs. Queen Alexandra's son did not have the heart to displace her from the Norfolk home she loved, so the whole family, with their much increased retinue, crammed into the cottage. The family loved the place and were quite content; the opinion of the servants ("I suppose they live in the trees," George once said when asked about their accommodation) was not sought. It certainly made a contrast with BP.

David suffered the biggest changes in his life. After his grandfather's funeral he went back to Dartmouth to continue his training for the Navy. But, as he recalled, "My term mates welcomed me back with appropriate condolences; yet, in a way difficult to express, there had grown up unconsciously among them a subtle respect for my new position." On the material level there came about a ridiculous change with the death of the old King: as heir to the throne, David now took the title Duke of Cornwall automatically, inheriting vast wealth and estates in Cornwall, and much urban property in London. In the spring term at Dartmouth his sole income had been one shilling a week for sweets and little luxuries; now his fortune was in millions.

David claimed indifference to all this money and possessions; and by contrast with his father and grandfather and his sister and brothers, he developed an antipathy towards the increasing ceremonial inevitably and inseparably associated with his life. Since he had become aware of his future role, from about the age of six, he had reacted with self-consciousness or anger to any reference to being set apart from the mass of British people. He longed to be an ordinary boy able to mix equally with other boys, just as he wished ardently for a normal adult life.

Although David never openly expressed this view, he considered, more clearly with every passing year, that there were important things in life above being a king, and he resented that he should have this role thrust upon him. "What have I done to deserve to be heir to the throne?" he confided, soon after the death of Edward VII, to a diary he kept intermittently. Only Finch understood this feeling of anger and resentment in the boy who was already almost a man, and silently sympathized.

However much in later years David's dutifulness and sense of responsibility may have faltered, at this stage it overcame the reluctance he felt towards the grand ceremonials in his life. To this was added the real fear he felt for his father, who remained as short on understanding as with words. "You are now old enough to take part in the forthcoming state ceremonies," George told his son crisply one day soon after he became King, "when many eyes will be upon you. Remember to conduct yourself at all times with dignity and set a good example to others. You must be obedient and respectful and kind to everyone." That was all.

David endured without complaint the Order of the Garter ceremony and the coronation, where in brilliant Garter robes, and a heavy coronet, he was obliged to kneel at his father's feet and swear, "I, Edward, Prince of Wales, do become your liege man of life and limb, and of earthly worship; and faith and truth I will bear unto you, to live and die, against all manner of folks. So help me God."

But before the formal investiture as Prince of Wales, which followed three weeks later at Caernarvon Castle, David's patience cracked. Shown for the first time the white satin breeches, mantle and surcoat of purple velvet edged with ermine, he refused to put them on. What he called "a family blow-up" then ensued, with raised voices and the use of expressions that were later regretted by all concerned. "What do you think my friends in the Navy will think?" David thundered. "No, I'll have nothing to do with this pantomime."

But, with a mixture of entreaties and threats, May overcame her son's objections. "Your friends will understand, David. Now come along and be reasonable . . ."

And so the Home Secretary, Winston Churchill, proclaimed his titles, and George invested him. It was a boiling hot day in mid-July, with the crowds as oppressive as the weather, but David carried off everything very well, earning even a word of praise afterwards from his mother, but not of course from his father.

On this day, too, David made his first public speech, "half fainting with nervousness," having been instructed by the radical, nationalist Chancellor of the Exchequer, Lloyd George, in the pronunciation of the Welsh phrases:

> I thank you with all my heart for your cordial welcome, and with you I wish that this may be the first of many visits to our beautiful country.
>
> As your address reminds me, the many links of the past, my Tudor descent, the great title that I bear, as well as my name David, all bind me to

Wales, and today I can safely say that I am in *"Hen wlad fy nhadau,"* the old land of my fathers.

I assure you that I shall never forget today as long as I live, and I hope sincerely that it will always mark a happy day in the Principality, one which brought you a new friend. He is, it is true, a young friend—I am very young—but I have great examples before me. I have my dear father and my dear mother, and good friends to help me; and so, bearing in mind our ancient and beautiful saying *"Heb Dduw, heb ddim; Duw a digon,"* * I hope to do my duty to my King, to Wales, and to you all.

Bertie, meanwhile, had acquired a hero in his life. He was Lieutenant Louis Greig RN, and Bertie first met him at Osborne in 1909. Greig was popular with all the cadets. He was twenty-nine years old, and a rugby football international, who held the post of assistant medical officer at the college. A graduate of Glasgow University, he had played for Scotland while a student there. At Osborne he was chiefly known, and admired, for his prowess as coach, which he practised "with a wealth, ferocity and lucidity of language which left no illusion as to his meaning." He was a young man of high spirits and total fearlessness, who took pity on Bertie. He was rewarded by an affection which developed into a close relationship. This lasted far into adulthood and provided a steadying influence and a steel girder of support as strong as the one Finch had given since infancy.

Meanwhile, Finch himself accompanied Bertie, well wrapped-up after another illness in spite of the August heat, in a reserved carriage with sleeping compartment from Portsmouth, through the night to an estate called Alt-na-Guilthasach above Loch Muick deep in the Scottish Highlands. His other companion for the weeks ahead was James Watt, the head of the science department at Osborne, a fine teacher, and by happy chance an equally brilliant fly-fisherman. The daily struggle with mathematics was made that much more palatable by the other instruction, in fishing, which Bertie loved

*"Without God, without anything; God is enough."

as he learned "many of those touches which distinguish the accomplished fly-fisher from the ordinary water-flogger."

The fact that David was not with him signified more than the inevitable separation of brothers during different stages of education—in this case Bertie still at Osborne and David at Dartmouth. Although the two boys had derived much mutual comfort during what would otherwise have been a very lonely early childhood, they were not alike in spirit or temperament. David was irritated by Bertie's apparent slowness of mind and non-comprehension even of trivialities in their everyday lives, and was sometimes alarmed by his brother's exasperation and sudden fits of rage and violence. He did not find him an easy or comfortable companion, although there were many times of shared jokes and laughter, especially when they were younger and Mary was present and taking part in their high jinks.

For his part, Bertie had mixed feelings about David's superior academic record, though, goodness knows, it was nothing to write home about. There was also a touch of jealousy of his easy, un-shy manner which always attracted the first attention when meeting people. For David, everything seemed to come easily. A less determined boy than Bertie might have given up; he was saved by a concealed grittiness which often surprised people, but which irritated David when it showed itself. "He may not seem much just now," a shrewd admiral once remarked, "but he'll get farther in the end—you mark my words."

Possibly the relationship between the two boys through their teens is best expressed in terms of their missing one another less than many brothers only eighteen months apart in age would have done. Affection remained, but it also remained muted. The distance between them grew wider as David became closer to his lively, daring and uninhibited younger brother George. Then, in later life, other influences played their part, most particularly the women who came into the young men's lives.

Finch's role remained that of the neutral, mutual friend and guide, never discriminating between the boys, never speaking ill of either of them, but cherishing, beneath a cloak of confidentiality, a deeper faith in the younger boy.

Bertie returned from his Scottish convalescence as well as he could ever expect to be, and joined his class at Osborne several weeks late. His academic career proceeded on its undistinguished course. When he was not bottom of his class he was second from bottom. Had it not been for his rank, he would certainly long since have been "warned," the preliminary to being "sacked." As reports arrived for the King and Queen, George became more and more alarmed and enraged. "He is always very penitent with me," the commanding officer, Captain Christian, wrote to him, which only served to enrage George further, especially as his son seemed to show a marked lack of interest in his poor record. "I am sure the boy has determination & grit in him but he finds it difficult to apply it to work, tho' with games it comes out strongly," the good Captain tried to reassure the father.

In fury and despair George seized his pen and wrote to his son:

> My Dearest Bertie,
>
> . . . I am sorry to have to say that the last reports from Mr Watt with regard to your work, are not at all satisfactory, he says you don't seem to take your work at all seriously, nor do you appear to be very keen about it. My dear boy this will not do, if you go on like this you will be at the bottom of your Term, you are now 71st & you won't pass your examination & very probably will be *warned* this time if you don't take care. You know it is Mama's & my great wish that you should go into the Navy & I believe you are anxious to do so, but unless you now put your shoulders to the wheel & really try & do your best to work hard, you will have no chance of passing any of your examinations.

The final examinations were in December 1910, and with no indication of improvement in the performance of their royal charge, the teachers began to show the first signs of panic.

How could they fail him? Yet how could they pass him for Dartmouth, where he would be more inadequate than ever, and make all too clear the special preference over more competent cadets that he had been given?

"I am afraid there is no disguising to you the fact that Prince Albert has gone a mucker," teacher Watt at Osborne wrote in confidence to teacher Hansell at Buckingham Palace. "He has been quite off his head, with the excitement of getting home, for the last few days, and unfortunately as these were the days of the examinations he has come quite to grief . . ." Indeed he had, Bertie's final position being sixty-eighth out of sixty-eight.

"Another year will produce a great change in him," the authorities predicted more in hope than conviction. But it was enough to pass him into Dartmouth.

By contrast with his elder brother, Harry was for a while an academic success. "It is *wonderful* how well he has got on here so far," reported the headmaster of St Peter's Court at the end of the boy's first term. And to Hansell, Harry boasted, "I think I have got a chance of winning a prize at the end of the term for arithmetic." And he did. No one was more pleased than Hansell, who, after losing the battle to send the first two boys away to school, now saw his recommendation justified.

Harry was not quick on the uptake but, like Bertie, was doggedly persevering. Also like Bertie, he suffered poor health and from knock-knees. But Harry refused to let this get him down, and letters home, and records, show that he was back on the games field with remarkable speed after another dose of flu or mumps or whooping cough.

There were ups and downs at St Peter's Court, but the place suited this boy and he made several lifelong friends. Harry was a kind, generous-natured boy, and nothing underlined this more than his reaction to the arrival of George in the summer term of 1912. George, nearly three years younger than Harry and known at this time (to avoid confusion) as Little George, was academically already on the same level as his older brother. To say that Little George was intellectually privileged by contrast with the rest of George and May's children may not sound very high praise, but in fact by any standards this fourth boy was unusually bright, and where he found his natural culture and instinct for music, besides his sharpness at languages and the sciences, is a mystery.

Hansell was as astonished and mystified as anyone:

> Buckingham Palace
> S.W.
>
> 2 March 1912
>
> My dear Gladys [he wrote to his sister],
>
> I was so glad to hear of the success of Nona [her daughter, who had just passed her examination with flying colours]. Please give her my congratulations. I wish I had as responsive children in my care: she must be so satisfying to teach.
>
> Having said this, I must except young Prince George from my strictures. He is as bright as the proverbial button. Thank goodness, H.M. has agreed that he should join Prince Harry at St Peter's Court next term. I shall miss him but it will be best for him. I can even imagine his getting a scholarship into Eton College, if such were needed.
>
> The weather is terrible in London. And H.M. is worried sick about this coal strike. The miners will be the only losers, I fear, in the end.
>
> Your affectionate brother,
> (signed) Henry

So little George arrived at St Peter's Court in late April 1912 and Harry revelled in showing him round, introducing him to the other boys and revealing the tricks and secrets of a mildly mischievous nature so beloved of prep school boys. In no time at all Little George had settled in, making many friends through his charm and sprightliness, and astonishing the teachers with his academic precocity. One of them wrote to Hansell, "Judged by the performance in the classroom of Prince Henry, we were not expecting too much of his younger brother, but he turns out to be a clever little boy who is already showing himself more advanced than his contemporaries—and his brother. I congratulate you on turning out such a nice and bright lad."

Some boys would have become jealous of a younger brother who shone so brightly. But Harry was of a tolerant nature and took things as they came. By his standards, and by Bertie's standards, Harry was doing well, but he got precious little encouragement from home. Harry loved games, and like Bertie again, found that he could make his mark on the cricket or football field and compensate, in his own mind at least, for inadequacies in lessons. At cricket, he never quite made it to the first eleven, but in one match alone he took three wickets and scored no fewer than sixty runs. And how did his father react to the news of those sixty runs when Harry proudly told him? "The bowling couldn't have been very famous," he commented caustically.

Football was very much on his mind in the winter term especially, and so he quite reasonably wrote about it, like most boys of twelve. Clearly bored and exasperated, his mother wrote back, "All you write about is your ever-lasting football, of which I am heartily sick." And, told by letter that he had a cold, May, who was soon bored by health matters, too, commented "You always seem to have one, which is tiresome."

Harry's prep school life ended on 29 July 1913. A few days before, he wrote to his sister that he had bowled eighty-one wickets, caught ten catches and made two hundred and sixteen runs.

After some slack periods at St Peter's Court, Harry had pulled himself together for his final examinations. In a last letter to Hansell, the headmaster wrote that "he has come on a great deal. I have got really to like him very much [he continued]. He has developed so much in seriousness & thoughtfulness, without losing any of his love of fun. Everybody likes him."

It is certain that this was true. It can truthfully be said that Harry, in adult life as well as boyhood, never made an enemy. He was not the brightest of company but it was very difficult not to like him.

It was Eton for Harry in September 1913, and Mr Samuel Lubbock's house, widely regarded as the best. At first Harry showed himself very much Bertie's brother, and there were reports of "listlessness alternating with restlessness." His division master, George Lyttelton, also commented on his "fits of giggling which sometimes overcome him and play temporary havoc with his attention."

But Eton was undoubtedly the right place for Harry and Lyttelton and Lubbock on the whole gave good reports of his progress. Only his parents remained dissatisfied with his performance. It was a ridiculous, if typical, contradiction that George and May should single out their third son for the relatively gentle treatment this public school offered rather than the more rigorous education provided by one of the services, and then pour scorn on any achievement or improvement he recorded. Between them they found fault in almost every department. A lot of people asked for his photograph, as they frequently asked his elder brothers. Prints were given freely to David and Bertie, but his mother warned Harry that they cost one shilling each, which he did not have. May wondered how he spent his money "for it seems to go very quickly."

Harry let all this petty and almost non-stop niggling wash over him and remained cheerful. From the begining, he enjoyed himself at Eton, and after visiting David at Oxford, even conceived the ambition of going to university himself.

3

David and Oxford would appear to be incompatible, and certainly Harry's eldest brother was not at the university by choice. In fact, since the death of his beloved grandfather, Edward VII, David had found himself frustrated in almost everything he wanted to do. On completing his last term at Dartmouth, he and his fellow cadets were to take part in a final training cruise, after which they would graduate and automatically qualify for the dirk and white patch of a midshipman.

"No cadet," David wrote, "yearned for this proof of success more than I. Now, without warning came a letter from my father explaining that, since I would naturally be obliged to play a prominent role in his coronation in June, I would have to forgo the training course in North American waters upon which my hopes were set."

So, instead of sharing informally the advantages of an Atlantic crossing with his friends, it would be the embarrassments of pomp and ridiculous costume at his father's coronation! On coronation day itself, David was rated a midshipman anyway, but it was of little satisfaction to him because it was clear to him and everyone else that he had not really earned this qualification. Then there was the investiture as Prince of

Wales. "When all this was over, I made a painful discovery
about myself," David wrote. "It was that, while I was prepared to fulfil my role in all this pomp and ritual, I recoiled
from anything that tended to set me up as a person requiring
homage."

Then there was a brief reprieve from his new responsibilities and duties. At last he was to go to sea!

His father arranged for David to join the *Hindustan*, commanded by Captain Henry Hervey Campbell; an old friend
and shipmate of his, Captain Campbell often stayed at York
Cottage with the family, becoming friends with all the children. In his determination to ensure that David was not
going to be offered any special privileges (and no doubt at the
King's request), David was worked unusually hard. "I was
soon to discover," he wrote bleakly, "that the Captain Campbell with a deck under his feet was a wholly different man
from the genial guest at York Cottage."

Four days before the coronation of her son George and her
daughter-in-law, Queen Alexandra learned that David, Bertie,
Mary, Harry and George were all to ride together in one
carriage, *without an adult*. Her peals of happy laughter caused
her lady-in-waiting to look up from her embroidery and ask
what she found so funny.

"My dear, just look—all the Georgie pets together in one
carriage! There will be chaos and pandemonium. It will be
like the knockabout act at the music hall. Such mischief!"

"Don't you think we ought to speak to HM about it,
then?" asked Lady Treadgold seriously.

"Oh no, it will be lovely."

And so it was.

David and Mary had been given pride of place in the
open carriage on the back seat. David was in his Garter
clothes and robe with coronet, Mary was dressed in a robe of
pale blue velvet with an ermine train and coronet. Bertie,
Harry and Little George sat opposite, with strict orders to
behave themselves and do as David told them. (John was no

more than a distant observer, peering over the Palace wall with Lala.)

The "Georgie pets" received an even louder reception than their mother and father from the massed crowds lining the route from the Palace to Westminster Abbey, and all five of them responded as they had been instructed—smiles and waves all the way. Even David had to admit (in spite of his "ridiculous" clothes) that he quite enjoyed this part.

The ceremony was very long, and, especially to the younger children, extremely tedious, and by the time they were back in their open landau, they were fidgety and anxious to let off steam. As the bells rang out, the horses picked up speed, and a massive cheer arose from the thousands outside the Abbey, Harry and Bertie decided that they were overcrowded and began to dispose of Little George under the seat. The youngest was certainly not "little" any more at the age of eight and struggled against the indignity, while the crowds they were passing at that moment burst into spontaneous laughter at the unscheduled scene.

David and Mary at first pretended not to notice, and "were behaving with admirable propriety." Mary's biographer continues:

> The Princess soon became very shocked as matters grew worse, and sharply remonstrated with her unruly small brothers; but her words were totally unheeded, and it was soon obvious that at any moment the obstreperous three might land in a heap on the floor of the carriage.
>
> At last the Princess reached forward and firmly separated them and sat them up in their seats. She lost her coronet in the effort, which was not surprising; but the Prince of Wales picked it up, and she calmly replaced it upon her head, while the quintet proceeded for the rest of the procession in a state of rather greater harmony.

Queen Alexandra missed all the fun and games she had predicted would take place. But she heard about it at Sandringham (it was kept from George and May) and rocked

with laughter and asked her informant to repeat her account
in full detail twice before she was satisfied.

A special relationship was now developing between the second youngest and oldest "Georgie pets." George once recalled:

> There was nothing I enjoyed more than accompany-
> ing David up to the Big House. David was eight
> and a half years older than me but we got on
> famously. He used to tell me everything. He had
> completed his sea experience and Oxford was loom-
> ing in his mind like a black cloud on the horizon.
> Meanwhile, we had a lovely winter at York Cottage
> together.
>
> Our parents had gone away to India for the
> Coronation Durbar at Delhi, a very grand business
> indeed. Bertie was away on his naval instruction,
> Harry was at school, leaving David, Mary and me
> at York Cottage with Hansell and Finch. Mary had
> a few lessons, mostly French and German, but
> spent most of her time out riding as I remember
> and I had to spend mornings in the schoolroom, but
> it was really a very free and easy time. I am ashamed
> to recall how relaxed we all were with our parents
> away. You could see the difference in Hansell and
> Finch, too. Not only did we have the run of the
> cottage but there was never any fear of bumping
> into Papa or Mama unexpectedly.

The fourteenth of December was a wet and cold day up in
north Norfolk, too wet even for Mary to ride and the hunt
that day had been abandoned. But shortly before darkness set
in—at around four in the afternoon—the skies suddenly cleared
and there was a brief glimpse of the low sun in the west
before it disappeared finally, leaving a scarlet sky over the
fields and woodlands towards King's Lynn.

As the little clock in their mother's drawing room tinkled
out four chimes, the two boys got up from the chairs where
they had been reading. "Time to go," said David. It was not

an urgent appointment, but their grandmother would be expecting them and neither David nor George wanted to disappoint her. Besides, as George once remarked, "It's always jolly up at the Big House."

Finch helped them on with their overcoats. "Just you see you don't catch cold," he said to them in the hall. "No, Finch," said David, laughing. "We won't if you promise not to nanny us. We're big boys now."

There was still light enough to guide them to the Big House but in any case they could have completed the short walk blindfolded. The lights were going on—so much brighter now that Queen Alexandra had reluctantly allowed electricity to be installed—and the curtains in the tall windows were drawn as the two boys crunched across the gravel of the sweep of drive in front of the house.

The front doors were opened as they walked into the porch, Sanders welcoming them with a smile and a slight bow. "Good evening, Sir. Good evening, Sir. What a dreadful day it has been."

"You never spoke a truer word, Sanders," said David as he turned to allow the butler to take his coat. "I trust it has not depressed Her Majesty too much."

"It would take more than a drop of rain to do that, Sir."

Queen Alexandra was in her usual chair before a blazing fire in the small drawing room—"Much cosier, my dear!" In front of her was a square inlaid table covered with the pieces of a jigsaw puzzle, only a few of which had been fitted together. She was dressed in a long brown velvet afternoon dress, fastened at the back, and featuring the new "figureless" shape. Her hair, as always, was built up into a high coiffure, diamonds sparkled in her elaborate ear-rings, and she had on her favourite necklace, a double chain of rubies. She was sixty-seven years old now—her birthday had been two weeks earlier—and it was forty-eight years since she had arrived from Denmark to be embraced by her fiancé at Gravesend and become Princess of Wales. At that time the Crown Princess of Prussia described her future sister-in-law:

> She is a good deal taller than I am, has a lovely figure but very thin, a complexion as beautiful as

possible. Very fine regular white teeth and very fine large eyes—with extremely prettily marked eyebrows. A very fine well-shaped nose, very narrow but a little long—her whole face is very narrow, her forehead too but well shaped and not at all flat. Her voice, her walk, carriage and manner are perfect, she is one of the most ladylike and aristocratic-looking people I ever saw.

Now as an elderly woman, her skin was still fine and "enamelled," and there was no dimming of the sparkle in her deep blue eyes. "Ah, boys, how lovely of you to come," she greeted her two grandchildren. "Come and help me, this is too difficult for my old brain."

On the Queen's right side, in an upright chair in order to acquire a more favourable view of the table, sat a woman who did show her years—white-haired and heavily lined, with fingers heavy with rings of ruby, diamonds, and sapphires. She was the Hon. Charlotte Knollys, the sister of the late Edward VII's secretary, Lord Knollys, who had given almost all her adult life in the service of "dearest Alix," inseparable companion, closest friend, for almost fifty years, *without a single break.*

Next to her sat another woman of about the same age and having a great air of the patrician about her—tall, grey-haired, with positive features, especially her nose, which had a hawk-like configuration. She appeared indifferent to the jigsaw puzzle and its progress, and acknowledged the boys' greeting with a faint tilt of her head. The Queen called her Louise—"Louise, dear, do pay attention . . ."—and she was in fact Louise Jane Hamilton, Duchess of Buccleuch, and Mistress of the Wardrobe to the Queen.

Then there was Sir Dighton Probyn, a massive and formidable figure, with a full head of iron-grey hair and a flowing white beard to his lower chest. He had won the Victoria Cross in the Indian Mutiny in an action the boys' grandfather had recounted to them many times, and had formed King Edward's Own Lancers, otherwise "Probyn's Horse." He was a man who had certainly never experienced fear in his life—a life that had spanned almost eight decades.

The Queen loved him and depended on him, partly
because, as her Comptroller, he shared her eccentric and
extravagant views about money and expenditure. "Those two
will have us all in the workhouse!" David had once heard his
father exclaim in despair.

Now this ferocious if ageing figure stood with his back to
the fire surveying the jigsaw puzzle table as if he were a
general planning a battle. "We've a sticky situation here,
boys," he greeted David and George. "You'd best come up
on the right flank with reinforcements."

The only other figure in the drawing room was a visitor
from the Cottage, a little boy, pretty and fair-haired and not
unlike David, who appeared to be no more than three but in
fact was six and a half. He was the boys' youngest brother,
John, sitting on his grandmother's lap and giving his whole
attention to her necklace. When he heard David's voice, he
turned his head slowly, smiled and bounced himself up and
down, picked up a piece of jigsaw before Alix could restrain
him and threw it to the ground in celebration.

"There, little Johnnie's always pleased to see you, boys.
He would love to play with you but I think it is bathtime."

At that moment the ample figure of Lala Bill appeared at
the door with Mary, dressed in the starched white uniform
she had worn indoors for as long as David and George could
remember. She bobbed a curtsey to the company and smiled
at the two bigger boys. "I hear Prince Harry's due home from
school tomorrow," she said. "Then it will be Christmas in no
time. Won't it, my beautiful boy," Lala said as she reached
for John and plucked him with muscular arms from the Queen's
lap—"Thank you, Ma'am. And Finch will be putting up the
Christmas tree in the hall tomorrow, too. He ought to put
you on top of it, shouldn't he, my little angel." Lala held John
to her chest and he put his arms round her neck as if she
were the only secure rock in a hazardous and mystifying life.

"Good-night Lala," called George. "I've got your present—
I hope you like it. And Mary's."

It was a typical winter evening at Sandringham House.
The General creaked down into a chair at a side table and
played double patience with George, very slowly, complaining about the light (which was perfectly adequate) but sur-

rendering gracefully when defeated: "Too good for my ol'
brain." David concentrated for a while on the jigsaw, asking
his grandmother how his parents were getting on. "The last
telegraph was dated yesterday and it recounted the day of the
Durbar, and that was on Tuesday. Tomorrow Papa is laying
the foundation stone of India's new capital." The Queen
slipped in a different piece and clapped her hands. "They
sent their love to you all."

Games ceased with the arrival of tea and *petits beurres*,
there was teasing laughter when David confessed he had not
bought anyone's Christmas present yet. Then the mah-jongg
board was brought out, and the players were presently joined
by the Queen's rather tiresome and bossy sister, the Dowa-
ger Empress of Russia, who had long overstayed her welcome
after the coronation.

It was, as always, a happy time, until 7.15 p.m. when
the grown-ups had to retire to dress for dinner, and the boys
to return to the cottage for supper. "I insist that you take the
carriage home," Alix said. "But, Grandmama, it is only . . ."
A raised hand: the Queen had spoken. The coachman was
aroused, the horses harnessed, the lamps lit, and in ten
minutes David and George, apologizing to old Boston, climbed
into the carriage for the short cold journey down the drive.

4

The following morning Louise Duchess of Buccleuch took
the same journey with Boston down that drive, but this
time the coach swept on past York Cottage, past the lodge, to
the railway station. The Mistress of the Wardrobe was beginning her long journey home to Drumlanrig.

Drumlanrig Castle in Dumfriesshire, the Scottish seat of
the Buccleuchs for many centuries, is a magnificent and
perfectly proportioned edifice of pink granite, on which, after
rain, the sun picks out the flecks of mica, causing it to glitter
like a fairy-tale castle. Within the towers at each corner are
dark winding staircases, perfect for ghostly children's games,
while by contrast the drawing rooms of the main building
look out over beautiful gardens, many-shaped flowerbeds,
box hedges and gravel paths. A park stretches away to the
River Nith and, far beyond, the moors rise up to meet the
sky. The land covers nearly half a million acres; the castle
makes Sandringham seem like a cottage.

Louise's husband was a gnarled giant of a man, dark-
eyed, black-haired, deep-voiced, almost a caricature of the
popular impression of a brutal Scottish laird. He dressed the
part, too, in the roughest of tweeds and the heaviest of boots.
But he had a loving heart and a gentle and hospitable nature.

With his vast wealth and acres, he could offer his guests everything, and did so generously. He liked nothing better than having droves of relatives and friends about him, the younger the better, shooting and playing.

And now, as the Christmas of 1911 approached, the Duchess was on her way to help her husband William entertain the guests at Drumlanrig before they all returned to their own homes for the festivities. There would be much shooting on the moors, while the castle in the evening would echo to the voices and laughter of the young and privileged.

Among the very young was the Duke and Duchess's granddaughter, Lady Alice Scott, who one day would bind even closer the Buccleuchs' ties with the royal family. And many years later still, as an old lady, she wrote of those innocent days at Drumlanrig, recounting how every day started with prayers in the chapel, with the Reverend Mr Smith Dorian acting as private chaplain.

Within three years the old Duke had died of cancer and Alice's father succeeded to the title in the last summer of peace. The summer of 1914 evokes memories for anyone still alive today. Alice Scott remembers particularly the great number of congenial people who came to stay, many of them friends of Alice's brother, Walter, then at Oxford: Prince Paul of Serbia, Count von Beiberstein, "Bobbety" Cranborne, the Bowes-Lyons, and many more. Mike and Rose Bowes-Lyon were great favourites, and their younger sister Elizabeth was there, too, as a special concession, sweet as the nectarines in the greenhouses, with a complexion like the peaches on the south-facing wall, and eyes as blue as the summer sky. Elizabeth was nearly fourteen and older than Alice: curly, dark hair, a ready smile and charm-tilt of the head. She did not slip into their more robust games very easily although there was no sign of nervousness in the girl as soon as she was in the saddle, and she could manage a fresh little colt with confidence and skill.

"What is Glamis like? Is it full of ghosts?" Alice asked Elizabeth about her home. "Papa says Glamis is full of spooks and ghosts and is the most haunted castle in Scotland."

Elizabeth Bowes-Lyon, destined to be the first to marry one of the Windsor boys, looked coolly at Alice Montagu

Douglas-Scott, who would one day marry another of these boys, and in a dismissive voice said, "Oh no, there are no ghosts or any nonsense like that. Glamis is a very nice home. Bonnie Prince Charlie once slept there, so did your ancestor, Sir Walter Scott."

"A very nice home." So that was the definition of Glamis, one of the biggest, boldest castles in Scotland, as defined by the pretty Elizabeth, youngest daughter of the Earl and Countess of Strathmore. If it could be called a nice home in 1914, it was not so when James V regained the castle for the crown by ejecting the widow Glamis and having her burnt as a witch in Edinburgh. Then there was the mad son of the house who, in 1707 when his father was absent, broke free and descended to the kitchens where a boy was turning the spit for dinner. When the father returned it was the boy who was on the spit, with his son turning it.

This and other blood-curdling tales of the past were very remote from the highly respectable and kindly Bowes-Lyons whose first residence Glamis Castle was—Claude George Bowes-Lyon, Earl of Strathmore and Kinghorne, Viscount Lyon and Baron Glamis, Tannadyee, Sidlaw, and Strathdichtie, Baron Bowes of Streatham Castle . . . and so on; and his wife Cecilia, who by this time had borne him six hefty sons, and four daughters (little Violet died at eleven years), with Elizabeth the last daughter.

The only association with violence in this pleasantly civilized family was through the Army, father having served in the Life Guards, his son Fergus serving in the Black Watch. And shooting and fishing, of course—Elizabeth taking an instant and early interest in fly-fishing especially. The Bowes-Lyons, indeed, were a thoroughly decent lot, so un-patrician and unassuming in their manner and style of living that they could have been transported to an upper-middle-class house in the English home counties without being regarded as above their station. And they would have been perfectly comfortable there.

"The first thing about the Bowes-Lyons," one of their contemporaries said, "is that they give no sign of consciousness of rank, while taking their responsibilities very seriously indeed. It was unspoken outside the family, and rarely mentioned within the family, but they did regard the Sutherlands and the Buccleuchs and a few more of the monumentally rich and massive landowners among their fellow Scots as a bit ostentatious in their wealth, and the frequent travelling about from one palace to another of some of them as just a teeny bit vulgar. The Strathmores, like Alfred and Nina Douglas-Hamilton, tended to keep themselves to themselves, thought all this Scottish patriotism a bit 'off,' and the Royal Family, while perfectly respectable, really rather foreign—and *German* at that."

The Strathmores' London house reflected their style more appropriately than multi-turreted Glamis, and strongly contrasted with the Buccleuchs' Montagu House in Whitehall. Number 20 St James's Square was a relatively recent acquisition, deep in the heart of clubland, a few hundred yards from Piccadilly, with convenient stabling and the use of the square gardens for nursemaids and children as well as a sizeable garden of its own. It was an Adam mansion, built in 1771, with Adam ceilings, drawing rooms decorated by the Swiss painter Angelica Kauffmann (1741–1807) and a beautiful broad staircase.

St James's Square was the Bowes-Lyon home for much of the year, although St Paul's Walden Bury, in Hertfordshire, all red brick and careful gardens, was the house that Elizabeth and her brother David remembered most clearly. David, almost two years younger than Elizabeth, idolized his sister, who returned his love in full measure. "The Benjamins," after the two youngest children of Jacob and Leah, their mother called them, or "The Benjamina," always together, or so it seemed, under the management of their nursemaid Clare Cooper Knight, or "Alah."*

On an early autumn day in 1905 a carriage drew up outside their London residence, with two large trunks and one young lady, a Frenchwoman, Mademoiselle Lang, who

---

*Daughter of a farmer, James Knight. Later nanny to Mary Bowes-Lyon's (Lady Elphinstone) children, and Elizabeth's Elizabeth and Margaret-Rose. Died Sandringham 2 January 1946.

had been appointed governess to "The Benjamins." She was to exert an influence over the two children out of proportion to her diminutive size and modest opinion of herself. She was astonished to be met in the hall, after her long and rather tiring journey from the other side of Paris, by one of her charges. "She was an enchanting child with tiny hands and feet, I remember," she later recounted of this meeting, "and rose-petal colouring. She advanced to meet me with out-stretched hand, the five-year-old murmuring politely, 'I do hope you will be happy here.'"

It was Mademoiselle Lang's early evidence of the precociousness and total unselfconsciousness of Elizabeth Bowes-Lyon, the perfect hostess from toddling age.

I had never met a child so advanced. She read *me* stories instead of the other way round! She recited psalms and passages from the Bible and recited poetry like a bright ten-year-old. What was left for me to teach her? In fact, quite a lot, including the French tongue, although she already had a smatter-ing of that. *Un enfant extraordinaire!*

When David found it difficult to pronounce "Mademoiselle" Elizabeth decided that "Madé" was easier for him, and that is what the children called me for all the time I worked for Lord and Lady Strathmore.

Elizabeth was so full of life and contrasts, one minute like a grown-up, a grand hostess in com-mand, the next playing with her pets, and with David like any six-year-old. I remember so many stories of her soon after I arrived. There was the day of the garden fête, complete with the lady palmist. Elizabeth strode in to the tent without hesitation and demanded that her hand be read. When she came out I asked, "What did she say?" She made a face. "Oh, she was silly. She said I was going to be Queen one day when I grow up." I laughed and said, "Then they will have to change the laws of England for you." "Who wants to be

Queen anyway," she sang out, and began dancing
to one of my nursery rhymes, *S'il fleurisse je
serai reine*— "If it blossoms, I shall be Queen."
Then there was that time when she began to go to
school . . .

Cecilia Strathmore had enlightened beliefs on education and
was determined that her youngest and exceptionally bright
daughter should be educated to a standard to match her
mind. It was thanks to her mother that the child who had
opened the door to Madé on arrival already had a smattering
of French and German and could read fluently. Her sister
Rose, ten years older, once wrote:

> Indeed, Lady Strathmore "brought her up" in ev-
> ery way. As David wrote: "My mother taught us to
> read and write. At the ages of six and seven we
> would each of us have written a fairly detailed
> account of all the Bible stories. This was entirely
> due to our mother's teaching. She also taught us
> the rudiments of music, dancing and drawing, at all
> of which my sister became fairly proficient."

David used also to recount this anecdote about their mother's
attitude to punishing Elizabeth:

> As Elizabeth was the youngest daughter, she was
> very much with our mother. She was such an at-
> tractive little thing that an old friend asked my
> mother, "What *can* you do to punish Elizabeth?"
> My mother said, "It is quite enough just to say
> 'Elizabeth!' in a very sad way; then she will hang
> her head and be sorry." It is quite true; I have
> heard her myself. My father adored her too, but it
> was really my mother who brought her up.

When in London Elizabeth attended dancing and music lessons with special tutors. Then, in the spring of 1909, when
she was eight, Cecilia decided that Elizabeth should spend

two terms at a Froebel day school in Marylebone High Street, as a supplement to the lessons of her governess.

Cecilia insisted on receiving weekly reports on Elizabeth's progress from the headmistress, Miss Constance Goff. Then came the afternoon of "the visit." Elizabeth, now nine years old, had not been told that Miss Goff was to return home in the carriage with her to St James's Square in order to discuss her pupil's progress with Lady Strathmore.

Then, as Elizabeth ran out to be met by the coachman and helped into the carriage (as if she needed it), she saw that Miss Goff was already installed in one of the seats. Miss Goff greeted her with a laugh. "I hope you don't mind sharing your carriage with your headmistress."

"It's a great pleasure, Miss Goff," Elizabeth replied at once. "Are you visiting Mama?"

"Yes, my dear. We are to have a little chat."

As the horses clip-clopped down Bond Street, busy with fine ladies observing and buying the latest autumn fashions, Elizabeth said, "There is only one thing you and Mama will wish to talk about—and that is *me*." She turned towards Miss Goff beside her and smiled sweetly and then laughed. "Is that not so?"

"Yes, of course. You are quite right."

Then Elizabeth asked conversationally, "What do you think of the higher hemlines this season, Miss Goff?"

And they talked ladies' fashions all the way down Piccadilly and Jermyn Street and into St James's Square. At Number 20 they were received by the butler, who at once spoke to the headmistress. "I am extremely sorry, madam, Lady Strathmore has been delayed but asks me to tell you she will be home as soon as possible."

On overhearing this, Elizabeth took immediate command and, as soon as the butler had taken her own and Miss Goff's coat, led her into the front drawing room where she installed her by the fire. "I know it is rather early, but I do think fires so cheer up a room, don't you?" she remarked as she pulled the bell and ordered tea from the maidservant. "And ask Mrs Manders to put plenty of cream on the scones"—the only clue to the age of the stand-in hostess. Miss Goff played her part perfectly and never once allowed herself an indulgent smile as the conversation continued. Elizabeth poured out the tea and began to speak of the purpose of Miss Goff's visit. "Well, Miss Goff, as Mama appears to be unduly delayed, for which I am sure she is so very sorry, perhaps you should tell *me* about my progress. And please don't hesitate to include any shortcomings requiring correction." She smiled conspiratorially. "I assure you, whatever you say shall be passed on truthfully."

At this point Lady Strathmore entered the room. "Oh, Miss Goff, I am too terribly sorry . . . Ah, I see Elizabeth has been looking after you. Quite the little princess . . ."

And from that moment, encouraged warmly by Elizabeth herself, she was known in the family as "Princess."

To the north and west of Glamis Castle the Grampian mountains loom dark and lowering in heavy summer weather, white-dashed with snow in winter sunshine, dividing Scotland as the Apennines rear up to splice Italy. Distantly on the western side of the Grampians, almost one hundred miles from Glamis, and beneath the massive peak of Bidean Nam Bian, lies Glencoe.

Mademoiselle Lang had, farsightedly and sensibly, read some Scottish history before taking up her appointment with the Strathmores, and partly to satisfy her own curiosity and to add a note of reality to her pupil's history, had suggested to Cecilia that she should take Elizabeth and David to see the valley and the place where the dreadful massacre of 1692 had taken place.

This expedition was carried out, after much careful planning, shortly before Easter 1914, when there were heavy drifts of snow in the valley. The two young Bowes-Lyons never forgot that day, and Madé's graphic description of the treacherous massacre of the Macdonalds by their hereditary enemies, the Campbells. Some weeks later Elizabeth, still full of that day at Glencoe and all that she had seen, rather bored the older Scott children at Drumlanrig, all of whom had seen the valley and heard the history often and long ago in their education.

5

Some three thousand miles away, across a particularly storm-tossed Atlantic that spring, another child would have listened more eagerly to the "Princess," especially as she was at that time deep into the novels of Sir Walter Scott, and she was at a school in a town called Glencoe, named after the Scottish valley.

The school was Oldfields, and its address was simply Glencoe, Maryland, USA. It was an estimable school, like Elizabeth's in Marylebone High Street, for forty girls, but was certainly not run on Froebel lines. It is almost certain that Miss Anna G. McCulloh, who ran it jointly with her brother, had never heard of Froebel, although she knew all about the Scottish Glencoe, and more Scottish history than all the Strathmores and Buccleuchs.

Oldfields was run on traditional lines for the daughters of gentlefolk, and "Gentleness & Courtesy" governed the conduct of teachers and pupils alike. Notices proclaiming "Gentleness and Courtesy are Expected of the Girls at all Times" were posted above every doorway. Even the games teams were called Gentleness and Courtesy, although there was as much realistic shoving and tripping at Oldfields as in any other basketball team.

The pupil at Oldfields who was deep into Walter Scott's novels at the time when Elizabeth "the Princess" Bowes-Lyon was visiting Glencoe, was Bessie Wallis Warfield, sometimes called "the Duchess" by her doting mother. Bessie Wallis, whose father Wallis Warfield had died of tuberculosis when she was still an infant, loved Oldfields, Glencoe. Later she wrote of "Miss Nan" as the headmistress was called by the girls: "She was sixty-two years old, tall, spare, precise of movement and speech; her iron-grey hair was brushed into a severe pompadour; and she unfailingly wore black dresses with little white turn-down collars."

And of the school itself, she wrote:

> Along with its emphasis upon the rules of etiquette and comportment, Oldfields also attempted to inject a reverence for God. Every morning, after the rising-bell and before breakfast, five minutes were given to school prayer, which followed the Episcopal Book of Common Prayer. Grace was said before meals, and in the evening, after study hall, we sang hymns. Sunday morning each of us was required to memorize the Collect and the Gospel of the day before marching off to church. At five-thirty there was Evensong and then, after supper, an extra-long session of hymn-singing. Miss Nan looked upon Sunday as a day to be devoted to instilling into her young girls the meaning and obligations of the Christian faith.

Bessie Wallis also did rather well academically at Oldfields, and the school liked and admired "the Duchess" as warmly as she admired Oldfields. By odd chance, on the very day that Elizabeth Bowes-Lyon was admiring the beauties, and shivering at the horrors, of Glencoe, Miss Nan wrote to the girl's mother:

Oldfields School
Gencoe, Md.
31 March 1914

My dear Mrs Rasin,

We will give Wallis the privilege of going into town on Wednesday afternoon on the 2.20 train to have her skirt fitted.

She has been such a faithful student and her averages have been so good we feel that she deserves some extra privilege.

Our chaperon will be at the Union Station waiting to bring Wallis back to school on the 5.10 train.

Hoping that you are feeling much stronger.

Yours sincerely,
A.G. McCulloh

Bessie Wallis's mother had become "Mrs Rasin" on her marriage to a particularly nice and, fortunately, well-off man called John Freeman Rasin. He had accepted his stepdaughter as if she were his own, and a loving relationship developed between Bessie Wallis and her stepfather. He admired her spirit and vivacity, and loved to watch the dark-haired, pretty girl at play. Later, he witnessed her development over the years into the striking young woman of eighteen she became in that spring of 1914.

Bessie Wallis knew that her stepfather was unwell when she had gone back to school—poorly enough for her mother to insist that they should move from their apartment in Baltimore to Atlantic City with its healthy sea airs. Then on a day in early April while she was in class, Miss Nan came up to her desk and asked her to come outside. "Please come to my room," she said gently. "I have bad news for you, I'm afraid."

There Bessie Wallis was told, "My dear, I am so sorry. But your mother has telegraphed to say that your stepfather has died and that she would like you to come home to the funeral." Then she held the weeping girl in her arms until she ceased sobbing, and dabbed her eyes with her handkerchief.

"But he was such a good, kind man, Miss Nan. How could God be so cruel as to take him from me and my mother?"

"God is not cruel, my poor girl. He is all-wise, and there is a reason for everything, however hard and unwelcome it may be. God's will be done."

Two days later, on 6 April 1914, Miss Nan took Bessie Wallis, dressed all in black, to the railroad station and put her on the train to Baltimore where the funeral was to take place at the home of her stepfather's sister.

Bessie Wallis wrote of this first great tragedy in her life:

The maid who let me into the apartment showed me into a front room. The curtains were drawn, and in the process of trying to adjust my eyes to the abrupt change from bright sunshine outside to the interior gloom, I thought the room was empty. Then in a corner I noticed a dark shadow—it was my mother, enveloped in a black crêpe veil that fell to her knees. She looked so tiny and lost and pathetic that my heart broke. As I started towards her a sound of weeping made me turn towards the other side of the room. There, on a window-seat, all in a row in front of the drawn shades, were three quite shapeless shadows—three of my stepfather's sisters, draped alike in heavy black veils and sobbing quietly in unison. They made me think of the Fates, and I was glad to find my mother's arms.

That sad day was a long time running its course. I spent the night with my mother at the apartment where I had found her.

6

At Athens, Greece, on the other side of the world, and some twelve years before the death of Bessie Wallis's stepfather, the marriage took place of Prince Nicholas of Greece and the Grand-Duchess Helen of Russia, bringing together two dynasties. Prince Nicholas was the brother of Prince Andrew, father of Prince Philip, today Queen Eizabeth II's consort.

As the Tsar's niece, Grand-Duchess Helen was among the last Russians entitled to bear the resounding title of "Imperial and Royal Highness." She was also quite breathtakingly beautiful. As for Nicholas, he "loved painting, poetry, books, the theatre, and beauty in all its guises. He had a rare sense of humour, a devout sense of duty, a firm faith in God."

They had three daughters, equally gifted and quite as lovely as their mother. The third, Princess Marina, was born in Athens on 13 December 1906. The upbringing of these privileged girls, full of culture and laughter, was in stark contrast with those of George and May's children in England.

The two families of cousins met when Edward VII died in 1910 and the Greeks were invited over for the funeral, staying at Buckingham Palace with "dear Georgie and May." They arrived complete with an entourage of twenty on an afternoon early in August, just before the Cowes regatta.

Besides the new King and Queen, all the boys, and Mary, had been summoned to greet their Greek cousins.

The children had met before, but the proceedings had always been stiff and self-conscious, only Mary showing any initiative among the English children. The age gap was too great and their time together too brief for any intimacy to be formed. This time, with three days together at the Palace, it was different. The Greek Princesses, with their irrepressible high spirits and spontaneous charm, managed to relax the stiff and selfconscious boys; and Mary, bearing the responsibility of hostess, fought and won against her own shyness.

A game of croquet after tea, which got more and more out of hand, had them all laughing. George, seven now, and closest to Olga and Elizabeth in age, tore up the hoops and placed them in a row. He was the first to attempt to leap them all, and fell laughing three hoops short. In spite of her slight lameness, Marina was next.

She fell, too, managing only four of them. "I remember George gallantly helping her up and then both of them falling on the grass, consumed with giggles," David later wrote. "After that, I remember, we started playing bowls with the balls and that, too, soon became somewhat out of hand. One of the balls went into the lake, floating because it was made of wood and Princess Marina took off her shoes and began to wade in, while at the same time Bertie and I, as qualified sailors, launched the rowing boat.

"All this nonsense was halted by the arrival of the Greek Princesses' nanny. She only had to call out the names of her charges once and they all came to her, Princess Marina with her white dress soaked. Bertie and I apologized, and so did Mary. The nanny admonished Princess Marina but was soon smiling as she took the girls inside. They called her 'Foxy.' "

The Greek Princesses had not expected to enjoy such a carefree time on their English visit because the Court was in full mourning, and they had previously associated London with rain and coolness of weather as well as their cool reception by George and May and the children. This time it was quite different.

But, as for so many of the royal families of Europe, the first decade of the new century, appropriately represented in

Four generations—four sovereigns. At the christening of the future Edward VIII, Queen Victoria is flanked by her son and grandson

Smiles for the photographer from Bertie (left), David and Mary

"Our poor darling little Johnnie," wrote May on hearing of the death of her last born.

Harry

George

"Childbirth is a great bore for me & requires a great deal of patience to bear it," declared May. Her sextet in 1906, John in her arms and (l to r) Mary, Harry, George, David and Bertie

Bertie in 1908 with Mr Hansell ("Mider") and Lord Desborough

David in what he called his "preposterous rig" for his investiture as Prince of Wales

Growing up: Bertie (left) and David with their mother

David the horseman

Britain by the extrovert, life-enhancing Edward VII, slipped swiftly into a new era of unrest, violence and anxiety. In England there were crippling strikes, ever-increasing worry about the naval rearmament of Germany, the Irish question and the intractable suffragettes. Germany's problems were no fewer, while the press and government whipped up the militarism and incipient paranoia of the people. The troubles in Russia were even deeper seated, with revolution becoming an increasing threat while the Tsarina blocked any efforts towards reform.

In Greece the tranquillity of the lives of Nicholas and Helen and their three pretty girls was abruptly smashed with the outbreak of war against Turkey in 1912, and the assassination of King George on 18 March 1913. The shot that killed the good and fearless Dane who had ruled Greece so wisely for so long was echoed by another shot, at Sarajevo this time, the following year; and for Marina and her sisters presaged a time when they were to lose their home and their fortune. It was a time when violence and the news of deaths of friends and relations became commonplace. Travel from place to place was now forced upon them instead of being undertaken by choice to enjoy the company of smiling friends and relations.

PART THREE

WINDSORS AT WAR

Vain, mightiest fleets of iron framed;
Vain, those all-shattering guns;
Unless proud England keep, untamed,
The strong heart of her sons.

Sir Francis Doyle

1

In July 1914 the British Foreign Secretary attempted to mediate in the wars and crises in the Balkans. But already events elsewhere were getting out of hand after the assassination in Sarajevo of Archduke Francis Ferdinand of Austria and his wife at the end of June. Ultimata flew from chancellory to chancellory and the armies of France, Russia, Germany and Austria were mobilized. The Great War, which the people of Europe had for so long feared, appeared inevitable by the end of July. Germany declared war on Russia on 1 August and on France two days later. On 4 August Britain declared war on Germany, amidst great patriotic demonstrations in both countries.

On that evening, Princess Mary went to bed early at Buckingham Palace, weary from the emotions of the day and the non-stop chatter at the dinner table. It had been a small dinner at Buckingham Palace; besides two of her mother's ladies-in-waiting, and her father's naval ADC, there was only David and herself. The shouting and cheering of the crowds outside the Palace could clearly be heard, and the talk was all of the war and of how quickly it would be over and of Sir Edward Grey's speech in the House of Commons the previous afternoon. At one point in the conversation Mary heard her father say, "There is nothing else we could do. It will be a terrible war and we must put all our weight behind winning it quickly."

Towards the end of the meal, May said to her husband, "George, don't you think we ought to go out on to the balcony again? They have been calling for us ever since we last appeared."

"Yes, my dear, we will go now. Come, David."

Mary stood with the rest but spoke quietly to her father. "Papa, will you mind very much if I do not come this time? I am so tired and have a headache."

May heard her appeal and turned sharply, about to utter a rebuke, including some use of the word "duty." But Mary's ever-indulgent father just smiled and said how sorry he was. "You have shown yourself once to them, my dear, and I think that will do."

They had dined in the small dining room on the northwest corner of the first floor of the Palace, and now George and May and David, in that order, left the room and set off to walk to the Balcony Room at the front of the Palace facing down The Mall. The cheers that met their appearance as they stepped out through the open doors echoed throughout the Palace.

Mary and Else heard them from Mary's suite on the other side of the Palace, overlooking the gardens. When the maid drew the curtains back and opened the window wide in response to Mary's complaint of the heat, the sound was louder than ever. "The whole of London is out there, Else," Mary exclaimed, collapsing into a velvet-covered armchair and kicking her shoes off. "When I went out with the King and Queen and the Prince of Wales before dinner, they stretched as far as you could see up The Mall, but I hear there are many more now."

"What do you suppose will happen to me, Ma'am?" Else asked anxiously, "I mean, as a German, will I be imprisoned?"

Mary reassured her. "They'll not worry about you, Else. But of course the King is worried at the death and destruction. And he is worried about my brother in the Navy. And there'll be no Cowes Week—and no Balmoral either, not for a while anyway, and no grouse shooting for the King, which will be a great blow for him."

Mary at seventeen was now fully grown, and was the same height of five feet seven inches as her two elder brothers, less awkward than in adolescence and less un-handsome, though her Hanoverian chin precluded any idea that she would ever be a beauty.

Else helped her mistress out of her long dress and the corsets that so unnecessarily held tight her newly formed satisfactory shape. She had been with Mary for ten years now. "All of us loved her for her devotion and warm-hearted personality," David once wrote.

"At least it means I shan't have any more threats from Germany," Mary said with a laugh, "whatever the Navy and the Army have to suffer."

Else did not follow her mistress's line of thinking and asked for an explanation. "You *must* remember the threat of Cousin Ernest, Else," Mary reminded her. "The Queen wanted us to be betrothed. But luckily he married the German Emperor's only daughter. The Queen was very put out, but I was *not*."

Else did indeed remember those anxious months, with her mistress threatening to have nothing to do with the young man—or any other young man. How many times she had heard Mary say, "I shall *never* get married, Else. Fancy having to share a bed with a *man*. I would rather sleep with my horses in the stables."

Mary was shyer than anyone her maid, and her lady-in-waiting, had ever known; only really comfortable with them and in the company of her horses, and perhaps with her two elder brothers, and a little bit with her father. It was Bertie who was later overheard to say, somewhat disloyally but affectionately, "Oh Mary—Mary *was* a horse until she came out!"

No, there would be no threat of betrothal to any German relative until Britain and France had won the war. That was true. But, sweet, selfish seventeen though she might be, Mary had been deeply affected by the threat of war, and was deeply fearful of its consequences.

On the first night of war, after remaining on the Palace

balcony for a full fifteen minutes with May and David, George retired to his study to read some papers and write up his diary:

> Tuesday August 4th. I held a Council at 10.45 to declare war with Germany. It is a terrible catastrophe, but it is not our fault. An enormous crowd collected outside the Palace; we went on the balcony both before & after dinner. When they heard that war had been declared, the excitement increased & May & I with David went on to the balcony; the cheering was terrific. Please God it may soon be over & that he will protect dear Bertie's life. Bed at 12.0.

While her father was composing this entry shortly before midnight, with the war against Germany nearly one hour old, his daughter slept in her room not far distant from him in the Palace. It was an uneasy sleep, the sleep of the weary but anxious, broken by numerous dreams. Her father had told her a few days earlier of the Royal Navy's battleships and battle-cruisers racing up-Channel through the night, all lights extinguished, guns manned and look-outs straining for any sign of an attack by the enemy. "They are proceeding to their Scottish bases," George had confided to his daughter, "far to the north in Scotland."

It was a scene that provided the subject for one of Mary's most fretful dreams that night. She saw Bertie in his gun turret on board the dreadnought *Collingwood*. In spite of the half-light, she had a clear picture of him. Only a few weeks earlier, when the battleship was anchored off Brighton, she had gone on board and he had proudly shown her his action station in the control cabinet of "A" turret, and the fire control instrument called a Dumaresq for which he was responsible. Bertie, not stuttering at all, had explained about "rate of change of range," of "estimated change of course and speed of enemy," and other technical expressions and phrases which Mary had tried her best to understand because dear Bertie was so enthusiastic about his instrument and his newly-learned skill.

Now, in this dream, the *Collingwood* was racing through the water, pitching and rolling as she knew (to her cost) even the biggest ships did, the breeches of the huge guns angled low in accordance with the elevation of the barrels—just as Bertie had shown her. There were many more dim figures at their action stations in "A" turret, a shell poised ready in its cradle for insertion into the breech when the gun had been fired.

None of this was too clear in Mary's dream-picture; only Bertie's figure, bent over his instrument, legs apart, eyes glued to the lenses, familiar and vulnerable. It was a moving picture, like *Quo Vadis* which she had been taken to see, but no piano music, no sound at all, until she suddenly heard Bertie's voice, clear, unhesitating, loud and authoritative: "Enemy in sight!" he called, repeating "Enemy in sight!"

Then Mary heard a tremendous crash which threatened her ear-drums as the brilliant white light that accompanied it almost blinded her. And she knew at once that it was not Bertie firing those two 12-inch guns, but an enemy shell striking his ship—and striking his ship with deadly accuracy on "A" turret.

Mary cried quietly at the savagery and the suddenness of the catastrophe, awoken by the explosion of a celebrating rocket above the Palace, crying for her lost brother who was so gentle and had never done anything really bad in his life. She wished that Lala Bill still slept in the room with her. Mary might be seventeen and grown-up really, but she would have liked those big soft arms to hold her at that moment.

Reality was altogether less dramatic, although the last days of peace and the first days of war were memorable and tense for all those at sea with the Royal Navy. Thanks to immense perseverance, Bertie had completed his naval training in 1913, and was appointed midshipman on 15 September. Like his father before him, as only the second in line to the throne, he believed that the Navy would be his lifetime career. But unlike his father, who loved and lived for the RN, Bertie had discovered, once in it, that he was less keen on it than he had thought. At this stage he was only tolerating it,

knowing that no other career was open to him so he had
better make the best of it. It was typical of his philosophy of
patience and acceptance. He called it "bowing to the inevitable." He liked the comradeship all right, but he really did not
care for the sea, which always made him terribly sick. And,
far from improving his health, sea air seemed only to exacer-
bate the gastric troubles stemming from his infancy.

In Bertie's diary there were frequent entries like "Sick
all day," and "Very seasick the moment we got out of harbour . . ." But he carried on somehow with his duties, except on one or two occasions when the sickness was so severe
that he lapsed into unconsciousness.

Now that he had fulfilled George's ambition to have an
actively serving son in the senior service, relations between
George and Bertie took on an entirely different complexion.
George wanted to hear every detail of his life at sea, including all the "snotty skylarking."

> Sorry that with the help of someone else [he wrote
> to Bertie on hearing of a mishap] you fell out of yr.
> hammock & hit your eye on yr. [sea] chest, it must
> have hurt a good deal . . . I should do the same to
> the other fellow if I got a chance.

Life in the Royal Navy for young members of the royal family
was an oddly contrasting mix of roughing it in the gunroom
and enjoying the luxuries and privileges of high rank. It had
been the same for Bertie's Great-uncle Alfred, for his father
and for the Battenbergs, father and son. It all added a further
strain to a demanding life. Within days of having his ham-
mock cut down* Bertie, as Midshipman His Royal Highness
Prince Albert, was sitting down for dinner with sixteen
admirals.

The Navy's last peacetime summer manoeuvres in 1914
ended with a grand review of the fleet, the like of which
would never be seen again. Bertie had been proudly expect-

---

*A highly dangerous "sport," incidentally, which was only stopped
when one unfortunate midshipman broke his back and was paralyzed
for life.

ing to be among the other seven hundred and fifty-seven members of the *Collingwood*'s company when his father inspected the fleet; instead he received a message a few days before the event commanding him to join his father on board the royal yacht.

It was typical of the false position in which he so frequently found himself, obliged against his earnest wishes to forsake his shipmates and "hang about with the nobs," as they would have put it. So Bertie inspected several of the ships in company with his father, and on 18 July 1914 was obliged to sit next to him in the state dining room of the *Victoria and Albert* for dinner, with Admiral Colville on his right. All the flag officers, including the most venerable and senior of them present, paid much attention—too much by his reckoning—to him, enquiring after his training and progress.

The fleet was about to put to sea on exercises and preparation for war at the time of the assassination of the Archduke Franz Ferdinand. And so for the last time in peace the fleet steamed past the *Victoria and Albert* and their sovereign, who stood on the bridge to take the salute. The gigantic armada of hundreds of men o'war of all sizes and classes took more than six hours to pass before steaming out into the Channel. "We cheered ship when we passed Papa in the royal yacht," Bertie recorded tersely.

A few days later George wrote from Buckingham Palace to Bertie. The letter indicates more clearly than any other evidence the temporary halt to the harassment of his second son, coinciding ironically with the advent of the giant conflict, involving millions, with his cousin Kaiser Wilhelm II. There was indeed to be no Cowes in 1914, the racing in which the Kaiser had so strongly competed year after year; peacetime yachting for a week in the Solent was to be replaced by more than four years of bitter fighting at sea, in which Bertie, so recently unsure of himself, was to take his confident part.

Dearest Bertie [wrote his father]

Many thanks for your letter of 26th. I was also sorry not to have said goodbye to you last Sunday before leaving the "Collingwood." I quite understand you were in your turret. I also missed you on bd. the Yacht, as we were late in getting into harbour & it was raining so hard. I have just heard from yr. Captain that for the moment all leave is stopped on account of the European situation & he has asked for my instructions concerning your coming on leave on Friday as arranged. I have answered that of course you could not have leave until the situation became normal again. I am sure you would be the last to wish to be treated differently to anybody else. But I do hope that things are going to come right & that there will be no war & that you may be able to come on Friday or very soon after . . . I have had to give up my visit to Goodwood where I was to have gone yesterday & up until now, on account of the political situation, I have made no arrangements yet for going to Cowes on Saturday. I shall indeed be disappointed if we are unable to go. I hoped to have raced in the "Britannia" at least 4 times next week. Harry who has had a chill comes home tomorrow & George on Thursday. Our weather has been quite cold & blowing hard each day, a great change to all the nice warm weather we had before.

I shall be most disappointed if you are unable to come on Friday, but hope we shall meet very soon.

With love from Mama
          Ever my dear boy
          Yr devoted Papa
          G.R.I.

Bertie's father was due for the disappointment he feared, and it was a long time before he saw his sailor son, who became the subject of his nightly prayers for his safety rather than for an improvement in his academic progress. Bertie was suddenly a man, and a man at war.

In his usual prosaic style, Bertie recorded that night

passage of the fleet up the Channel and then north up the North Sea to its battle stations.

> We left Portland at 7.0 a.m. and went to General Quarters during the forenoon to try all the navy-phones. The Captain gave us our war stations before lunch. We started war routine at 1.0 p.m. . . I kept the afternoon watch alone, as I was one of the 3 midshipmen of the watch. After tea everything was rigged for night defence, and all boats were placed on the deck, and cables and wire hawsers were lashed and stowed below. After dinner . . . we went to night defence stations. The 4″ guns were all ready for a destroyer attack. We passed the Straits of Dover at 12.0 (midnight).

No "enemy in sight," no sudden explosion of enemy shell, as Mary's dreams had depicted. All that was still to come . . .

2

David steadied the Lee-Enfield, forced himself to relax, held the sight on the distant figure, aiming for the heart . . .

It could hardly be a greater contrast with Folly Hang at Sandringham, the beaters moving forward in a steady line, the beautiful pheasants rising, sometimes in pairs, sometimes in groups of four or five, climbing laboriously for height, their combined cry echoing back from the next covert. A steady right-left, two birds, one male, the other female, faltering in flight, feathers scattering and floating down, but soon outpaced by the heavy bodies, turning over and over before landing with a thud.

Now David was lying down in the butt with his "long" charger-loading Lee-Enfield. "Commence rapid fire!" Squeeze the trigger, right hand to the bolt, plunge it home, lock, fire again . . . ten times in quick succession, punching holes in the target, ten close together, every one "fatal." Those years out with the guns, often with his father at his side, instructing, encouraging, were paying off now, here, out on the range at Warley. It was supremely satisfying to counter any hints of privilege in being gazetted to the King's Company Grenadier Guards, even if five inches short of the statutory minimum height, by proving to be one of the finest shots in the lst Battalion.

A great deal had happened since I had stood on the balcony with my father and mother after dinner on the night the war broke out [wrote David of that time]. The very next morning my father signed my Army commission and in the afternoon I took the train to Brentwood in Essex where the battalion was stationed at Warley Barracks. The toughening process began at once. There were long route marches, breaking into the double every now and again, about the Essex countryside. Then there was squad drill on the square under the barked orders of a six feet four inch sergeant-major, gymnastics, swimming, field exercises, and every day out to the range.

I loved it all. Suddenly life had hard purpose behind it, with the clear goal of beating the Germans before Christmas. But in fact the war was not going well. The French and Belgians were being driven back, and no sooner had the British Expeditionary Force landed in France than it was forced to retreat. I knew it would not be long before the battalion was sent to France to give support, and I could already see the headlines in the newspapers: "First Battalion Grenadier Guards in Action: Great Heroism: Germans forced Back."

Then we were moved back to London, to Wellington Barracks. The sudden granting of forty-eight-hour leave in mid-September was a sure sign that the battalion was going overseas. But my immediate transfer to the 3rd Battalion, stationed at the same barracks, confirmed my earlier suspicions that I would be left behind.

It was a terrible blow to my pride. I went at once to see my father at the Palace, trying to conceal my bitterness. I asked why this had to be. My father answered that it was not his wish but Lord

Kitchener's. "Lord Kitchener," he said, "does not want you to go to France just now."

In 1914 Field-Marshal Lord Kitchener was a national hero, the victor of Omdurman who had avenged Gordon's death at the hands of the "Mad Mahdi," and a hero of the Boer War, too, virtual ruler of Egypt and the Sudan. He was a commanding figure with piercing blue eyes, an impressive waxed moustache, and a florid complexion. His authority was total. David had often met him, and always been deeply impressed by him. Now he decided without more ado to confront the lion in his den—the den being the War Office where Lord Kitchener now worked as Secretary of State for War.

Very few people would have obtained an interview at short notice with this great man just now. David pulled his rank without any scruples, as near as did not matter commanding the Field-Marshal's time; and then walked alone, without even an equerry, across St James's Park, rehearsing in his mind what he would say.

An ADC led David into Kitchener's office where the Field-Marshal was on the telephone issuing orders in the same tones, and almost at the same volume, as the sergeant-major at Warley. When he had finished he stood and dropped his head in a brief formal bow. "Your Royal Highness."

"It is good of you to see me, Field-Marshal," David said, sitting down and trying to keep his voice steady. "My father tells me you do not wish me to go to France with my battalion. I would like to serve my country like any other Grenadier—or any other young man for that matter."

"You, Sir, are a rather special case."

"I am a loyal patriot and a servant of my father's people. And anxious to do my duty, Field-Marshal." There was a huge painting of the Battle of Omdurman on the wall behind the Field-Marshal's desk with natives falling in scores, clutching their bare breasts or heads, and by contrast only one or two troopers spreadeagled in the dust of the desert. Beside it was a highly flattering portrait in oils of Kitchener himself, in full dress uniform.

"I appreciate your patriotism and your wish to serve your country, Sir. And you may be sure work will be found for you which will be as valuable as fighting in the front line. But I scarcely have to remind you that you are heir to the throne."

"What does it matter if I am killed," David pleaded. "I have four brothers."

Kitchener stood, his bearing adding further weight to his authority. "If I were sure you would be killed, I do not know if I should be right to restrain you. But I cannot take the chance, which always exists until we have a settled line, of the enemy taking you prisoner."

This was a contingency David had not allowed for, and he was temporarily at a loss for words. Then, clutching at a straw, he asked "And when the line is settled?"

"I do not wish to make a promise at this stage, Sir, with everything so undecided, but perhaps a staff appointment in France . . ."

David knew that he could pursue the subject no longer, and stood up, a sudden smile on his face of such warmth and charm that the iron Field-Marshal was forced to respond, though his smile was more like a stiff grimace. "It is kind of you to see me when you are so terribly busy, Field-Marshal Kitchener. May I wish you every success." And he stood to attention before turning to leave.

But David had not entirely wasted his time, and Kitchener's, by seeking that interview. As a result of following it up with a message reminding the Secretary of State of his half-promise of a staff appointment in France, he received a signal on 14 November 1914, ordering him to the staff of Field-Marshal Sir John French, the British C-in-C at St Omer in northern France. David was beside himself with excitement:

Buckingham Palace
14 November 1914

At last! So I am not to be disgraced by inactivity after all! I am to go to France the day after tomorrow & report to Sir John French. Then I trust that I will rejoin my battalion at the front. The whole prospect fills me with pleasure & satisfaction after my long fight. I have thanked Papa for giving his

permission & I think he is pleased & proud. But
Mama lamented having *two* sons at the fighting &
said she would pray earnestly for Bertie's & my
safety every day—& many times. I went to see Sir
Dighton Probyn with the news. "You will be a
credit to your country, dear boy," he said. "I only
wish I could be at your side. I would like to get a
bayonet into the guts of a Boche." Mary came to
my room & insisted on polishing my Sam Browne
belt which Finch had already made so that I could
have shaved in it. "Just to show how proud I am of
you," she said.

The next day, Sir Dighton wrote to an old friend about
David's visit:

> I saw the dear . . . Prince of Wales yesterday. He
> came to wish me goodbye—and it was really de-
> lightful to see the change that had come over him
> since he had last been in this room. On the last
> occasion he really *cried* with sorrow at the idea of
> "being disgraced," and he said he was not being
> allowed to go to the war. Yesterday his face beamed
> with joy. Do let Lord Kitchener know this.

In the early morning of the day before David was due to
leave, Finch brought him his usual tea in bed, drew back the
curtains to reveal a dreary November dawn, and seemed
disinclined to leave.

"What's the matter, Finch?" David asked from his bed.
"You look as if you're going to confess to stealing the crown
jewels."

"Well, Sir, I know it's rather short notice, Sir, and I am
getting on. But . . . Sir, is there any chance that I might
accompany you to France as your servant? It would please
me very much."

David smiled over his cup of tea. "How old are you?" he
asked.

"Forty-five next birthday, Sir. But fit as a fiddle, as you
know."

David said nothing for a moment. Then he suddenly smiled more broadly than ever. "By Jove, Finch, will you really? I don't see why not. After all Sir John French is sixty-three at his next birthday and he's running the show! You will have to go to the barracks this morning, ask to see the adjutant and give him the letter I will write for you when I get up."

And so it came about that the man who had been with David almost all his life, could be seen carrying a soft leather bag with the Prince of Wales's insignia on it in each hand, striding at his side up the platform at Charing Cross Station on the morning of 16 November, heading for the Dover troop train.

Lieutenant Prince Edward of Wales and Private Finch were welcomed at the Field-Marshal's HQ at St Omer that evening. French had commandeered a luxury hotel in the centre of the little Pas de Calais town, where he and his staff lived in style and comfort, while David was offered a house which he shared with five other officers.

David was seated on French's right hand in the mess on that first evening. He had met the Field-Marshal only once before, at a lunch at Buckingham Palace before the war, and had thought him a pleasant enough old buffer. He was of medium height, stout, with a florid complexion and bristling white moustache. He had made his reputation in the Boer War and thought entirely in terms of that protracted uprising, in which the British had as a rule heavily outnumbered the enemy. When he began to outline the present situation on the western front, he talked the language of that campaign, of kopjes and cavalry charges, guerilla raids and ambushes, burgers and Maxim guns: he even, on one occasion, had to correct himself when he confused "burger" with "Boche."

Above all, the Field-Marshal was full of optimism, which infected the whole GHQ, David soon discovered. Almost his opening remark to David was, "I'm glad you've got here in time. Another few weeks and there would be nothing for you to do."

"How do you mean, Sir?" David asked, mystified.

"The war would be over if you'd come any later. It'll all be finished by Christmas—you mark my words."

David's only explanation of this extraordinary claim was that GHQ was so distant from the fighting—some thirty miles and out of earshot of the artillery. He knew that reality was quite different, that the French Army and the BEF had suffered defeats and retreats from the outset, with terrible casualties. While still in London David had learned of the death of his equerry, Major Cadogan of the 10th Hussars, of no fewer than seven of his fellow officers of the 1st Battalion, of two of his father's equerries, of Prince Maurice of Battenberg, the First Sea Lord's nephew. "I shan't have a friend left soon," David had written despairingly in his journal.

David was assigned an office, a desk, a secretary and a pile of forms to check. His heart sank. "There would be nothing to do," the Field-Marshal had said. It now became increasingly clear that there was nothing to do anyway, that work was being "made" for him, and that Kitchener had sent him here to silence him and meet his wish to come to France. David had been warned by his father to keep out of danger as far as possible; now it became evident that he was not going to have the opportunity of doing anything else.

During these first dismal weeks David was a witness to the arrival of almost unrelieved bad news at GHQ, which was then reprocessed to emerge as optimistic war bulletins for consumption at home.

"It is very depressing," David confided to Finch one evening after returning from the usual prolonged and luxurious dinner—the port still circulating when he excused himself. "We are losing the war. We are short of everything—of men, guns and shells, and every day we are retreating at terrible cost. I don't flatter myself that I can do much to turn the tide, but at least I could shoot a few Germans before they shot me. And, Finch, there are seventy or eighty young men like me back here at GHQ who could be up there fighting instead of feeling guilty and doing nothing but eat all this French food and drink fine wines . . ."

Finch was sympathetic but, suspecting that his master might do something dramatic (for no one understood his character so well), felt impelled to issue a mild warning. It did no good. The next morning, after writing yet another letter to his father pleading to be transferred to a fighting unit, David "borrowed" a despatch rider's motor bicycle and sped off east. He could have used his car, and his driver, too, for that matter. He had formed a fatherly affection for his driver, Private John Green, an innocent wide-eyed farmer's boy who shared his master's wish to fight but was quite clearly unfit for the rigours of the trenches. No, the motor bicycle would provide him with fast, discreet mobility, where his Daimler would be recognized everywhere.

For the first time, the heavy guns could be heard at St Omer, indicating a big enemy "push." Daid wanted to see for himself what was happening. He had no intention of taking himself to the front line and embarrassing officers with his unwanted presence. But he did also believe—quite rightly—that to be seen would give moral support as soon as the news went round.

Before he had got very far, it began to rain and the dark clouds created a premature dusk. He knew he was going in the right direction because the sound of the guns could be heard above the engine of his motor bicycle, and their flashes lit up the sky like a continuous thunderstorm. David pressed on, soaking wet, past marching troops, horse-driven ambulances and the ghostly shapes of shattered houses and barns . . .

Back at St Omer the word had got around that the Prince of Wales was missing! It reached Sir John French himself, and in a state of near-panic orders were issued that all motorized transport must be commandeered, including David's own big Daimler which he rarely used, and search parties must be sent out to find him and bring him back.

The search continued for hours. Messages were passed down to platoon level. Field telephones rang. Word spread throughout the BEF—"The Prince of Wales must be found— believed to be somewhere near the front lines—inform immediately . . ." Thousands of infantrymen, fighting a German attack with everything they had, heard the news. And their fighting spirits rose.

No one will ever know exactly what effect on morale the knowledge that the heir to the throne was somewhere among

them had on the men in the line. But the line held that
night, and the following morning the true story flashed from
unit to unit about how and where the Prince had been found.
By chance it was one of his fellow officers in the 1st Battalion,
Grenadier Guards, who found him, almost within rifle distance of the front line trenches. A faint light attracted Lieutenant Gibbons-Crosby to the shattered stump of a tree just
off the road he was driving along. The Prince of Wales,
soaking wet and covered in mud, was playing, and winning, a
game of *vingt-et-un* with some *poilus*, and talking in French
with rapidity and fluency. They had no idea who he was, and
were not told when Gibbons-Crosby crawled under the sheet
of canvas they had strung up. "Excuse me, Sir, Field-Marshal
Sir John French is very anxious to see you."

David made his excuses in impeccable French, gave
them back their sous, and apologized to his fellow officer for
the trouble he had given. Lying beside the road were the
bent remains of a Rudge motor bicycle. "I think I hit a shell
hole," David explained laconically.

This was the most spectacular of a number of unofficial
visits to the front made by David—visits that led to his being
nicknamed "Dynamite" because "we never knew when he
might go off." Recognizing that he could not be stopped,
French gave in and regularized these expeditions.

A memorandum signed by the Field-Marshal:

> Your Royal Highness, Field-Marshal Sir John French
> would appreciate it very much if HRH would be
> prepared to make informal but prearranged visits to
> French divisional headquarters close to the front line.

These were a great success and kept David out of mischief for
a while that winter. But he was soon fretting again to be
allowed into the front lines and to be risking his life along
with his fellow officers and their men. His letters to his
father, and to his old friend Lord Stamfordham, the King's
Private Secretary,* took on a pathetic note as they were met

*Rt Hon. Arthur Bigge, created 1st Baron Stamfordham 1911. Pri-
vate Secretary to Queen Victoria 1895-1901, to George as Duke of
York, Prince of Wales, and King 1911. Died 31 March 1931.

with sympathetic but unyielding replies. With the publication of each new casualty list, many of them including officers
he had known in peacetime, his anguish increased. There is a
bitter note in the letter to his father dated 19 May 1915:

> I never see anything or go near the front . . . I feel
> that in later years I shall ever regret the fact that
> I was out so long in N. France & yet saw practically
> nothing of the fighting or got any proper idea of
> what our troops had to go thro. I shall have to
> remember the war by the various towns & places
> far back which were headquarters of generals I
> was attached to, of meals, etc!! But I have said
> enough!! . . .

But David knew that he had not "said enough." His tor-
mented emotions spill across his letters. Later, he was able to
write more coherently of his feelings during this most difficult
and tortured time of his life so far:

> It took me a long time to become reconciled to the
> policy of keeping me away from the front line.
> Manifestly I was being kept, so to speak, on ice,
> against the day that death should claim my father.
> But in the midst of all the slaughter of the western
> front, I found it hard to accept this unique dispen-
> sation. My generation had a rendezvous with his-
> tory, and my whole being insisted that I share the
> common destiny.

3

A measure of relief from this misery and guilt was provided by David's transfer to the staff of Major-General Lord Cavan, commanding the Guards Division. Frederick "Fatty," 10th Earl of Cavan, was a typical product of his times and rank, and—alas—of the senior generals running the war on the western front. Forty-nine years old, not privileged with a razor-sharp mind, Cavan was known as a "good sport," was as proud of being Master of the Hertfordshire Hounds as of his service in the Boer War, was utterly fearless and expected his officers and men to be utterly fearless, too. Although his opportunities for front line action were strictly limited by his HQ responsibilities, "Fatty" Cavan earned the honour of being mentioned in despatches no fewer than seven times.

David's arrival at Cavan's HQ coincided with the final preparations for General Haig's attack to deprive the enemy of an important ridge beyond Loos. These were days before total disillusionment had set in, and expectations were high. David at first shared the excited optimism—until the day before the offensive opened, 24 September 1915. He was on traffic duties, ankle-deep in mud, directing men, wagons and vehicles. It was pouring with rain. Soaked and half-dead with

weariness, units of Kitchener's "New Army," the volunteers
trained since the outset of war, marched by and up to the
front line. They had been on their feet for twenty-four hours,
David discovered, without anything to eat. The following
morning, they were ordered into the attack. The result was
inevitable and catastrophic. They were mown down in thousands as they stumbled across open, muddy ground, the
survivors finally halted at the German barbed wire.

It took the Guards Division to drive back the Germans
the following day, again with awful casualties. And on 29
September David accompanied General Cavan on a tour of
the battlefield. An extract from David's journal:

> Of course the dead lie out unburied & in the pos-
> tures & on the spots as they fell & one got some
> idea of the horror and ghastliness of it all!! Those
> dead bodies offered a most pathetic & gruesome
> sight; too cruel to be killed within a few yards of yr.
> objective after a 300 yrds. sprint of death!! This was
> my first real sight of war, & it moved and im-
> pressed me most enormously!!

Earlier on this same day David acompanied his general to the
ruined village of Vermelles. They arrived in two cars, John
Green driving David's and both drivers remaining behind to
guard their vehicles. Then the party walked east up a slight
hill towards the front line for over a mile, while rifle fire
cracked and bursts of machine-gun fire sounded like the rapid
tearing of linen sheets, and occasionally there were bursts of
enemy artillery fire—"a spot of Hun hate" as the troops called it.

"How do you rate our success, Sir?" David asked Cavan.

"Pretty bloody good so far. We've got the quarries and
we're on the ridge in parts—thanks to the Guards." Cavan
pointed his stick at a pile of German corpses, lying like grey
sacks of corn for collection after the harvest. "You can see for
yourself the Boche has taken some punishment."

They continued through a farmyard surrounded by shattered buildings. A single German shell whistled overhead.
No one took the slightest notice.

"Did the gas kill many of them?" David asked. The

Germans had first used gas almost a year earlier, and again at
Ypres back in April, gaining a massive advantage. The Western Allies could no longer flinch from using this new, vile
weapon themselves. This battle marked its advent.

A staff colonel intervened and told David that evidence
of the effect of the gas attack which had opened the offensive
had been found on some three hundred German corpses.
"What we discovered at Ypres, Sir, was that it blinded our
men and made them vulnerable to small arms fire."

The party was approaching a British battery which was
firing intermittently at a German position. David, like all the
HQ party, held his hands over his ears when a gun fired. A
sudden shout from a sergeant caused the guns' crews to
throw themselves to the ground, and as David saw them do
so, an enemy shell burst scarcely forty yards from them,
sending up a mass of earth and debris, some of which spat-
tered them. David felt the sting of a small stone against his
cheek. A captain commanding the artillery stood up and
called in their direction:

"There'll be more of that, Sir. Will you please take cover."

With evident reluctance, and slowly, like a recalcitrant
child obeying his father, "Fatty" Cavan led David and the
rest of them to an old communication trench, which they
then followed to HQ 1st Guards Brigade in a ruined farm. At
this point David's journal becomes somewhat technical:

> . . . after a short pow-wow, forward to an observa-
> tion sta. at point G.23 b 5.5 in our present 2 line.
> To get there we had our original system of trenches
> round "Triangular Fence" to traverse & then climbed
> out over to the original German front line past
> "Lone Tree" . . . In doing so we were able to see
> exactly what the assaulting parties of the Div. had
> to undertake on the morning of the 25th . . .

"Four hours later," David wrote, "the 4 most interesting hrs.
of my life!" Cavan and his party were back at the church, all
worn out by the physical effort, except the ever-fit, keen
Prince of Wales. Cavan paused as the cars came into sight.
"See what's going on, Eric," the General ordered. There was

a crowd round David's Daimler and no sign of either driver.

David ran towards the spot under the trees. There were branches and twigs scattered about the dusty earth and a clear but indefinable sense of death in the hot air. "Where's my driver?" David demanded of a corporal, who stood to attention and saluted. All those peering inside the car turned and shuffled away as if nursing a guilty secret. Among them David was relieved to recognize Cavan's driver.

The corporal, a young man no older than David, with a soft moustache and pale cheeks, said, "I'm afraid there's been an accident, Sir. Enemy shell, Sir. Shrapnel."

David could see that his car was punctured with numerous holes of various sizes ranging from six inches to half an inch, over the bonnet and fluted radiator and, more ominously, the leather seats, front and back. He did not need to ask more. "Where is Green, Corporal?"

"He's in Number 4 Field Ambulance dressing station, Sir. Just over there." He pointed in the direction.

John Green's body lay with several more at one side of the tent. David drew back the blanket from his face—that good, straight, honest Somerset face. He was told by the doctor that he had been hit by a piece of shrapnel through the heart and death was instantaneous. "Poor fellow," David said aloud but very quickly. "His mother and father will miss him. He was an only son, he told me."

The news of David's escape reached Buckingham Palace with the speed of a telegraph, and inevitably in exaggerated form. To begin with, David's driver had been killed with David beside him in "a miraculous escape." And so on. David had expected repercussions from the incident. But he did not expect the first communication to be so mild, and to be from Lord Stamfordham, who had just lost a son himself, rather than his father:

Buckingham Palace
Octr. 1. 1915

Sir,

You may like a line to say that while the King grieves to hear that your chauffeur has been killed

and realizes that your car, and I expect, Cavan and
yourself were exposed to heavy fire, His Majesty
received the news quite calmly and without blaming any one; and by His Majesty's orders I have
written to Cavan saying that he is content to leave
it to C's decision where and when you go into the
front with the object of seeing the ground over
which the Division is fighting. But, Sir, you who
are so thoughtful of others, will not, I feel certain,
forget Lord Cavan & the heavy weight of responsibility resting upon him in his Command & remember that your safety, your Life, so precious to your
Country, is another care which circumstances has
devolved upon him. Make it as light for him as you
can Sir! . . . God bless and keep you Sir is the
prayer of your humble and devoted servant.

Stamfordham

David's other "humble and devoted servant," Frederick Finch,
shared his master's anguish over his deliberately restricted
activity in the war and provided him with all the comfort and
support his role allowed him to assume, never for one moment as much as hinting at criticism of the powers-that-be
responsible. Finch was always ready with a match for David's
interminable cigarettes, perhaps a whisky and soda at the end
of an arduous day (never a large one, for David at that time
was the lightest of drinkers), offering him warmer clothes
when it became cooler in the evenings, taking his tunic when
the fire overheated his private room. When David wearied of
the drinking and sports in the mess in the evening and
returned to his room, Finch would be ready with a pack of
cards to relax his master's mind.

Imagine, then, these two men, more than a quarter
century apart in age, and as distant from each other as possible in class, education and wealth, sitting down late in the
evening opposite one another, separated by an upturned
wooden box for a table, playing two-handed whist, competi-
tively but with the utmost cordiality. Their conversation is
relaxed as if they are brothers, sometimes reminiscing about

boyhood pranks at Sandringham, fishing expeditions in Scotland, Osborne when the "Good Queen" was still alive—personalities among the staff or David's relations, skirting round only the delicate subjects, like David's relations with his father.

A hurricane lamp hangs from the ceiling; the flash of distant artillery fire penetrates the curtains; sometimes the lamp swings from the concussion of a British battery firing half a mile distant. It is November 1915, this is the western front in the biggest war in history, and it is nearly a year since the Christmas when the war would certainly be over. But then Field-Marshal French's time would be over, too, in a few weeks when he would be relieved by Field-Marshal Haig.

David's absence at "heavy" evenings in the mess was not remarked upon. It was generally understood that his position was a delicate one, and all the officers, from General Cavan down, liked the Prince for his modesty and winning ways, and admired his clear desire to get into the fighting. Small incidents were recounted about his determination not to accept any special privileges because of his position. It was recalled that a number of the HQ staff ended a weary day far from their base and had to make do with borrowed accommodation.

When what billets that were available had been apportioned to the senior officers [ran one account] it was discovered with dismay that the Prince was without a bed. When the fact became known, several of the officers at once offered to resign their billets in order that their royal colleague might rest in comfort. But the Prince refused all such offers. "I have been unlucky," he remarked with a wry smile, "but I can manage quite well on the floor," and throwing his knapsack down for a pillow, he laid down on the floor, covered himself with his "British-warm," and was soon fast asleep—tired out.

David's aversion to accepting any special privileges led to frequent sniping from his father, which was much worse for David than sniping from enemy lines. The wearing of ribbons for bravery was one point of contention which led to bitter feelings in David. One day he received a letter from his father which infuriated him. When he reached his room that evening, he threw himself on his bed. Finch was there, laying a fire in the minute grate. "Take a look at this, Finch—what am I to do?"

Buckingham Palace

Dearest David

. . . Ld. Cavan has written about your wearing the ribbon of the Legion of Honour. It is very silly of you not doing what I told you at Easter time, which was to wear the ribbons of the French and Russian Orders that were given you. I know the French order was given you in peace time, but I explained that if you had not had it, you would have been given it for war service, the same as Uncle Nicky sent you his order especially. The French naturally are hurt if you don't wear it. So get both the ribbons sewn on your khaki at once . . .

Ever my dear boy,
Yr devoted Papa,
G.R.I.

When Finch had finished reading the letter and passed it silently back to his master, David repeated, "What am I to do, Finch? Kings and Emperors are always giving one another decorations, like Christmas presents. If I were to wear the Legion of Honour today it would falsely suggest that I had been given it for bravery, as a French officer would be awarded it. And the same with the Russian order."

"It is very difficult for you, Sir," was all Finch felt able to say. "I am very sorry. Perhaps a mild response, Sir?"

What Finch was prepared to say was all that David

expected from him, and all he needed—the sympathy of an old friend. "If I write a reply now, Finch, it will not be mild."

"Perhaps you could wait a day?"

"I'll do that," David agreed, the beginning of a wistful smile on his face.

22 September 1915

My dearest Papa,

. . . First I must apologize . . . I think you know how distasteful it is to me to wear these two war decorations having never done any fighting & having always been kept well out of danger!! I feel so ashamed to wear medals which I only have because of my position, when there are so many thousands of gallant officers, who lead a terrible existence in the trenches and who have been in battles of the fiercest kind (many severely wounded or sick as a result) who have not been decorated. No doubt I look at this thing from a wrong & foolish point of view but this is the view I take . . .

Ever yr. most devoted son,
David

In mid-October 1915, after the limited success at the Battle of Loos, David heard from his father that he was coming to France for discussions and inspections—"to help the spirits of my troops." George left London on 21 October with his party, excluding Lord Stamfordham but including Sir Charles Cust, his equerry for twenty-three years and old navy comrade. He stayed at first at the Château de la Jumelle at Aire, conversing with high ranking officers, and incidentally learning of the disquiet felt about French's leadership. After that he toured a number of areas and inspected troops in great numbers, always with David at his side, and wearing his French and Russian decorations.

King George preferred to use his car, and when he reached a unit scheduled for inspection he would get out and walk down the ranks. He claimed that this was the most intimate and personal way of letting himself be seen, and it allowed him to stop for a chat now and again.

On 28 October George and David and their party, including Field-Marshal Haig, drove to Labussière to inspect the First Army. Then the party drove on to Hesdigneul and the aerodrome of the lst Wing, Royal Flying Corps.

Here Sir Douglas Haig asked the King if he would care to borrow his horse for the next inspection. "I think the men would appreciate it, Your Majesty. And they would be able to see you better."

There was an awkward pause. David, knowing his father's aversion to riding at any time, and especially on formal occasions on a horse he did not know, awaited his father's response anxiously. He would want to please the Field-Marshal, and perhaps the troops had been told he would ride down their lines? "The horse is mine, Sir," continued Haig. "I have ridden her for many years and she is completely quiet and crowd-trained."

"Very well, Field-Marshal. I will do as you suggest."

The mare was produced, and there was no further delay. All went well. George inspected several lines of troops, responding to the salute and looking easy and comfortable mounted on the mare, the field-marshal and David riding at his side. At length they reached the aerodrome, where the entire wing was drawn up, and flying had ceased for some time.

Fifteen minutes later, the inspection completed, the station commander called for "Three cheers for His Majesty!" The RFC response was magnificent, far exceeding in volume any achieved by the Army. And it was too much for the King's mare, which reared up, lost her balance, slipped on the wet ground, and fell back on top of her rider.

"Oh, my God!" someone shouted. "Call an ambulance." The horse had got up, leaving the King still prone on the ground. More than two thousand men had witnessed the catastrophe. "He's dead—our King is dead!" a voice cried out; it was Corporal John Squire from Brentford, an ardent

royalist, like most of his chums. "We've lost our King!"—
"Someone pick 'im up!"—"Oh, Gawd save im!" one or two
broke ranks and began to move towards the prostrate figure—
their lord and master. Then someone blew a whistle and
an authoritative voice shouted, "As you WERE. Stand to
ATTENTION!"

"For a few terrifying seconds I thought he was dead,"
David recalled. "We all rushed towards the limp figure; to
our immense relief it moved, and our worst fears were further allayed by our hearing groans mixed with indignant
rage."

No ambulance had arrived, so a group of officers, and
David himself, lifted the gravely injured King into his car,
propping him up in his seat. David and Cust got in behind,
and they set out for the château, George intermittently crying
out in agony.

"Why are we going so slowly?" he demanded crossly at
one point.

"We are held up by battalions of the Guards Division,"
David explained. "You were going to inspect them this afternoon." The King groaned, and David leant over to try to
catch his words, still unsure that his father was going to live.
George seemed to be expressing disappointment.

"I suffered great agonies all the way," the King later
dictated for his diary. "During 29, 30 and 31 October I
suffered great pain and hardly slept at all as I was so terribly
bruised all over and also suffered very much from shock."

On 1 November the King's Physician, Sir Bernard Dawson, decided that he could be brought back to England. An
ambulance train was provided. Before the King was taken
from his bed, he recalled that he had been going to decorate
a sergeant with the Victoria Cross. He felt wretched about
missing this occasion. Sergeant Oliver Brooks had held a
redoubt during the Battle of Loos for twenty-four hours almost single-handed and with a meagre supply of hand gre-
nades as his only weapon. "Please bring him to me," whispered
the King.

Before the train drew out, the sergeant was brought to
the side of his cot. Sir Charles Cust read out the citation, and
smiling through his pain, the King was just able to pin the

award to the kneeling hero's tunic and whisper his congratulations and express his pride. The word of this ceremony spread wide and swiftly through the ranks, doing as much good to morale as if the King had been wounded beside them in the front line trenches.

"The injuries were more serious than could then be disclosed," Dawson wrote later. "Besides the widespread and severe bruising, the pelvis was fractured in at least two places and the pain was bad, the subsequent shock considerable, and convalescence tedious."

And, as his official biographer noted, "Those closest to him realized thereafter that he was never quite the same man again."

Then there was the unfortunate business of "the pledge." The need for war materials of all kinds had sent thousands of men and women flooding into the factories. Their new-found wealth led to much heavy drinking, which in turn led to absenteeism and inefficiency. David Lloyd George, chairman of the newly formed Munitions of War Committee, considered that one way of reducing drinking would be by example. He then sounded out the King—would he lead the way? Inspired by Lloyd George's Welsh enthusiasm and power of persuasion, George very reluctantly succumbed. "His Majesty feels that nothing but the most vigorous measures will successfully cope with the grave situation . . . the King will be prepared to set an example by giving up all alcoholic liquor himself and issuing orders against its consumption in the Royal Household . . ."

Thus came about the "King's Pledge." Despite all the publicity, very few people conformed and "Mr Lloyd George's crusade left His Majesty and his Household high and dry."

4

In spite of Mary's reassurance to Else, a few days later the Queen had to call her to her sitting room and, almost in tears herself, told her she could no longer remain in the Princess's service. "My dear, you will have to choose between internment here, or return to your home. The King and I are heart-broken, but it is one of the terrible results of war."

Else chose to return to Germany and, with everyone in floods of tears, left with her trunks for the station on 7 August. Mary was grief-stricken and was seized with loneliness. Other people, she felt, were filled as never before with a sense of purpose. Also they had plenty of friends with whom to share the excitements and sorrows of these stirring days. She herself had nothing to do and no close friends of her own age. The familiar faces, the family intimates, and now Else, had all scattered, David completing his military training in the Guards, Bertie at sea with the fleet, Harry and George out of London. Her mother and father were overwhelmingly busy and preoccupied with things to do with the war—so busy that they had not noticed the emptiness of the life of their only daughter. But, then, imagination was never their strong suit. Whereas, by odd contrast, Princess Mary had a well-developed sense of imagination, and was perhaps too strongly inclined to self-analysis. Sandringham, beloved Sandringham, she judged, might prove at least a partial cure.

George and May made no objection to Mary's proposal to go to Norfolk for a while. In fact they were rather relieved at the prospect, being vaguely aware that there was nothing for her to do at BP. But for the war, preparations would be proceeding for Mary's eighteenth birthday the following April, and her taking her place in the royal circle. But state functions had all ceased with the firing of the first shot and would not take place again until victory was achieved.

"We shall miss you, Mary," George declared at the end of dinner before he stomped off to his study. "I will warn Cousin Louis where you are so that the Navy will be alert for any sudden incursion. We have been warned to expect bombardments off the east coast. It would be a feather in the Kaiser's cap to claim his Navy had bombarded a royal palace but I think von Tirpitz would see that it would be too dangerous to penetrate so far west along the Norfolk coast."

May was more concerned about her daughter's luggage and personal arrangements. Since the departure of Else, Mary had had the use of one of Lady Katherine Coke's maids. "She will be coming with you. She is very experienced at travelling. Do you find her satisfactory, my dear?"

Mary confirmed that she was "very pleasing," and at the same time wondered if her mother or father would ever ask her if she missed Else. She thought probably not. "Be very gentle with little Johnnie," May instructed her. "The least excitement causes him to have one of those terrible fits. And the doctor says they are very bad for him."

Prince John had been diagnosed as having *le grand mal*, the worst type of epilepsy, and the seizures had become so frequent that he lived all the time at Sandringham, looked after by Lala Bill and an under-nurse, beloved by all, but a constant anxiety.

York Cottage provided no escape from the effects of the war. There were soldiers with rifles on the railway bridges *en route*, and at all the stations, including Wolferton, where a carriage awaited Mary and her new maid. At the gatehouse two marines were on duty, presenting arms as the carriage clattered through and up the drive.

The housekeeper, Mrs Ridgeway, met them at the door. The butler, although over-age, had tried to join up, and Mrs Ridgeway apologized for the unraked gravel and the untrimmed lawn outside the front door. "We've only two gardeners left and they're both over sixty," she explained. "And now the coachman is threatening to leave us. I don't know what the world is coming to, Your Royal Highness, I really don't."

But at least the house smelt the same—of furniture polish and the scent of flowers—and for Mary it was lovely, as soon as she reached her room, to stretch out, still in her travelling clothes, on her familiar bed. There were paintings and smaller brown photographs of some of the ponies and horses that had filled her childhood, Leach hunting prints— and a reproduction Rossetti which Uncle Adolphus had given her for her twelfth birthday, in a premature effort to woo her from the equestrian to the artistic world.

After tea, she took Kate, her new maid, down to the stables and introduced her to two of her favourite old ponies in the paddock, long since put out to grass, to her two fine hunters, to Bobby and Beatrice, and to the dear old mare she used for hacking. There was much whinnying and whickering and stroking of noses, jealous shovings aside and proffering of chopped carrots and small handfuls of oats.

Here, at least, amidst this heady scent of straw and dung and horse sweat, the world was magically unchanged, and Mary was thankful that she had come. "Will you be going out before breakfast?" Rogers asked. "Like the old days?" And Mary smiled and said. "Yes, please, seven o'clock if that is not too early."

Nor had Johnnie changed very much, and Lala Bill not at all. Mary went to Prince John's room before dinner as he was being prepared for bed by Lala. He was just past his ninth birthday, and Mary noticed again what a sweet-looking boy he was, almost girlish with his fair hair allowed to grow long (it was always a business cutting it). What a tragedy about his epilepsy! Lala had prepared him for Mary's appearance so that it would not be a sudden surprise. The boy was clearly delighted to see her, putting his arms around her neck and saying her name over and over again. Then he ran to his

toy cupboard and pulled out the box of bricks which she had
given him many Christmasses ago and which he always showed
her when she visited him. Correctly arranged, they formed
into pictures of zoo animals. He needed a little help but not
much.

For several days—warm, sunny days, with the merest
breeze off the North Sea—Mary revelled in the curative
qualities of Sandringham, riding two or three times a day,
once swimming in the sea, visiting her old friends among the
staff at the Big House, and on one afternoon going down to
the railway station to greet Grandmama Alix, freed at last
from her duties in London.

Mary found her much changed by the war, and she was
certainly in no state of mind to enquire how Mary was managing without Else. It was "the filthy, cruel Hun" who had
invaded her beloved Denmark back in 1864 and "stolen half
the land God had given to us." "And now they are doing the
same thing to poor little Belgium, murdering all the women
and babies . . ."

There was no more violent hater of Germany than this
widowed Queen, and Mary, who had loved her ever since
she could remember, felt embarrassed for her and in her
company. This only added to Mary's sense of isolation and
loneliness. If only, if only, she had someone in whom she
could confide, someone to whom she could open her heart—
like dear Else, so steady and understanding.

But for Johnnie, Mary would early have consulted Lala
about her unhappiness, as she always had done as a small
girl. But her youngest brother, who occupied almost every
waking moment of Lala's time, presented an obstacle, a bar-
rier which Mary found difficult to surmount.

Mary had been at York Cottage for some ten days when
her maid brought her a message that Lala would love to see
her in her room if HRH could spare the time. Spare the time
indeed! Mary laughed to herself ruefully, and made her way
up the stairs. Lala's room, next to Prince John's, was on the
second floor, where bars had been secured across the windows, and a wooden wicket gate with a special latch was a
safety measure against a fall downstairs.

Lala, dressed as always in white linen with starched cuffs

and collar, greeted her warmly. "I've scarcely seen you since you arrived, Ma'am," Lala said, with a hint of a curtsey. "It is kind of you to come."

"You're always so busy, Lala. I didn't like to intrude."

"Well, now, Johnnie's sound asleep, and I have some cocoa ready if you would like some. And we can have a bit of a talk."

It was warm in Lala's room, close under the roof, and the window was wide open to the dusk. The familiar objects of a lifetime's service with the York family were to be seen everywhere—pictures on the walls, hand-made presents from the children—including a badly knitted doll Mary had made when she was about four, and a model battleship from Bertie. Lala's wickerwork armchair, with the faded blue cushion carrying the York arms, was like something out of a fairy tale retold after many years.

Never a one for delay or for mincing her words, Lala quickly got round to the subject that was clearly weighing on her mind. "You're looking peaky, Mary dear. I don't like that. What is it? You're missing Else, I expect?"

Mary nodded and sipped her sweet cocoa. "Yes, I do miss her. Second to you, she was my dearest friend. And you are always so far away and so busy, Lala."

Lala smiled sympathetically, and Mary waited for the inevitable aphorism. "The trouble is not only loneliness, and *that* is not easy to cure overnight. It's not like medicine for a cough. It's having nothing to do. And you know 'Satan finds some mischief still / For idle hands to do.' There is none of Satan in you, Mary dear, but you do need occupation. And our country has never needed busy hands like it does now."

"But Lala, I'm not allowed to do anything. It is easy for David and Bertie, they just have to go away and fight. I wouldn't mind fighting, too. But . . ."

"Listen to me, I have an idea for you." The chair creaked as she leaned forward, putting down her mug.

Mary waited. Darling Lala, always so practical, always with a solution . . . "I know Christmas seems a long way away but you know how time flies and waits for no man. And it may take a little time to get ready, too."

Mary listened, enchanted, to Lala's proposed scheme,

wondering at the ingenuity of this nursemaid who gave the impression she had little knowledge of the outside world. And at the end she said, "Now I want this to be *your* idea. No one will listen if they know it's Mrs Bill's scheme. It has to be Princess Mary's—her contribution to the war effort."

"Oh, but that wouldn't be fair, Lala. Not honest either."

"You need not say, 'I have thought of this idea.' Just write it down in clear words, I am no good at that anyway, and give it to Lord Stamfordham. Just ask him, 'What do you think of this, Lord Stamfordham? If you think it is a good idea, will you please present it to my father.' "

5

One week after Mary returned to London and Buckingham Palace, Lord Stamfordham was making his regular 10 a.m. visit to King George in his Study, with two family items on the agenda. They came at the end of a list which included half-family and half-state business. The position of Prince Louis of Battenberg* as First Sea Lord was becoming more and more difficult, with increasingly hostile public and private attacks on him personally as a German-born prince leading the nation's first arm of defence against the German enemy.

"It might have been all right, Sir," remarked the King's Secretary, "if the Navy had not suffered so many early misfortunes. But as Your Majesty is aware, there have been cries of treachery from the lower class newspapers, blaming for example the escape of the German battleship *Goeben***to secret signals she received from Prince Louis by way of the German Admiralty."

George, frowning deeply, and stroking his beard as he

*The King's cousin and father of Dickie Battenberg, future Lord Mountbatten.
**Actually a battle-cruiser of 23,000 tons armed with ten 11-inch guns.

always did when he was agitated, asked what Winston Churchill had to say on the matter. "Not that I trust that fellow. Prince Louis is not just my cousin—he's worth ten of that man."

"The First Lord believes he will have to go, Sir."

One day in the future, George was to write of Lord Stamfordham, "He taught me how to be a King." His advice was always wise and considered, and George almost invariably followed it. "And you?"

"I fear I agree with him, Sir."

George grunted and remained preoccupied as his Secretary continued: "And now for a more agreeable matter, Sir. It concerns your daughter." He paused.

There was a brief silence, then the King's face suddenly lightened. "And what has she got to say for herself?"

"A proposal has been made that every man serving in the Royal Navy and the Army should have a Christmas present, wherever he may be. May I suggest, Sir, that it should be called 'Princess Mary's Christmas Present for our Fighting Heroes'?"

"What have you in mind, Arthur?"

"Perhaps a brass box of tobacco or cigarettes, a pipe and a tinder lighter, with a suitable inscription like 'Imperium Britannicum,' and perhaps a medallion bearing the Princess's portrait."

"An excellent notion. We must start an appeal, and Mary must head it. Mary has not had much to do in this war and seems in low spirits. Well done, Arthur, you are a genius. I will tell the Queen at lunch, and my daughter too, if she is present. You have made my day."

The Princess Mary Appeal was launched on 16 November 1914. Part of it ran:

I want you all now to help me to send a Christmas present from the whole nation to every sailor afloat and every soldier at the front. On Christmas Eve, when, like the shepherds of old, they keep their watch, doubtless their thoughts will turn to home and loved ones left behind . . . I am sure that we would all be the happier to feel that we had helped

to send our little token of love and sympathy on
Christmas morning . . . Could there be anything
more likely to hearten them in their struggle than a
present received straight from home on Christmas
Day? Please will you help me?

[signed] Mary

The target was £100,000* and it was soon subscribed. The
brass boxes were manufactured, and in each, besides the
contents, was a printed card— "From the Princess Mary and
Friends at Home," and on the reverse: "With best wishes for
a Happy Christmas and a Victorious New Year." (Indian
troops in France got sweets instead.)

Mary loved every minute of the campaign, from attending committee meetings (and giving her opinion when asked),
to visiting provincial towns and cities for meetings. She never
spoke—would never at this time have dared to speak in
public—but her mere presence on the platform ensured a
good audience, and a good collection.

From a shy seventeen-year-old girl, she started to become a more confident young woman. Every day there was
something important to do, people needed her, asked her for
her opinion. The correspondence, beginning as a trickle,
became a flood, so that at one time she was employing three
secretaries. Then, after Christmas:

Dear Princess Mary,

Your cigarettes are much appreciated by me and
my mates in 4 Troop who have arskd me to rite on
their behalf. A good smoke does your spirits something wunderful in the trenches.

Thank you Madam
(signed) Len Atkinson, Private

Hundreds of letters like this arrived at Buckingham Palace in

*Say £3,000,000 today.

January, and continued well into the early spring of 1915. Mary read and answered every one, signing "Mary" at the bottom in her sensible rounded hand. For Private Mike Brabston of the lst Battalion, Irish Guards (and for how many more no one ever knew) the brass box proved a life-saver as well as a comfort. During the fierce fighting at Givenchy, Brabston was struck right over the heart by a German bullet. Mary's cigarette box was in his top-left tunic pocket and it deflected the bullet harmlessly.

In later fighting, Brabston was struck in the eye—a "Blighty"* this time. When he had recovered sufficiently he proudly presented his life-saving memento to the hospital matron, Miss Virginia Morrell.

Miss Morrell examined the tortured piece of brass with its disfigured likeness of Princess Mary on it. "Would you like me to send it to her, Brabston?" she asked him, and he agreed at once—"if you think it's all right, ma'am."

A few days later a letter arrived at the hospital, with the embossed crown and "Windsor Castle" at the head:

> Her Royal Highness is delighted to hear that Private Brabston is safe, and the box has been shown to their Majesties, who hope that Private Brabston will soon recover from his wounds.

Mary's war work became so demanding and time-consuming that she rarely got to York Cottage now. At one time four months passed without her once getting into the saddle. Public duty had taken over her life, as it had for so many other women, in the munitions factories filling shells, in the women's auxiliary services, nursing and in many other special war jobs.

One of Mary's biographers has written of the deep sense of responsibility that this young woman developed:

> She showed quite clearly during this period that those qualities of strength and endurance which as

*A wound bad enough to send you back to Blighty—or Britain.

yet had remained passive in her could pass the test of active experience.

Lord Kitchener, seeing her on one occasion talking and smiling with a draft of troops about to leave for the Front, said to General Haig, who happened to be with him:

"There's a little 'soldier' whose example has done more than anything to rally the women of England to the Colours."

Kitchener, terse and a man of few words, never wasted praise, and this tribute to Princess Mary is therefore all the more striking.

Princess Mary's education now took an important turn. No longer was she called upon to study with her governess, but to take the initiative in countless activities and to undertake the responsibilities of a leader. Her days became crowded with engagements and the few hours that were allowed for rest and recuperation she employed in the planning of schemes and the making of bandages for hospitals and comforts for the men at the Front. It was with the greatest difficulty that the Queen was able to make her daughter relax and take the rest that her additional activities as her mother's deputy demanded.

Take a day in July 1917, a time when the third Battle of Ypres (or Passchendaele) is about to open, with thousands dying in the mud from exceptional rainfall, and many others succumbing to the new German mustard gas. In a beautiful position high above the River Thames at Richmond, a hospital for totally disabled war wounded has been established. It is called the Star & Garter.* Here men who have lost limbs, or are paralyzed and immobilized, or blind, are being offered some purpose, some activity, to help make what life is left to them supportable. Here men in their wheeled chairs, supporting themselves on crutches or lying on couches, bear silent witness to the fact that they have given of their best in their country's service.

*Continuing its good work today in the same building.

These crippled wrecks, many of whom will never reach even middle age and for whom the thankfulness at being alive at all is sometimes very limited, have been working for months on handicrafts within their limited ability.

To raise funds for this splendid institution, an exhibition is to be held of over two hundred examples of the men's handicraft, all of it made painstakingly.

> The Star & Garter Home
> Richmond
> Surrey
> 12 May 1917

Your Royal Highness,

I am writing to Your Royal Highness at the suggestion of Sir Arthur Stanley of the Red Cross in order to enquire whether you might honour us with your presence at a special exhibition of the work of the gravely wounded ex-servicemen at this hospital.

Perhaps Your Royal Highness might also consent to present badges to those whose work for the hospital has been of exceptional value. The badges, one of which is enclosed for Your Royal Highness's approval, show the figure of Mercy tending the helpless with a suggestion of a Red Cross in the background.

If Saturday 14 July might be convenient for Your Royal Highness, the Committee members and I would be most honoured to greet you here at about 2.30 p.m.

> I remain Your Royal Highness's
> most humble and obedient
> servant,
> (signed) Frederick Treves

This was the sort of engagement that Mary found most rewarding. "I am looking forward to this afternoon," she told Lady Bertha Dawkins, her lady-in-waiting, on the morning of the presentation and inspection. "But this is your first visit, Bertha, to a very severely handicapped home," Mary continued to the much older woman, "I hope that you won't find it too upsetting. You will see that some of the men look alarming, and of course one must not give the slightest hint or indication of shock at their wounds and disabilities."

Bertha Dawkins had been with Mary for nearly three years now, and had witnessed at close quarters the rather gawky, shy girl of seventeen grow into the practised public figure of twenty years, prepared to address several hundred people, and, like some veteran of hospital visiting, actually warning in advance her lady-in-waiting of sights that might shock her.

The visit to The Star & Garter Home was a great success. Mary, looking at her best in white voile and a leghorn hat trimmed with blue ribbon and small flowers, was received by Sir Frederick Treves and Major John Dickie, the medical superintendent. The visit was widely reported.

All through that summer of 1917 Mary was busy with a wide range of functions—"a concert in aid of minesweepers" on 13 July, a visit to a munitions factory on 21 August, a baseball match between Canadian teams two days later. But by far the most important engagement, one that both hardened her resolve and changed her attitude to life, was her visit to Southend. In many ways it was no different from any others, although (according to a contemporary report) it was somewhat unusual that when her train left Liverpool Street Station she was "accompanied by a fleet of aeroplanes."

Mary was met at Southend by a Guard of Honour mounted by the RFC and the 4th Essex Volunteer Regiment. But it was the reception by the VAD and the subsequent tour of a hospital accompanied by these nurses, which hardened a resolve in Mary to take a new, independent step in her life.

The responsibility of attending functions like these over several years, of making many speeches and many decisions, of direct contact with the real world—moreover the real world at war—outside the protective walls of castles and palaces, had brought a new strength and a new edge to Mary's character. For this reason, when she made up her mind that she had carried out enough inspections, made enough speeches, presented enough medals, and received *quite* enough obsequious addresses of welcome and gratitude, she did not hesitate to make her views and plans clear.

"I have decided," she told her mother at breakfast one morning in April 1918 (a time when the war was going badly and it looked as if the Germans might enter Paris at any day), "to become a nurse."

" 'Decided,' my dear?" the Queen said in shocked puzzlement, as she poured the tea, unaccustomed to the use of such a verb in the past tense by her children, least of all her daughter.

"I am twenty-two years old, Mama, and quite capable of making my own decisions. I have watched for too long the wonderful work of healing and caring performed by VADs and I would like to become one myself."

"Well, I don't know my dear. I shall have to speak to Papa about it. It is very . . ."

"I have spoken to him. Last night." Mary was sitting up very straight in her chair, a set expression on her face—a face which had gained strength in its features in line with the new toughness of her personality. "And he thinks it is a very good idea."

Silence. May was not at all pleased but for once was lost for words. At last she said, in pathetic defiance but totally without conviction that it would influence the decision: "You know you will have to have your *hair* cut short."

Mary suppressed a smile. She had not expected to win her battle so easily. Her hair indeed!

6

Bertie's war battles had been of two kinds, mostly of a dispir-
iting nature, but finally—ah, the memory of that great fight!
It would remain with him all his life, to be recalled in times
of depression or at times when his frail self-confidence faltered.

But in those early days of August 1914, while David
fretted with frustration at being kept out of danger, Bertie
shared the pride and satisfaction of standing guard over his
father's United Kingdom and Empire with thousands more
sailors. Britain's Army might be puny by contrast with the
armies of France, Germany, Austria and Russia, but her
Navy, which secured the trade and the island shores, was the
largest in the world; and in 1914 "Britannia Rules the Waves"
was more than the title of a patriotic song.

And now Germany was threatening this rule with a navy
that was modern and powerful and determined, built in little
more than a decade by a great military power that had
defeated France less than half a century ago and was about to
attempt to do so again.

At dusk on the first evening at the anchorage of Scapa
Flow, north of Scotland, Bertie made his way up to the
bridge with Lieutenant Campbell Tait, the officer of his tur-
et and a friend of both David and himself. The scene was an

impressive and reassuring one. Anchored in long lines, the dreadnought battleships of the Grand Fleet gave an impression of strength and invincibility.

One of the nearest battleships to the *Collingwood* was the *Téméraire*, a powerful twin-funnelled dreadnought with two tripod masts so characteristic of British battleships and battle-cruisers, and—like the *Collingwood*— with ten 12-inch guns in six armoured turrets. "I served in her when she was first commissioned," Tait remarked. "And a dashed fine ship she is, too."

"Did you ever read Sir Henry Newbolt's 'Fighting Téméraire'?" Bertie asked. "It was one of the very few poems my tutor made me learn by heart that I really enjoyed. Wonderful poet, Newbolt." And, for the first and probably the last time in his life, Bertie quoted poetry to suit the occasion . . .

> *Now the sunset breezes shiver,*
> *And she's fading down the river,*
> *But in England's song for ever*
> *She's the Fighting Téméraire.*

"Let's hope we don't have to wait for too long before we *do* fight," Lieutenant Tait remarked earnestly.

At that moment Captain James Ley arrived on the bridge and Tait and Bertie stood to attention and saluted him.

"A nice evening for the first night of war," the Captain said. "And, gentlemen, I approve your sentiments. And the poem, Your Royal Highness." And he laughed.

"Sir Henry Newbolt, Sir. Not me," Bertie confessed.

The Captain strolled over to the officer-of-the-watch, exchanged a few words, and returned. "I don't know about action, gentlemen, but we've had one surprise already. You will hear about it officially in the morning, but there's no harm your knowing now. We have lost our Commander-in-Chief."

"Admiral Callaghan, Sir? You mean . . . ?"

"He has been superseded," said Captain Ley. "Sir John Jellicoe is taking over. And we've got a new name. 'Grand

Fleet.' Frankly, I don't like this idea of changing horses in mid-stream, but I do like the name, don't you?"

Other officers came up on to the *Collingwood's* bridge as dinner in the wardroom finished—the Commander, Horace Watson, Lieutenants Maxwell Napier and Horace Herbert, Midshipman The Hon. Bruce Ogilvy, son of his mother's lady-in-waiting, Lady Airlie, and a particular friend of Bertie's—and conversation became general. Admiral Callaghan, it was agreed, would be sorely missed. The fleet was accustomed to him as C-in-C and although Admiral Jellicoe's name and reputation were well known, it seemed odd that the change should have taken place at such a critical time. But on one subject there was complete agreement, and Bertie swelled with pride: King George had sent a telegram to the fleet wishing them all well, and everyone savoured it:

> At this grave moment in our National History I send to you and through you [i.e. Sir John Jellicoe] to the officers and men of the fleets of which you have assumed command, the assurance of my confidence that under your direction they will revive and renew the old glories of the Royal Navy, and prove once again the sure shield of Britain and of her Empire in the hour of trial.

Bertie soon left the bridge to turn in as he was on the middle watch—midnight until 4 a.m.—and by contrast with his sister who went to bed at the same time to the sound of cheering and clapping, all Bertie heard were the creaks and groans of a man o'war at anchor and the occasional cries of gulls.

Trained as every man in the Grand Fleet was for war, the sudden sense of vulnerability, the knowledge that their ships were now targets, that it was the intention of the enemy to take their lives, was a new sensation. It was a condition that no manoeuvres, no amount of peacetime training could prepare them for completely. In the hearts of many of these sailors there was felt a chill shaft of fear, mixed with indignation and determination to hit at the enemy first.

This was a time when supportive comradeship and disci-

pline counted most strongly, and it was demonstrated when
the Grand Fleet put to sea, division after division of battleships, preceded by scouting cruisers and escorted by flotillas
of darting destroyers, beneath a great pall of black smoke, as
if Scapa Flow were a suddenly active volcano. Bertie was not
on watch, but, like everyone else, he was on deck to witness
the stirring sight of the fleet putting out through the narrow
channel of Hoxa Sound between Hoxa Head and Flotta, and
then east into the grey wastes of the North Sea. Bertie
decided that he had never felt so excited, so well, and so
fulfilled in his life.

There was no contact with the enemy on this Grand
Fleet sweep and they returned to Scapa Flow on 7 August.
The German battle fleet showed no signs of wishing to chal-
lenge the Royal Navy, despatching only minelayers and
U-boats, one of which was rammed and sunk by the cruiser
Birmingham on 9 August.

Two weeks later Bertie's own private war, a war against
ill-health that had flared up time after time in his short life,
broke out again. With a sinking heart, he wrote in his diary
on 23 August:

> After lunch I kept the afternoon watch, I then went
> to the sick bay with a violent pain in the stomach,
> and I could hardly breathe. They put hot fomenta-
> tions on it, which eased it . . . Morphia was in-
> jected into my arm. I was put to bed in the
> Commander's cabin at 8.0 and I slept the whole
> night.

This time it was not his old gastric complaint but appendicitis, which was a relief, although it entailed transfer to a
hospital ship, and a nursing home in Aberdeen. Here Bertie
lay, awaiting an operation, when Jellicoe with part of the
Grand Fleet steamed out of Scapa Flow again and raced
down the North Sea towards Heligoland Bight, where the
first surface action of the naval war took place. Bertie read of
the British victory—three German cruisers and two destroyers sunk—in the newspaper as he lay awaiting an operation.

The *Collingwood* had not in fact been present—but how Bertie wished he had been there!

Bertie was operated on on 9 September by Professor John Marnoch of the University of Aberdeen, Hon. Surgeon in His Majesty's Household in Scotland. It all went off well, without much pain, and Bertie had every expectation of rejoining his ship after convalescence. Meanwhile, there were visitors, Mary and Mademoiselle Dussau, and on another day David and Mider arrived at eleven o'clock to see him and both thought he was looking well.

In spite of the most careful convalescence, spent mainly at York Cottage, Bertie's recovery was slow and interrupted by relapses and sudden outbreaks of gastric trouble as well. All through that autumn of 1914, while David at last got his way and went to France with Finch, Bertie remained out of the war, far distant from his ship, lamenting his ill-health. The heavy casualty lists, with many familiar names, and the capture of Louis Greig at Antwerp, added to his depression.

Privately, the King's Surgeon, Sir Frederick Treves, thought he should never go to sea again. It was as well that Bertie was not informed: it would have lowered his spirits even further. But by mid-November Bertie was physically very much better, which inspired him to start a campaign, quite as intensive as David's to get to France, to return to his ship, the symbol of his manhood and purpose in life.

Bertie sent notes to Treves and to his father telling them how fit he felt and asking for a remission from what he regarded as his prison sentence, although it was really quite the reverse. At last he heard from his father that the Surgeon would now allow him to return to service duties ashore and that if he did not suffer another attack, he could, after a period, return to his ship.

The shore duties were the most interesting that he could ask for, and, thankfully in uniform again, Bertie reported to the War Room at the Admiralty on 2 December 1914. His task was to keep up to date the great wall charts which showed at a glance the position of every major British warship, and as far as possible those of the enemy. It was a stirring time to be where he was. The Royal Navy had suffered a humiliating defeat off the coast of Chile when a German squadron had all but wiped out a weaker British cruiser squadron searching for it. Counter-measures were being taken, and the task of tracking down and destroying the German ships entailed the movement of many men o'war, including three battle-cruisers from the Grand Fleet.

King George was at Sandringham when news began to arrive at the Admiralty of a great British victory in the South Atlantic. The two big German armoured cruisers which had sunk the British squadron were sent to the bottom south of the Falkland Islands, along with the German admiral, and two of his three smaller cruisers had been sunk, too. Bertie, glorying in this triumph, and in his early and secret news of it, got a message through to his father on 10 December.

I have just returned from the Admiralty, and have heard that the *Nürnberg* has been sunk by the *Kent*, one of the *Cumberland* class. There are very few people who know this, so please don't tell anybody as I don't know whether it will be in tomorrow's papers or not. I thought you would like to know, and I am so glad to be the first person to tell you.

But Bertie was not the first person with the news; Winston Churchill had sent a personal message some hours earlier. George had no intention of allowing his son the satisfaction of boasting of "inside" news and told him so—"crushingly" according to Bertie's official biographer.

It was only a few weeks since his father had shown how proud he was of his son serving in the Grand Fleet and enthusiastically preparing to lay down his life for his country—a brave new Bertie. Now it became increasingly evident that his father had reverted to his old attitude, shared with his mother, of disdain amounting almost to contempt for this frail young man of nineteen.

By contrast, Bertie's affection and respect for his parents never wavered. He had been so proud of gaining for the first time their full respect; now he was more than ever determined to recover it. How strong this feeling was became evident later in his life; it was shown at the time only by the unremitting letters and memoranda so appealingly stating his case for being allowed to serve at sea again.

On 3 February 1915, while Bertie was on duty in the War Room, the fearsome Admiral "Jackie" Fisher, who had taken over from Battenberg as First Sea Lord, came in with Winston Churchill to study the charts together. They were discussing the condition of the German battle-cruisers, which had been damaged in a running battle with Admiral Beatty's battle-cruisers at Heligoland. "They are working day and night to repair the *Derfflinger* and *Seydlitz*, Jackie," Churchill was saying. "I have the news from Germany. We must be ready to meet them again before long."

Bertie was impressed to be in the presence of the two national heroes who were running the war at sea, and with his fellow officers stood to attention until they were told to return to their work. It was Churchill who recognized Bertie first, and at once expressed concern that he was not with his ship. "I thought you were with the *Collingwood*, Your Royal Highness," he said with his faint but characteristic lisp.

"I have been, Sir. But I had my appendix removed. Now that I am quite fit again, I find it hard to get back."

Churchill muttered something to his Private Secretary, and to Bertie said, "We'll see what we can do. I am sure the King is anxious for you to be at sea—he'd be there himself if he could—and wouldn't he love it!"

The next day Bertie was summoned to the office of the Second Sea Lord and was told that he should rejoin the *Collingwood* at Portsmouth the following week. That evening he wrote triumphantly in his diary, "I went to the Admiralty for the last time!"

In these early days of March 1915 Bertie was experiencing for the first time in his life a sense of fulfilment and hard purpose. He was now a senior midshipman and did not keep watch at sea. Instead, he was in control of the searchlights at night and in charge of submarine look-outs by day. While in harbour he worked as an assistant to the Gunnery and Tor-

pedo lieutenants, and ran the steam pinnaces and picket-
boats. He was still not allowed to take part in any of the
rougher sports like football and hockey, but he was able to
play golf on the course that had been laid out for officers.

German U-boats continued to preoccupy the fleet, just
as they were begining to cause havoc among merchant shipping, including the liner *Lusitania,* sunk with the loss of
almost 1,200 of her passengers, many of them women and
children, including 128 neutral Americans. "A terrible catastrophe with so much loss of life," Bertie wrote in outrage. "It
makes one so angry to think that after a thing like [this] we
cannot do anything in revenge. Here we are absolutely ready
the whole time and still we have to wait."

To keep the spirits of the thousands of men of the Grand
Fleet at a high level for month after month of inactivity was
one of the most difficult and important tasks of Admirals
Jellicoe and Beatty and the ships' commanders. But it was
wonderfully successful, as witnessed by Bertie's letters and
diary entries. Also, he was revelling in his renewal of good
health. "I have been very fit since I returned here," he wrote
to Hansell.

Unfortunately Bertie temporarily ceased to keep his diary after 5 May 1915, but it was some time during this month
that, with a sinking heart, he recognized the return of his old
gastric trouble. After a series of increasingly bad attacks,
Bertie had to bow to the inevitable; and there began another
period of semi-invalidism, which always left him with a sense
of shame as well as physical weakness.

At length, it was back to the Admiralty for "light duties"
and then three months of sick-leave. Then suddenly, and
thankfully, there occurs a break in the tedious and disheart-
ening routine of medical tests and instructions to "take care."
Like a sudden shaft of light in the gloom of war and personal
unhappiness, there came a letter from David in France.
Come out and join me, it said in effect. "Papa has telegraphed to say it is all right, and it will be jolly to see you
after all this time."

On 24 January 1916, in the grip of winter, Bertie arrived by motor at the HQ of the Guards' Division at La Gorgue. In the privacy of David's tent the two young men, in khaki and navy blue, embraced one another.

"How are things, Bertie? Papa says you have had a rotten time, but you don't look too under the weather to me."

They exchanged cigarettes, David sitting on the single folding camp chair, Bertie on the bed.

"I'm very well—perfectly all right to rejoin my ship. But the doctors are terrified of letting me do so in case something goes wrong and they get the blame. They think that even if the *Collingwood* blows up they'll be held responsible for my death. Anyway, who cares? I'd rather have a fine death than be wrapped in cotton wool like this."

"I agree," David declared warmly. "Do you remember Mider quoting Dr Johnson to us when he took us to the Tower of London years ago? I think of it often out here: 'Every man thinks meanly of himself for not having been a soldier, or not having been to sea.' "

"But it's even worse being a soldier or a sailor and ducking out of the danger. I think Papa would like us to be in the firing line," Bertie added in defence. "But he is surrounded by these doctors and advisers—"

"And Kitchener," David broke in, using the name like an expletive. "But Papa could overcome this opposition if he wanted to. He's just thinking of himself as usual, with Mama urging him on."

Bertie was shocked at his brother's bitterness and lack of respect for their parents but did not protest: above all, he wanted this visit to be a success.

And so it was. The next morning Bertie greeted Finch, known as Grandpa among the other servants, whose familiar features and steady manner Bertie found as reassuring as ever. Later, General Cavan allowed them to go off on their own in David's motor, with only David's ADC, cautioning them of an imminent bombardment of an enemy position later in the morning. Bertie looked about him in wonder, asking his brother questions, as they drove up a rutted frozen road with many deviations round shell holes and piles of rubble of smashed buildings. He had read a great deal about conditions up at the front, and seen hundreds of photographs in the newspapers, the *Illustrated London News* and *Graphic*. Reality was even worse. In one village, only a part of the church remained standing; every other building had been reduced to rubble. And yet, amazingly, the inhabitants—or some of them—still lived among these ruins, in makeshift huts or tents, in spite of the danger of a fresh bombardment.

"Why are they allowed to?" he asked David.

"They're moved out from time to time," he said. "But they always come back. And a great nuisance they are, too, poor souls."

They reached the summit of a slight incline, which allowed them a wide view over the landscape—if it could be called that—to the east and towards the German lines. A company of soldiers marched by, greatcoats buttoned to the neck against the cold, heads bowed like beasts on their way to the abattoir.

Their lieutenant looked up curiously at the officers standing in the back of the big Daimler, suddenly recognized the Prince of Wales and saluted, at the same time ordering his corporal to give the "Eyes left!"

David and Bertie returned the courtesy, and the officer suddenly doubled back to the car. "Excuse me, Your Royal Highness, Sir, I think I ought to warn you that the guns behind you will be opening fire in five minutes."

David thanked him and ordered his driver to drive on behind the party. "I think we may enjoy a little excitement if we are lucky," he remarked to Bertie with a confiding smile. "It's no good your coming all this way and not seeing a bit of Hun hate."

The car was fully half a mile from the well-camouflaged guns when they opened up. As a naval gunnery officer, Bertie had been present at dozens of practice "shoots" and had been inside a 12-inch gun turret many times, on a number of occasions firing the guns himself. He had taken part in "shoots" of a very different kind, too, on land and with game as the target, with as many as two hundred guns at a time. But he had never heard anything to compare with the volume and intensity of sound of half a dozen batteries of

18-pounders each firing eight rounds a minute. The percussive effect almost shattered the ear-drums, and they all held their gloved hands tight over their ears for the five-minute-long intensive bombardment, while the air about them was stirred into a half-gale by the rushing shells passing above.

David's driver was just beginning to give warning of enemy counter-action when, with a shriek and a final who-o-o-sh, a German shell landed between them and the batteries. David took out his binoculars and trained them on the skyline to the east, hoping to identify the position by the flash of the enemy guns. Bertie with his own glasses caught a glimpse of an artillery spotting plane, surrounded by brown puffs of bursting antiaircraft shells. A moment later a German observation balloon rose swiftly up into the sky on the end of its cable, and Bertie thought he could just make out the crew of two brave men in the suspended basket who would be spotting the fall of German shell.

"They are laying on a good show for us," David said, delighted at this evidence of enemy activity. At that moment three German howitzer shells landed close by, two on one side of their car, the third slightly more distantly to the left, just as if the audience of this "good show" had been identified. The ground shuddered as the stench and smoke drifted away in the wind . . .

Their driver, a good deal more rattled by this display of enemy "hate," had meanwhile got out of the car and was waving at them, "I think we ought to take cover, Sir," he called up, and David's ADC looked questioningly at him.

Other guns had joined in and the ground began to shake more violently and the air to fill with smoke and dust. These two young officers, the heir to the British crown and his brother, stood for a moment longer, utterly vulnerable to the ever-increasing volume of shellfire. Then David, understanding the dilemma of their driver and his ADC, who could scarcely run for cover without them, jumped out of the car.

"Come along, Bertie, we don't want your name on the blood list tomorrow—think how furious Papa would be!"

There was a disused trench a hundred yards away, and the four men ran towards it, a shell covering them with dust and sending fragments of frozen earth through the air. One of these caught Bertie on his right cheek, and when he put his hand to it he saw that it was smeared with blood. He had been wounded!

But Bertie's "wound" was no more than a scratch, and from the shelter of the trench and standing on an old ammunition box, he and David continued to watch the German bombardment, which now appeared to be concentrated on a point just south of the batteries, where a number of houses still stood flanking an already well-shelled road. At the same time, the British batteries opened fire again in double retaliation, which for several minutes caused an overwhelming cacophony of sound of both firing and bursting shells, as if the gates of hell had suddenly opened and all its inmates had set up a continuous roar of defiance.

Through the increasing clouds of smoke and dust, Bertie could still see the effect of the German explosions. "I saw several houses shelled by the Boches," he wrote that evening to a friend in *Collingwood*, "and the women and children running out by the back door. That makes one think of the horrors of war and those people who are shelled every day."

7

Four months later Bertie felt once again that he was the special target of German gunfire. Instead of a Daimler motor, this time Bertie was in his ship, sitting on the steel top of the foremost turret of the *Collingwood* with several others, including Lieutenant Tait and a distinctly overweight petty officer. It was just before 6.30 on the evening of 31 May 1916, and all this informal party on the roof were straining to obtain a sighting of the German battle fleet which they heard was rapidly approaching them from the south.

There was still nothing to be seen through the mist and black funnel smoke when two enemy shells "came out of nowhere, or so it seemed." They were heavy shells, probably 11-inch. As one struck the water to the starboard of the racing battleship, sending up a huge plume of water as high as the foremast, the second screamed like a banshee overhead and exploded on the port side with a similar effect—the perfect straddle.

This time Bertie made for safety more swiftly than he had back in January with David. "I was distinctly startled," he wrote later, "and jumped down the hole in the top of the turret like a shot rabbit!!" Immediately behind him the petty officer tried to follow him. But the hatch was too narrow for his girth and he became firmly stuck while Bertie and a midshipman pulled at his legs with all their might and Tait pushed from above. At the same time they heard distinctly the explosion of two more enemy shells, closer this time— "so close that the turret officer, who remained outside, could see the colour of the shells."

Perhaps it was the shock effect on the unfortunate petty officer that led him to succeed in extricating himself—or a good push from the turret officer. Anyway, his feet touched the top rung of the ladder below and he emerged, sore and rattled, but at once resumed his post along with Bertie and the rest. Tait took command and with Bertie's eye at his trainer's telescope, they prepared to open fire as soon as they had sight of the enemy.

Twenty-four hours earlier Bertie had been in the depths of depression. Ever since his return from France he had been locked into his own private campaign—to get back to his ship. As recently as 5 May, he had at last won, and was ordered to rejoin the *Collingwood*. Moreover, this welcome news coincided with his appointment to substantive rank of sub-lieutenant. It seemed that luck was at last on his side. He was sorry to leave his fellow midshipmen in the gunroom, but he had a warm welcome in the wardroom from the ship's officers. They knew how badly he had felt about his long absences, and his love of this battleship and loyalty towards all the ship's complement was transparently evident. Long since, he had let it be known that this was his real home. Here he behaved with total naturalness, and they all paid him the compliment of treating him similarly.

For more than three weeks Bertie had felt wonderfully well, and his spirits were high. Like his fellow officers, when at anchor in Scapa Flow, he visited friends in other ships, and on 28 May had taken a boat across to the battle-cruiser *Invincible* to take supper with an old friend from Dartmouth days, Derek Birch.

The next morning he was suffering from acute stomach pain, and his mercurial spirits sank as he reported sick and took to his bunk. He was greatly cheered when Lieutenant Tait visited him and told him that his friend was in the same condition. "Must have been something you ate!"

"Soused mackerel—that's it!" Bertie exclaimed, and groaned. "Too much of it."

"Well, at least it's not your old trouble."

It was indeed a very great consolation, but meanwhile the pain continued and he was sick time and again. He was still suffering pain and in his bunk when, at 5.16 p.m. on 30 May, the entire Grand Fleet was ordered to raise steam. One more false alarm! All it meant to Bertie was that, if they put to sea, the vibration and rolling would make him feel even worse, with the usual sickness as well.

Later that evening Admiral Jellicoe ordered his twenty-four dreadnought battleships, his battle-cruisers including the *Invincible*, and all the destroyer flotillas and scouting forces, to be ready to leave Scapa by 9.30 p.m. It was just midnight when the *Collingwood* followed her flagship, *Colossus*, into the blackness of the North Sea. In the cruising order which the battleships now assumed, *Collingwood* was second in line of the fifth of the six battle squadrons which now formed up. Like a double trident, this massive concentration of naval power sped east across the blackness of the North Sea, identifiable only by the white wash of bow waves and wakes astern.

At dawn Bertie groped his way to the wardroom in his dressing gown to hear if there was any news—not that there ever was. No doubt that, as usual, when they had made their rendezvous with Admiral Beatty's battle-cruiser fleet, they would turn about for base again.

"No, nothing to report," he was told. "Quiet as a bloody nun on the bridge."

Lieutenant Tait takes up the account of that day's proceedings:

Suddenly at about 2 p.m. a signal was received that the German High Seas Fleet was out and engaging our battle-cruisers only forty miles away and that the battle was coming in our direction. Huge excitement. Out at last. Full speed ahead. Sound of "Action"—you can imagine the scene! Out of his bunk leaps "Johnson."* Ill? Never felt better! Strong

*Bertie's *nom de guerre*

enough to go to his turret and fight a prolonged action? Of course he was, why ever not?

From the fore turret of the *Collingwood*, Bertie enjoyed as good a view of the engagement as anyone could have on this evening of rolling mist clouds and smoke from guns and burning ships. At about 6.15 p.m. the first evidence of the ferocious battle still being fought by Beatty and his surviving battle-cruisers came into the lens of Bertie's telescope:

> As we came up the *Lion*, leading our battle-cruisers, appeared to be on fire [Bertie recorded later], the port side of the forecastle . . . They turned up to starboard so as not to cut across the bows of the Fleet. As far as one could see only 2 German Battle Squadrons [in fact six] and all their battle-cruisers were out. The *Colossus* leading the 6th division with the *Collingwood* her next astern were nearest the enemy.

The *Collingwood* was turning to follow her flagship on to a new more southerly heading to cut off the German fleet when Bertie caught sight of a German cruiser, stationary in the water, already damaged and within range. The well-practised, complex but swift procedure of swinging the twin 12-inch guns of "A" turret on to the target, adjusting the elevation, was followed, and in less than a minute and for the first time in her life, the *Collingwood*'s guns fired in anger. Eight salvoes were fired, each causing the 19,000-ton ship to give a shudder like the shock of a boxer's punch.

"The *Collingwood*'s second salvo hit," Bertie reported, adding that the enemy was set on fire, "and sank after two more salvoes were fired into her."

Some minutes later the wreckage of a big ship came into view. She had broken in two, and so shallow was the water in this part of the North Sea that the bows and stern stuck out of the water like twin gravestones. Bertie heard the sound of cheering as some of the men decided that this was a German battle-cruiser or battleship, and confirmation of Admiral Beatty's earlier success. But, peering to port as they sped by this grim evidence of battle, Bertie was able to read the name-plate across the doomed ship's stern. She was the *Invincible*, in whose wardroom he had supped so injudiciously three nights earlier—and his heart went out to Birch, trapped with his shipmates in one or other half of this battle-cruiser.

They had already seen another big ship blow up, which was later identified as the armoured cruiser *Defence*. And then, at last, Bertie caught sight of the main enemy battle fleet through the mist which at one moment cut visibility to less than a mile, then as suddenly lifted so that briefly they could see a dozen miles to the south. Here the skyline seemed filled with the unfamiliar silhouettes of German battleships and battle-cruisers beneath a huge pall of smoke. After nearly two years of war there they were! Bertie felt a great surge of wonder and awe, soon giving way to a determination to destroy them.

The enemy battle-cruiser *Derfflinger* was barely four sea miles distant when "A" turret's guns swung on to her, and as the yellow muzzle flash of the German guns shone out like the ignition of giant matches, "A" turret's guns again opened fire. Through his glass, Bertie "could see huge holes torn in the enemy's side, exposing the main deck which glowed like a furnace, with flames leaping up through a rent in her quarter-deck."

Bertie's report continued: "One of the *Collingwood's* salvoes hit her abaft the after turret, which burst into a fierce flame . . ." But, like all the enemy fleet, she turned away on her track and was soon lost in the thickening mist.

In the German destroyer attack mounted to cover the battle fleet's retreat, the *Collingwood's* 4-inch guns opened an intense fire on the racing little German ships, and she managed to evade two torpedoes, one of which passed astern, the other just ahead of her.

None of the Grand Fleet's battleships took part in the spasmodic night fighting, which was mainly between the destroyers and light cruisers, and disappointment set in at dawn when there was no sign of the enemy and little expectation of finding his battle fleet again. For the battleships the engagement had been little more than a skirmish in the mist. Only the battle-cruisers were engaged for any length of time, and in the *New Zealand*, which survived with no damage and fired with greater accuracy and effect than any of the other battle-cruisers, Georgie Battenberg had had an exhausting time in his 12-inch gun turret. Like Bertie, he was mentioned in Admiral Jellicoe's despatches after the battle, an honour they both deserved and treasured.

It may have been an indecisive engagement, but the effect on Bertie was electrifying and, as with everyone who has seen action, it lasted all his life. "In a single summer afternoon," concluded his biographer, "he had passed into the full dignity of manhood . . . He had felt the excitement of battle . . . he had known the pride of sharing with others in victory and the sorrow that this victory had been robbed of its ultimate fulfilment."

Above all Bertie had passed a young man's ultimate examination, beside which the academic failures at Osborne and Dartmouth were negligible and now forgotten: he had been put to the test of fear and passed with flying colours. "When I was on top of the turret," he wrote to David, "I never felt any fear of shells or anything else. It seems curious but all sense of danger and everything else goes except the one longing of dealing death in every possible way to the enemy."

Bertie's attitude to death was the simple one of his generation, and it relieved the after-battle anguish which might otherwise have been unbearable. He lost other friends than those in the *Invincible*. But, "In a war on such a scale as this," he wrote, "of course we must have casualties and lost ships & men, but there is no need for everyone at home to bemoan their loss when they are proud to die for their country."

With "the blooding of Jutland," Bertie was reinstated in his father's esteem. "I am pleased with my son," he wrote; and determined to honour him with the Garter—"Remember it is the oldest Order of Chivalry in the world." Bertie was tremendously impressed, more for its significance as confirmation of his father's renewed regard for him than the insignia and robes of the order. "I feel very proud to have it, and will always try to live up to it." The event secured "a bare mention" in May's diary; none at all in George's.

A year after the battle Bertie, with the rank of acting lieutenant, reported for sea duty in the super-dreadnought *Malaya*, a 15-inch-gun battleship which had given a good account of herself at Jutland. Campbell Tait, now a commander, came too, along with other old friends. But above all, Bertie was reunited with Louis Greig, who had been released from a German prison camp in an exchange deal, and had been appointed as a surgeon in the battleship. "It is so nice having a real friend as a messmate and he is very cheery," Bertie wrote to his mother. The two men were to be inseparable for the rest of the war and for years after. Jutland had made a man of Bertie, and Greig was to polish and shape him for the remainder of his life.

8

"Well, it has to come," wrote Hansell to his sister. "It is a terrible future we face although many see the war as a brief inconvenience." He went on to say that he had Prince Henry and Prince George with him. Lady Beauchamp was teaching them French while he dealt with the other subjects. Eton had greatly improved Prince Henry, while his younger brother was industrious and intelligent. The youngest Bowes-Lyon boy, David, was to join Prince Henry in Mr Lubbock's house next half. The boys were craving for Scotland, but there was no question of the Court's moving to Balmoral for the present.

Harry and George were not the only young people who craved for Scotland in August 1914. Two others were staying reluctantly in St James's Square. At the Coliseum on the first night of the war Elizabeth and David Bowes-Lyon had watched Roshanara in Indian and Burmese dancing. They had enjoyed Lipinski's actresses, but best of all they had liked the turn called "Dog Actors." It was a fourteenth birthday treat for Elizabeth.

When they came out of the theatre at eleven o'clock the crowds were thick in the streets. David held Elizabeth's hand protectively as they wriggled through to their waiting carriage, their mother and father following them.

"Come on, kiddies—'ave a swaller—do yer good?" a leering drunk shouted at them, standing in their path. "Come on to the Palace—show you love yer King and Queen and yer country . . ."

David, twelve years and not tall for his age, pushed him aside and took Elizabeth past him, hurrying her on. "Everything seems to be happening on your birthday!" he said to her, smiling. Elizabeth felt well able to look after herself in a crowd, but she liked to see David in a protective role and knew how proudly he played it. Meanwhile their father had now caught them up and took charge for the last few yards to their carriage, to ensure that they were not interfered with.

There were people dancing on the top decks of the open buses and even in St James's Square, usually empty and discreetly quiet at this time of night, there were people singing and lying on the pavement against the railings of the centre gardens.

"Those first days of the Great War were very busy," Elizabeth recalled. "All my brothers, except David of course—he was too young—joined their regiments, and even my father, who would be sixty in March, put on uniform. For a time, our place in St James's Square was more like a barracks than a house, with Fergus, Patrick, Jock and Michael clattering about, leaving dirks, swords and even rifles in the hall. David and I took no part in all this preparation for war and had little to do." And to her biographer Elizabeth spoke of "the bustle of hurried visits to chemists for outfits of every sort of medicine and to gunsmiths to buy all the things that people thought they wanted for a war."

Then suddenly their mother seemed to notice their idleness and, to their delight, said they were to go to Scotland. Train services were already being disrupted by the movement of troops and sailors, and security measures against spies. "It was a wretched journey," David wrote. "The train was seven hours late and we had to sit up all night, and when we at last got to Glamis we discovered that it was expected we would be arriving with our mother in a week's time. Some of the men had already joined the local battalion, the 5th Black Watch, and the wives of the married men were worried sick—before they had even left for France."

David went on to describe "the eeriness of dear old Glamis," with no house party, no guests even. "The Glorious Twelfth passed with an uncanny silence." The maids had been told to look out comforts for the troops for the coming winter. Trunks were rifled and an assortment of old coats and shooting jackets, picnic rugs and woollen jumpers, were put in the hall. "The billiard-table was piled high with 'comforts'; thick shirts and socks, mufflers, body-belts and sheepskin coats to be cut out and treated with some kind of varnish." David and Elizabeth tried to bring back some of the old life into the place by playing tennis and croquet and riding their bicycles in their own invented game of polo on the lawn.

Their mother arrived from London with her maid on 23 August. Cecilia was full of news and plans, which she divulged over the lunch table soon after she arrived. "All the boys have left for their barracks except Fergus, and he is going on Saturday," she told them. "Papa will be remaining in London for the time being. He has some ridiculous notion of *fighting*, would you believe it? 'Every man will be needed,' he keeps saying, the dear old thing. But he may get some sort of staff appointment in view of his experience. Then there is what to do with Glamis."

"Are you going to close it down, Mama?" Elizabeth asked anxiously.

"No. But I am thinking of turning it into a hospital."

David could not believe his ears. "A hospital, Mama? with doctors and nurses and operating tables? But we're miles from anywhere . . ."

"More a convalescent home," Cecilia corrected herself. "Papa is making enquiries at the War Office. He'll have a word with Lord Kitchener, I expect, to find out what is most wanted.

"Then we're going to have two weddings next month. Jock is going to marry Fenella, if he's not sent to France first. And Fergus is going to marry his Chrissie."

Both boys had been engaged for some time, Jock to Fenella Hepburn-Stuart-Forbes-Trefusis, daughter of Baron Clinton, and Fergus to Lady Christian Norah Dawson-Damer, the twenty-four-year-old second daughter of the Earl of Portarlington. They had not intended to wed until the spring of 1915, but under the sudden pressure of war they had both decided to get married at once—perhaps before they were killed?

Now the idleness of the first days of the war changed to feverish industry. "Lessons were neglected," Elizabeth recounted, "for during these first few months we were so busy knitting, knitting, knitting and making shirts . . . My chief occupation was crumpling up tissue paper until it was so soft that it no longer crackled, to put into the lining of sleeping-bags."

By December the huge dining hall at Glamis had been turned into a hospital ward, with lines of beds along two walls, and two more rows down the centre.

David went off to Eton, leaving Elizabeth feeling lonely. Usually there were other children of her age at Glamis, visiting with their parents, but social life had come to a halt—except for the weddings of her brothers. Fergus was married far away south in Sussex. But on 29 September Jock married his bride in Scotland, and, while it was an austere ceremony to suit the times, Elizabeth as one of the bridesmaids was dressed in blue silk with late autumn flowers in her hair.

"It was a lovely wedding," Elizabeth recalled. "Fenella looked so beautiful, and there is always something specially moving about a wartime wedding with the groom in uniform soon going off to the front with all its dangers."

The crypt was turned into a dining room, the antlers and suits of armour and fearsome axes on the walls being retained, and later becoming the subject of much ribaldry among the patients. Elizabeth's older sister Rose had now completed her nurse's training and came up to Scotland to help to care for the wounded, while Cecilia took on Elizabeth herself as a sort of deputy hostess, confident in her daughter's skill in this role.

The first wounded were expected any day, and Elizabeth remembers "going out one day to the village shop not as usual, in search of bull's-eyes, but to buy unaccustomed things—Woodbines [cigarettes] and Gold Flake and Navy Cut."

The men arrived from Dundee in four motor ambulances on the afternoon of 12 December 1914, sixteen of them, all having been operated on and patched up from their wounds—mostly bullets and shrapnel—in the infirmary there. They were in need of peace and rest above everything else, and Glamis Castle, which had seen so much violence and bloodshed in the past, was, by contrast, to provide it.

Some of the men were not sure about that. One of them who survived the war, though wounded twice again later, recalls the misgivings he and his fellow wounded felt about going to stay "with the aristocracy in some bloody great castle." Private Mick McMahon said,

> I complained about it to the matron at Dundee Royal Infirmary, so did some of my mates. We all wanted to go home for Christmas, even if some of us was in a bad way still. It was a long drive, over the Sidlaw Hills and we was pretty knocked-up when we got there. It was snowing and bloody cold, I can tell you. The castle was the biggest building I had ever seen—bigger than f---ing Buckingham Palace, with turrets and things.
>
> We went through some bloody great gates and then drove up to the front door. There was two nurses and a middle-aged woman and a girl there. They said hullo and helped us inside. The woman, who was the Countess, talked to us all in turn when we was inside. Some of us was on crutches or in wheelchairs, and three including me on stretchers.
>
> Then the girl came up to us. She had a lovely smile—oh, it was lovely. And nice blue eyes. She really seemed to care about me as if I was the only one—where did I come from, and was I in much pain, that sort of thing. It lifted me right up, I'll tell you.

After that Elizabeth came and spoke to the men every day, learning their names at once, and remembering all their family details. She asked them if they wanted anything, wrote letters for those who asked, and gave them their letters—the lucky ones who ever had any—opening the envelopes for those whose hand injuries prevented their doing so. One victim had been blinded. Luckily, he had a letter from his mother nearly every day, and Elizabeth always read it to him, in a soft, gentle voice that no one else could hear.

David returned from his first half at Eton a few days after the wounded arrived, and played his part. He and Elizabeth watched carefully the arrival of Christmas parcels for the men, and on 23 December rode into Forfar to buy some simple emergency presents for those who had not received anything from home or friends—half a dozen fountain pens, some tins of pipe tobacco.

> On Christmas Eve, I thought we would have a lark [David recalled]. I dressed up as a lady visitor, in a skirt and cloak and buttoned shoes which had belonged to Rose. I wore a feather hat and veil, and then Elizabeth took me round the ward and introduced me as her cousin, a hospital visitor who had come to see how they were.
>
> I went round to each of them in turn, asking in a soft but high voice the sort of questions hospital visitors are supposed to ask—managing not to giggle once, though Elizabeth was on the verge of bursting at the seams.
>
> I think they probably knew really, but they were very kind and played up to my little joke, feigning astonishment when on Christmas Day I told them who "the lady" was.

It was curious for David and Elizabeth to spend their first-ever Christmas at Glamis with sixteen wounded men, some of them heavily bandaged or in plaster, others terribly disfigured and burnt. But everything had changed since the summer, which seemed worlds away now. One of the gardeners, too old for the Army, brought in a big Christmas tree from the estate, helped by his boy, and this was erected in the crypt with David's help, while Elizabeth piled presents around its trunk and decorated it with tinsel and candles.

Elizabeth Bowes-Lyon's formal academic education came almost to an end with the 1914 war; but the education preparing her for her life work began at what her elder sister once called "the University of Glamis." Rose Bowes-Lyon,* who eventually took over as head nurse at Glamis Convalescent Home, worked with her for much of the war. Elizabeth was friend and comforter to her elder sister's professional supervisor, although the two tasks, as in any hospital, sometimes lost their clear distinction.

Just as tens of thousands of young men who marched straight from the schoolroom into battle lost for ever any chance of higher academic education, but acquired strength, moral fibre and resolution from the experience of war, so Elizabeth, in the susceptible years from fourteen to eighteen, grew up at an unnatural speed while acquiring the toughness of spirit and also the tenderness and skill to communicate with people of any background and age.

An episode in the late summer of 1915 highlights Elizabeth's newly-acquired sense of authority, even if it was frustrated in this case. Corporal Ernest Pearne had been severely wounded in the shoulder, and after an operation was sent to Glamis just after Elizabeth's fifteenth birthday. The two had already become friends when, by chance, Pearne climbed to the top of the flagpole tower one hot afternoon, to find Elizabeth there with her black spaniel, Peter. They began talking to one another when the Corporal noticed that the flag was lying at the foot of the staff.

> I said it would look better at the top, so we decided to haul it up. We did so, and just as it reached the top the wind entangled it over the top of the staff, and try as we might it wouldn't right itself.
>
> I said that it had got to be put right and that I would climb up. She said, "Oh, no! Ernest, you must not attempt such a thing. Even with two good

*Born 1890, married in 1916 4th Earl Granville, a naval officer renowned for suppressing the slave trade and piracy in the Red Sea. They had a son and a daughter.

arms, it wouldn't be safe. With one in a sling it would be madness. You're not to do it."

I excused myself and said I was going to try.

At that she stamped her little foot, and called me "stubborn," "pig-headed," "foolhardy," anything to stop me. Then she ran away to get someone else to prevent me. It was a difficult job, but I managed to scramble up and slide down slowly dragging the flag with me. When I descended to the Crypt I met Lady Elizabeth coming back, and told her it was done. She stared at me amazed. "Well, Ernest," she said, "I didn't think you could have done it! You *are* stubborn!" Yes it was a sad day when it came to saying goodbye to her and all at dear Glamis.

Corporal Pearne was the most eloquent recorder of Elizabeth at fifteen years and of life at Glamis at this time. He seems to have worshipped her, in spite of disobeying her orders:

She had the loveliest pair of blue eyes I'd ever seen—very expressive, eloquent eyes that could speak for themselves. She had a very taking habit of knitting her forehead just a little now and then when speaking, and her smile was a refreshment.

I noticed in particular a sort of fringe at the front of her shapely head. Her teeth were even and very white and well set, and when speaking she would look ever so straight at me. Altogether she struck me as being a most charming little lady and a most delightful companion.

Elizabeth would usually come down after dinner with her mother and sister and talk to the patients, ensuring that they had tobacco and writing materials and other small comforts. Then she might have a game of whist.

I very often played as her partner, and when she was in doubt about what to play she would tap her forehead with a card and very often quite unwittingly expose its face, which to me was very amusing. Of course, at this time, she was just learning to play whist. When she was perplexed she would look at me and say, "*Do* tell me what to play, Ernest." Many a happy game we had together.

One reason why, as her sister Rose recounted, Elizabeth "took over more and more" from her mother was the occurrence of the first family tragedy of the war. Fergus came home on leave for a few days in September 1915, and visited his mother at Glamis with his wife and their two-months-old baby. He stayed only a few days before returning to his regiment on 20 September. It was the eve of the Battle of Loos.

While David, Prince of Wales, based at HQ a few miles behind the line, pleaded fruitlessly to join the attack, Fergus Bowes-Lyon led his company of Black Watch in the assault on the German "Hohenzollern Redoubt." He was struck down and killed on 27 September. He was twenty-six.

The news came as a devastating blow to the attenuated Strathmore family at Glamis. Fergus was the apple of Cecilia's eye, his death even more poignant for his recent visit with the baby. She went into a decline and retired to the privacy of her rooms.

Later, the reported death of Michael in action almost killed Cecilia. David, summoned home from Eton to give solace to his mother when the first news arrived from the War Office of his death, refused to believe it, and to be as downcast as the others. Elizabeth chided him for his cheerfulness. "You are not giving any comfort to Mama by whistling about the place and making jokes."

"But he's *not* dead. I know it. I've seen him twice. He's in a big house surrounded by fir trees. I think he's very ill, though, because his head is tied up in a cloth. I don't care what the War Office says. I *know* he's alive."

At last the news filtered through that Michael was a prisoner of war, though gravely wounded in the head, just as David had "seen" him. His mother was certain he would not

survive; "But, praise be to God," as Rose recalled, "Michael*
came home."

On Armistice Day, 11 November 1918, there were, as
there had been for almost four years, sixteen patients at the
Glamis Convalescent Home. Altogether some fifteen hundred men had sheltered here, been cared for by Rose and her
nurses, been comforted, entertained, enlivened, even en-
slaved, by "the wonderful Lady Elizabeth, not the Lady with
the Lamp," as one of her patients called her, "but the Lady
with the Smile." She was there as the minute hand of the big
wall clock in the one-time dining hall moved towards eleven
o'clock.

Elizabeth was firmly in command of the four bed-bound
men, the four in wheelchairs, and the remainder displaying
evidence of some serious injury. She stood on a chair her
eyes on the clock, and when it showed that the war was at
last over, she called out in her mellifluous but firm voice,
"We will now give three cheers . . ." And they did. "And
God save the King and Queen."

She was eighteen by now, with her hair up. She smiled
as they all looked at her, laughing and cheering. Then her
expression became solemn as she said, "Let us pray and
thank God for victory and for the end of this war." Those who
could went down on their knees, and Elizabeth knelt on the
floor, using the chair as a single-seat pew before her.

The war which had begun so noisily for Elizabeth in the
Coliseum Theatre in London, finished in silence and prayer
four years and three months later.

*The Hon. Michael Claud Hamilton Bowes-Lyon married Elizabeth
Margaret Cater in 1928, had two sons and twin daughters, and died
1 May 1953, aged 63.

9

As for Alice Scott, Elizabeth's neighbour at Drumlanrig, since they had met and played together in that last summer of peace she had been at boarding school. War work, during holidays, was limited to beating at shoots, most of the beaters having joined the Army, and moss gathering. Sphagnum moss was a good alternative to cotton for swabbing out wounds, because of its iodine content. "We would collect it in sacks," Alice remembered, "and then lay it across the lawn on dust sheets to dry. Afterwards all the bits of heather and peat, dead frogs and other foreign bodies had to be picked out before it could be sent to the hospital."

Alice was still at school when the war ended, better educated than most contemporaries of her class and wealth, but shy and diffident, comfortable socially only when in the saddle or in Girl Guide uniform. By now (1919) she was a close friend of Princess Mary, who shared her enthusiasm for the Guides. "I was very shy and rather plump. I made a miserable debut at a dance at Windsor for Princess Mary's birthday, uncomfortably squeezed into a white satin frock."

Mary's younger brother Harry was supposed to have been there but was prevented by illness . . .

The summer of 1914 that marked the outbreak of a great war in Europe, also witnessed the end of boarding school life for Wallis Warfield of Baltimore. "The class of 1914," she wrote, "went out into the world without fanfare or celebration . . . Not a single girl from my class at Oldfields went to college."

Instead, the fanfares and celebrations lay ahead, features of the struggle for a husband that now faced all the girls of Wallis's class just out of school. "Not only was marriage the only thing that we had to look forward to," she said, "but the condition of marriage had been made to seem to us the only state desirable for a woman—and the sooner the better."

Ahead lay presentations and balls, breathless speculations on the standing, eligibility and availability of young men, the significance of a gardenia, all the pageantry and protocol involved in the preliminaries to marriage for a well-brought-up Baltimore girl.

But even here, three thousand miles from the battle line, the gale of war was still felt, if only as a light breath. Baltimore was one hundred per cent pro-British, and as a gesture of support, thirty-four debutantes, including Wallis Warfield, signed a public pledge that, for the duration of the war, they would declare "an absence of rivalry in elegance in respective social functions."

This happened to be lucky for Wallis, for the trust fund which had largely supported her family ceased with the death of her stepfather, and "my mother's limited budget made a certain austerity necesary." For example, Wallis had to resort to the services of a black seamstress called Ellen rather than ordering her ball gowns from the fashionable couturier, Fuechal's.

During that first winter of war Wallis and her contemporaries "spent endless hours on the telephone, in prattle with our friends; a whirl of pre-debut luncheons at each other's houses; tea-time dances and chit-chat at the Belvedere Hotel, again with the same crowd—and always a mad rush from one enormously important trifle to another."

There was no one more attractive and more likely to come out well in the marriage stakes than Wallis; she was never short of handsome, well-off young beaux with their bouquets. But the war in Europe came home more seriously in the spring of 1915, when Wallis was expecting to give a coming-out party of her own—a tremendous ball that would be the talk of Baltimore. "Uncle Sol," S. Davies Warfield, a prosperous relative upon whom Wallis and her mother depended for financial bonuses, decreed that, as he was a leading figure in war charities and relief funds, it would not be appropriate for him to spend money ostentatiously on a ball. So that was that, "and a blow to me," Wallis complained.

However, a cousin took pity on the poor girl and put on an enormous tea-dance at the Marine Barracks in Washington, with the Marine Band, sixty strong, in gala red coats, providing the music. "The girls from Baltimore," noted Wallis, "had a glorious whirl." The glorious whirl, for Wallis, went on for month after month, as her confidence grew and she knew that when the time came she could pick her man and pin him down. In 1916, shortly before the Battles of Jutland and the Somme (one million casualties), Wallis wrote her mother a letter beginning, "I have just met the world's most fascinating aviator . . ."

Lieutenant Earl Winfield Spencer Jr, United States Navy, was a flying instructor at the nascent air station at Pensacola. They had met through Wallis's cousin Corinne Mustin, who was married to a captain in the Navy. Captain Mustin often had lunches for his junior officers at home, and it was at one of these that Wallis met Lieutenant Spencer. The first time she set eyes on him he was walking, "tanned and lean," towards the house with his superior officer, watched by Corinne and Wallis.

"He was laughing," Wallis recalled nostalgically, "yet there was a suggestion of inner force and vitality that struck me instantly. His close-cropped moustache gave a certain boldness to his features that was arresting."

At lunch, sitting opposite Win Spencer, "I felt excited and moved as I had never been before," Wallis remembered. "Here was a kind of man new to me, strong, assured, sophisticated—one who knew what he wanted and was confident of his ability to get it."

For his part, this pilot appears to have felt as strongly about Wallis at this first meeting. Other meetings followed. They walked the beach, collecting shells. He tried to teach her golf, which gave ample opportunity for close contact. Wallis did not much care for golf, but happily put up with it for the warm feeling of being with Win. The proposal of marriage came with startling speed, on the steps of a country club. Wallis begged for time, and Win was understanding. Her mother sounded warning notes—flying was dangerous, would she not find service life restricting? and so on—as did her future mother-in-law, wife of an affluent member of the Chicago stock exchange.

On 8 November 1916, a day when David, Prince of Wales, came close to being killed by a stray shell south-west of Beaumont Hamel, Wallis Warfield married Lieutenant Win Spencer in Washington. "It was a wedding with all the frills—hundreds of people, confetti, speeches galore, a cake as big as the White House or so it seemed. And Wallis looked sumptuous . . ."

To his fury, the bridegroom discovered that the hotel on the first night of their honeymoon was dry—"no alcoholic beverages may be sold on the premises." However, the far-sighted sailor had a bottle of gin at the bottom of his suitcase, and Wallis tasted alcohol for the first time in her life. Innocence was at an end.

10

Nothing signified more strongly the corruption of war than the mindless anti-German "hate" that was whipped up by the press and by certain members of parliament and influential and irresponsible individuals soon after war was declared. Integrity, moral courage and truth were all swept aside by a tidal wave of vilification and hatred, encouraged by such odious bodies as the Anti-German League. Few dared speak out against it for fear of being labelled unpatriotic, or even traitorous.

Nor was this campaign of calumny halted at the office of the First Sea Lord, or colleges with German-sounding professors or great London and provincial stores; slowly but with fearful implacability it crept up The Mall from the Admiralty like an advancing malodorous cloud to the home of King George and Queen Mary.

(no date, no address)

Dear Mr Lloyd George,

Isn't it about time we got rid of all these Germans in our land? I think so and so do my family and

friends. And I mean *all* Germans. It was bad enough
having our wonderful Navy run by a Germhun and
another Germhun as Lord Chancellor running our
law. But as our sovereign King and Queen—NO I
say. If we have to have a monarchy, then it should
be British. Send the King and Queen and all their
family back to Germany where they belong.

> Yours sincerely,
> (signed) Anonymous

In the spring of 1917 hundreds of letters arrived at 10 Downing Street. The reason was not hard to find. After more than
two and a half years of killing and destruction, the victory and
the end of the war appeared no nearer. One massive offensive after another on the western front ground to a halt with
tens of thousands of casualties. The Dardanelles had long
since been evacuated, leaving behind the bodies of thousands
of Australian, New Zealand, British and French soldiers.
British cities were bombarded from the air. Shipping losses
(nearly a million tons sunk in April) from U-boat attack had
brought the nation close to starvation, while the cost of the
war was threatening to bankrupt Britain.

Since the first days of the war the public had been
subjected to a barrage of anti-German reporting and senti-
ment, and feelings against the German people were now as
intense as the heat of a forest fire. The defeat of Russia was
widely ascribed to "the cruel and corrupt rule" of Tsar Nicholas, and in Britain republicanism ran alongside anti-Teutonism.
Hate was everywhere: against Jews, against young men not in
uniform, against scroungers as much as against war profiteers.

A mass meeting in the Albert Hall in London celebrated
the fall of tsardom, and the censor prohibited the publication
of any detailed reports. A letter from the famous writer H.G.
Wells published in *The Times* was, however, not censored. It
urged the formation of republican societies. He also wrote of
"an alien and uninspiring court." George was outraged by all
these seditious expressions at a time when his nation was
fighting for its life. His biographer's father later reported that

the King retorted, "I may be uninspiring but I'll be damned if I'm an alien."

If George V was not an alien, then what was he? No one was even sure of his name, but as the vendetta against him and his family grew, attempts were made to find out. Mr Farnham Burke of the Royal College of Heralds thought that his name might be Guelph, but more likely Whipper or Wettin. All that was certain was that he was a Hanoverian and descended from the Saxe-Coburg-Gothas, just as the reviled Kaiser was a Hohenzollern.

"This was the time," declared one cynic, "for the Prince of Wales to get killed by a German shell. It would have saved a lot of trouble then, and later." As it was, the Palace fretted and puzzled. Wise old Stamfordham initiated a new policy, and then a new name.

> We must endeavour to induce the thinking working classes, Socialist and others, to regard the Crown not as a mere figure-head and as an institution which, as they put it, "don't count," but as a living power for good, with receptive faculties welcoming information affecting the interests and social wellbeing of all classes, and ready, not only to sympathise with those questions, but anxious to further their solution. Regarding labour troubles and industrial disputes, I know, of course, that the role of arbitrator is not one which the Sovereign can adopt, but if opportunities are seized, during His Majesty's visits to industrial centres, in conversation with the workmen, to show his interest in such problems as employers and employed will have to solve, these men will recognize in the Crown those characteristics— may I say "virtues"?—which I have ventured to enumerate above.

A number of people close to the King came up with suggestions for a name which must appeal to the people as simple and rightsounding: Fitzroy, Lancaster, Plantagenet, and York, or just simply England, were considered. They all smacked of the past, and of past conflicts at that. But Stamfordham came up with the perfect name: Windsor, "the most appropriate, the most euphonious, the most economical, the altogether most delightful, dignified and appealing name."

The official announcement, a wordy, formal affair full of *do herebys* and *relinquish and enjoins,* was published on 17 July 1917, just before the murderous Battle of Passchendaele. Now, like the Hohenzollerns, the Oldenburgs and Hapsburgs, the King was King of a Castle.

But that was not all. Besides the removal of the Garter banners in St George's Chapel belonging to "enemy Emperors, Kings and Princes," there was to be more name-changing. The family name of Teck became Cambridge (although there was no greater German-hater than Queen Mary, except Queen Alexandra), the Duke of Teck becoming the Marquis of Cambridge, and Prince Alexander of Teck the Earl of Athlone.

"What a lot of nonsense is all this name-changing!" declared the ex-First Sea Lord, Admiral Prince Louis of Battenberg. But a few days later he learned that nothing was sacred and the honoured name of Battenberg must disappear, too, like those Garter flags. For a man proud of the Hessian dynasty, which he claimed could be traced back to Charlemagne, it was a terrible blow to add to his enforced resignation as head of the Royal Navy, itself "a cruel and unnecessary thing."

The "laborious new name" was Marquess of Milford Haven, Earl of Medina, and Viscount Alderney. The Admiral's wife, Victoria, a woman of radical and egalitarian, not to say socialist, views for a grand-daughter of Queen Victoria, was much put out, too. From a Princess she had descended to the peerage, and as she wrote to her lady-in-waiting, "I am unduly influenced by the recollection of brewers, lawyers, bankers Peers."

Her younger son, Dickie, now serving as a midshipman in the battle-cruiser flagship, *Lion,* (and no longer a Serene Highness), put on a brave face and, according to his mother, treated the whole thing as "a huge joke."

And so, with the end of the Great War still far beyond sight, Saxe-Coburg-Gotha became plain Windsor, and Battenberg became Mountbatten, and things were never the same again. They certainly were not for King George, ever-sensitive to criticism, and not only because of the public vilification he had suffered when he believed he was universally loved. The physical effects of his riding accident in 1915 remained, combining with continuing abstinence, for a man who had much enjoyed his drink, to deprive him of his old sparkle. And there were family worries, too, particularly concerning his youngest son, who now had to live in complete seclusion, and his eldest son, in whose future dutifulness he felt a growing lack of confidence.

"The year 1917 has not been a happy or satisfactory one," George wrote in his diary on the last day. "I can only pray that my poor country, and the Empire as well as my beloved family, will have a better year in 1918."

PART FOUR

THE WINDSORS WED

Oh woman! lovely woman! Nature made thee
To temper man; we had been brutes without you . . .

Thomas Otway

1

After four years and three months of the bloodiest war in history, there was a strong smell of revolution in Europe, and some of it drifted across the Channel to England. George was deeply shocked by the Army mutinies of early 1919, and the evidence of communist, republican forces at work. And then there was his Russian cousin and his family to be considered.

The question of what to do about "Cousin Nicky" and his wife and children, with his empire in chaos and ruins, had come up at the same time as the name crisis so ably solved by Lord Stamfordham. Only the Mountbattens (né Battenberg) had set eyes on the Romanovs since a state visit to Cowes and the fleet in 1909, but the attachment was strong and there was much concern for the safety of the imperial family as revolution broke out in Russia.

The Tsar had abdicated on 16 March 1917. Three days later the Foreign Minister of the Russian Provisional Government approached the British ambassador, Sir George Buchanan, about the imperial family seeking asylum in Britain. Sir George let it be known to the British Foreign Office that the Russian Foreign Office was "most anxious to get the Emperor out of Russia as soon as possible, the extremists having excited opinion against His Majesty."

This delicate matter did not reach George's ears for more than a week. The implications were numerous, and some of them dangerous. Chaos reigned in many parts of Russia with factions ranging from white Russians to Marxist extremists, all mobile and in conflict with one another. For Britain, it remained of critical importance to maintain friendly contact with the Kerensky government, which now, and sensibly, wished to rid itself of the embarrassment of the imperial family.

Buchanan hoped that "I may be authorized without delay to offer His Majesty asylum in England." This appeal was read out at a meeting at 10 Downing Street on 22 March at which Stamfordham was present. Afterwards, the King's secretary drafted a minute which read, "It was generally agreed that the proposal that we should receive the Emperor in this country (having come from the Russian government which we are endeavouring with all our powers to support) could not be refused." A message to this effect was at once transmitted to the Russian Foreign Office.

On his return to the Palace, Lord Stamfordham reported the conversation and the government's views on the matter to the King. And on that same evening George aired the subject at dinner—dinner still without whisky or wine. It was very much a family meal, with only Mary and Bertie, on leave from a temporary appointment at Portsmouth, and Lady Airlie, present.

Bertie found his mother still depressed and indignant about having to be called "Windsor." "What's the matter with 'Teck'?" she demanded. "It's as British-sounding as John Bull." And when his father came down to dinner he was looking poorly and worried. "I've been with the bloody Prime Minister most of the day, and Bonar Law* and Hardinge.** I was told—*told* I tell you—that Cousin Nicky and Alicky and the children are all going to be given asylum here." George's face began to turn white above his beard. "No one had thought fit

---

*Andrew Bonar Law (1858–1923), at that time Chancellor of the Exchequer.
**Lord Hardinge of Penshurst, Viceroy of India during the 1911 Durbar, and now Permanent Under-Secretary at the Foreign Office.

to consult me—me the King, and their friend and relation: I suppose because the buggers knew I'd say no."

May had long since become hardened to what George called his "salty language," but she was visibly distressed at her husband's state, and puzzled at the same time. She waited for a few minutes for him to finish his soup, and then said gently, "I don't quite understand, dear. Shouldn't we offer them hospitality, especially if they are in danger? All those darling children!"

George controlled himself sufficiently to explain in simple language the reason why they could not be allowed to come. They would, he claimed, be host to all sorts of trouble at a time when republican feeling in the country was rising. "A lot of people believe that the Russians are letting us down and losing the war because of corruption at the head of affairs. It's bloody disgraceful, I know, but there it is. We would become politically involved, there would be outrage among those buggers on the left—those socialist members of the House of Commons."

May murmured acquiescence: "Yes, I see dear." Bertie and Mary remained silent.

Lord Stamfordham therefore despatched a note to the Foreign Secretary giving the King's views. "He would be glad to do anything he could to help in this crisis," but thought it inadvisable to invite the Romanovs to Britain at this time. Then, when the Foreign Secretary appeared to be recalcitrant over the matter, Stamfordham was instructed to fire a heavier broadside—"Every day the King is becoming more and more concerned about the question," which the King knew had become public property with many "adverse opinions."

The Foreign Office finally capitulated, using as a facesaver the fact that their initial approval had not been taken up sufficiently speedily or enthusiastically by the Russian Foreign Office. A one-time Russian correspondent for *The Times* commented, "To what extent the King was thinking of his throne, and even the safety of his family, or was in his eyes representing the views of his people who believed that the Tsar was both a tyrant and had let in the German Army to save his skin, will never be known."

The appalling end of Tsar Nicholas and his family fifteen months later, on 16 July 1918, left a scar of guilt in the minds of George and May which was to throb intermittently for the rest of their lives. But to avoid any risk that the news might leak out that he had "sold the Romanovs down that pit shaft at Ekaterinburg" (as one unsympathetic commentator noted), George let it be known that his plans to send a British cruiser to rescue the Russian imperial family had been frustrated by the Foreign Office.

This myth was carefully cultivated by the family with the effectiveness that only those who hold great power (by rank, wealth or political position) can bring about. "It hurt my father that Britain had not raised a hand to save his cousin Nicky," his son David wrote. "Those politicians," George used to say. "If it had been one of their kind, they would have acted fast enough. But just because the poor man was an emperor . . ."

However effectively George deceived the world that all his efforts to save his cousin's family had been frustrated by his politicians, he could not deceive himself that the forces of radical anti-monarchism were not on the march in his kingdom. David and Bertie were both witnesses to a demonstration that confirmed this in a frightening manner.

At the height of the discontent in the Army, which was caused mainly by dissatisfaction at slow demobilization and the grievances of those who had been disabled, the War Office asked the King if he would attend a parade of discharged disabled soldiers in Hyde Park. George and his two sons rode out on horseback innocently expecting the customary adulation together with the playing of bands and the waving of banners. This time it was not the cheers of celebration and admiration that gave George trouble with his horse and threatened another serious accident.

David takes up the alarming narrative:

> The men, all in plain clothes, were drawn up in divisional formation. At first glance everything appeared in order, the men at attention, the bands playing, and so forth. Most of the men wore on their lapels the "Silver Badge," signifying their hon-

ourable discharge for wounds or other disabilities.
But there was something in the air, a sullen unre-
sponsiveness all three of us felt instinctively. My
father, steady as a rock, rode down the front line.
Suddenly there was a commotion at the rear; and,
as if by a prearranged signal, hitherto concealed
banners with slogans were defiantly unfurled. With
cries of "Where is this land fit for heroes?"—a
hurling back of Lloyd George's famous election
slogan—the men broke ranks and made straight for
the King, who was quickly surrounded and cut off
from me and my brother by a solid mass. For a
moment I feared he would be borne to the ground.

But the mob was less intent on committing bodily harm to
the King than presenting their grievances to him in person.
When the King, with the assistance of the police, succeeded
in extricating himself from the mob, he was white-faced and
thoroughly shaken. It was not only that "horsemanship was
not in him," as his biographer put it; for a moment he
thought he was going to be assassinated. He had experienced, for one moment, the same fear that must have overcome the Tsar when the revolutionaries turned on him, though
it was worse for the British monarch, who had had no warning of the hostile mood of the people.

"After my father dismounted," David recounted, "he
looked at me remarking, 'Those men were in a funny temper.' And shaking his head, as if to rid himself of an unpleasant memory, he strode indoors."

As if King George had not already an abundance of sorrows
and anxieties, in January 1918 he and May suffered a personal
and poignant loss which affected them deeply. Some years
earlier Prince John had to be taken from the care of Hansell to
be looked after by male attendants, with the ever-loving
attention of Lala Bill, who received in return the devotion of
the unfortunate boy.

Later in his short life of thirteen years, John had to be
segregated entirely from the rest of the family. A household

was prepared for him at Wood Farm on the Sandringham estate, where he lived—not unhappily—in complete seclusion. On 18 January 1919 Lala telephoned his mother to tell her "that our poor darling little Johnnie has passed away suddenly after one of his attacks. The news gave me a great shock," wrote May, "tho' for the poor little boy's restless soul, death came as a great release. I broke the news to George & we motored down to Wood Farm. Found poor Lala very resigned but heartbroken."

And to a friend May wrote, "I cannot say how grateful we feel to God for having taken him in such a peaceful way, he just slept quietly into his heavenly home, no pain, no struggle, just peace for the poor little troubled spirit which had been a great anxiety to us for many years, ever since he was four years old . . ."

A few days after the Hyde Park demonstration, George was having a general discussion about the state of the nation with his private secretary.

"Tell me, Arthur, do you think the country is close to revolution?"

"No, Sir," Lord Stamfordham emphatically replied. "I have great faith in the commonsense of the ordinary people in our country. But the disruption of the war has been greater than the politicians had expected. Very few of them, and none of your ministers except Winston Churchill, saw the war as it really was."

"David has, and he is as surprised and anxious as I am."

"It is not, I believe, merely the witnessing of the slaughter and the injuries to the body (as those misguided men in Hyde Park demonstrated), which has upset the country. It is new wealth for those who stayed behind, and uncertainty and anxiety among those who have returned home from the fighting, that is unsettling your people. It is a great and quite new division, Sir."

The King lit his third cigarette since breakfast, using the time to try to assemble his thoughts. "You mean jobs are hard to find?" he said at length. "And they have lost the comradeship of the services?"

"Those are two important factors, Sir," agreed Lord Stamfordham.

"What do you propose we should do, Arthur?"

"I have given this question some thought, Sir. What will regain some of the lost comfort of your people is a new family feeling—a feeling of imperial solidarity with our dominions and colonies, as a start. Your people in Canada, Australia, New Zealand, India and elsewhere have suffered greatly in this war. For you to go out and thank them would seal the imperial bonds and be popular with your people here at the same time. The pictures in the popular newspapers alone would be highly beneficial."

George, whose cigarette ash could reach remarkable lengths, watched it fall upon his waistcoat, and then brushed it aside irritably. "No, Arthur," he said decisively. "I am not strong or well enough. And . . . and—it would mean riding more beastly horses."

The shrewd Lord Stamfordham, who had anticipated his master's response, even to the words he would use, allowed the silence between him and the King to last for half a minute. Then he spoke again, respectfully yet firmly as always:

"Then, Sir, might I suggest that the Prince of Wales might carry out an imperial tour himself?"

"Excellent, Arthur! An admirable notion! I will speak to May about it this evening."

The sequence of events that now followed had been planned for by this servant of the crown. As long before as 22 December 1918, Stamfordham had written to David:

Sir:

. . . And now Sir, I am getting anxious about your securing a good Private Secretary . . . The reason for my anxiety is that I foresee a good deal of work ahead. For instance the King approved of an announcement being made at the annual half-yearly meeting of King E's Hospital Fund that you would take over the Presidency. [Other imminent duties

and engagements were then mentioned, together
with a first mention of *"Canada"*.]

I remain always your humble and devoted servant,
STAMFORDHAM

The Prince of Wales sailed for Canada and the United States,
with his private secretary, and an entourage of nineteen
more, in the battle-cruiser *Renown*, on 5 August 1919. It was
his first visit to the New World, which was to have such a
powerful influence on him.

2

The fact that Bertie had formed part of a team—a team of men, in the two battleships in which he served, who liked him and with whom he worked well, was as important a factor in his development as the discovery of his courage. Bertie's superiors "left it on record that his work was above the average, that he was zealous and hard-working, possessed of good common sense and upright character, and could handle men well."

Louis Greig, who was a wise judge of men and knew Bertie better than anyone else, believed that there had been four turning points in the young man's life. The first was in his infancy, when he and David had at last been rescued from the insane nursery governess, Mrs Green. This woman's treatment of Bertie had scarred him for life in mind and body, and things had improved for him greatly once she was gone.

Then there was his getting into the Navy. He had a bad time to begin with, but the sense of achievement was great—indeed the winning of that battle was as important as the winning of Jutland eight years later—and it had also taken him away from his parents, which was no bad thing in itself.

The third important experience was being under fire in the North Sea, and in northern France with David, and proving to himself that he was not afraid of death. While the more prosaic but still significant fourth turning point was the operation for a duodenal ulcer which Bertie underwent in November 1917. It was beyond Greig's comprehension why the Prince's medical advisers had not diagnosed the ulcer earlier. He himself had done so and had passed his opinion on to them many months earlier, but they had disregarded him, and even after the ulcer's existence had been recognized, several weeks passed before they decided to operate. Louis Greig was thankful that he and Campbell Tait, who had both left their ship when Bertie did, were able to be with him and try to keep his pecker up during the black period of uncertainty.

Bertie at this time thought his career in the Navy was at an end. While he had not been all that keen on it when he was a youngster, he had now become very loyal to it. "It has made a man of me," he used to say. Tait and Greig had a word about all this privately, and they agreed that the new flying branch might be the answer. He could be based on an aerodrome instead of a ship, and if he could pass his wings test he would be very proud of himself.

The next day Greig got round to talking about this in such a way that Bertie made the suggestion as if it was his own. So, while Bertie's medical future still lay in the hands of his doctors, his professional future as a naval airman was proposed to his father.

Tait and Greig's stratagem worked, and a few days later Bertie was writing to Hansell, "My own suggestion for once came off and Papa jumped at the idea. Greig is going there as well . . . he is a perfect topper."

Under pressure from Greig, the doctors had at last agreed to operate on Bertie's duodenal ulcer. Queen Mary's diary briefly tells the story:

November 28th 1917.

It is decided that poor Bertie is to have an operation tomorrow as he does not seem at all well & has constant pain. He is most cheerful about it . . .

November 29th 1917.

Dr Rigby performed the operation at 10, which was most successful. Sir Fred. Treves, Sir Bernard Dawson, Dr Hewett & Dr Greig were present & came to report to us later. The operation was very successful & they found the cause of all the trouble he has been having since 1915.

The moment Bertie came round from his anaesthetic, he began chatting merrily to Greig. "I was much amused," Greig said, "that he talked about his future as an airman with great excitement and *without the trace of a stutter!*" Whenever he was intensely interested in something, whenever he was professionally involved, Bertie's stutter always disappeared, which gave Greig confidence that one day he would overcome this handicap altogether.

As soon as he was fit enough, Bertie was appointed to a new "ship," HMS *Daedalus*. The first of this name had been a ship-of-the-line in Nelson's time; this one was a flat, exposed stretch of land in Lincolnshire, a training station for the Navy's aircrew, commanded by a great hero of the battles of Coronel and Falkland Islands at the beginning of the war, Rear-Admiral John Luce. It was Britain's Pensacola and the future site of RAF Cranwell. Here Bertie was to take command of Number 4 Squadron, Boy Wing. With Greig always near him to give him advice and assistance, and feeling fitter than he had felt for years, Bertie threw himself into this new task.

HMS *Daedalus* was very different from HMS *Collingwood*. First, it was a number of fields instead of a battleship. And the ship's company was quite different from "sailing Navy." Bertie had five hundred boys to look after, and they were very dirty. As he wrote to his father, "They live in small huts, 20 boys in each, & these give me the most trouble as they won't keep them clean without my constantly telling them off to clean them out of working hours."

Bertie had never lived almost cheek by jowl with the working class and lower-middle class and found the experi-

ence discomposing for a while. Of the petty officers, he wrote
to George, "One finds a tremendous difference between them
and the proper naval PO. But with a little persuasion I hope
to make them understand what I want." And as for his fellow
officers, who called him "PA," he thought them "very nice,
though a curious mixture of people, in every walk of life."

Louis Greig watched Bertie's reaction to "the ordinary
people," and decided that a bit of mixing with them was all
right, but "enough is enough," as he expressed it to his wife
Phyllis. Greig, now a major, rented a small cottage at South
Rauceby, four miles from the air base. It was over three
hundred years old and full of oak beams, charming and cosy
inside with log fires in large open grates. It did not bother
him or Phyllis that in the 1870s a mock-Gothic exterior had
been slapped on the outside.

"I think we ought to have HRH to live with us for a
while," he suggested one evening. "I don't think it is suitable
for the second-in-line to the throne to spend too long with that
rather rough lot in what they insist on calling their 'wardroom.' They're not really his sort and I think HM would like
him to be with us."

Phyllis, a daughter of the Norfolk Scrimgeours, was a
sensible down-to-earth woman. "Of course," she said. "Should
we move out of our bedroom?"

"Certainly not. At present he's sleeping in a corrugated
iron hut and the spare bedroom will be like paradise."

Phyllis had other questions of a practical nature, concerning Bertie's diet after his recent operation and so on.
They talked the matter over in detail, especially the matter of
visitors. Then they had a pot of tea, Phyllis went to bed and
her husband wrote to the King.

A few days later Bertie was able to report how happy he
was with the Greigs in their cottage, helping with the wash-
ing up and the gardening at weekends, "digging for victory"
and making a chicken run.

To begin with, Bertie's attitude to flying resembled the way
he had first felt about the Navy. He wanted to be a success,
he felt that it was his duty to fly, he would like to wear a

pilot's wings even though he knew he would never be a scout pilot in a Sopwith Camel on the western front. But if truth were told, he did not much welcome the idea of the actual flying.

The appointed day for his first flight, 5 March 1918, arrived. It was a wet and windy day, not really suitable for flying, as his instructor told Bertie.

"I'm not in the least anxious to go up," Bertie replied sardonically. "But I'll be no more anxious to do so tomorrow or the next day. We've arranged it for today and I'd like to get it over and done with."

With characteristic candour Bertie wrote to his mother that evening: "It was a curious sensation and one which takes a lot of getting used to. I did enjoy it on the whole, but I don't think I should like flying as a pastime. I would much sooner be on the ground! It feels safer!!"

After this, some time passed, and the Armistice was declared at last before he took a sustained course of flying instruction. Louis Greig knew that Bertie wanted very much to qualify but flinched from the risk of failure. He talked the matter over with Bill Coryton, a friend and flying instructor of great experience, and with Phyllis. To his wife he said, "I think it's very important for HRH's self-respect that he should earn his wings."

"Is there any chance that he might fail?" she asked.

"Practically none. He has good eye-brain-hand co-ordination and good timing. Judging by his shooting, his handling of a motor car and his standard of tennis he would make a good pilot. But if I suggest that he should take a full course of lessons he may think he's being pushed."

Phyllis gave the matter silent consideration. Since those weeks when Bertie had lived with them, she had felt a motherly understanding for him. Never a breath of criticism of his upbringing (about which she had learned much) did she utter, but she felt deeply that he deserved a better future than his past. If Louis thought that HRH would benefit from qualification as a pilot, then it was a matter of how best to set about it.

Her idea, when she voiced it, surprised her husband; it rather surprised her, too. "Why don't you take lessons with him, Lou?" she suggested. "Treat it all as a bit of a lark. And

if, as you don't think likely, he doesn't do very well or wants
to stop, then you can agree with him and say you're tired of
the whole business, too. It would make it easier for him. But
on the other hand the competition might spur him on—like
your playing tennis with him."

Greig thought about this silently. "But I'm forty next
birthday, dear. Flying's a young man's game."

"It's not like you to show hesitation, Lou." And Phyllis
laughed.

That settled the matter. And the next day, after the first
set of tennis and while they were resting, Greig said, "Phyllis
has suddenly told me she would like me to fly! How's that for
a surprise?"

"Indeed it is!" exclaimed Bertie. "And who's going
to teach this middle-aged man to be an intrepid aviator?"

"Bill Coryton said he would. He asked if you wanted to
have a go, too. He said he would bet you would beat me to
getting wings up." Greig laughed and headed for his end of
the court. "Come on—five-three to me, and you to serve."

Bertie pulled up to five-all and then took the next two
games. Flushed with victory, he walked towards the pavilion,
a towel wrapped round his neck, Greig at his side. Glancing
at the slim, fit figure, red-faced from the exertion and brim-
ming over with good health, Greig found it hard to relate this
Bertie to the pale, sick, wretched Lieutenant RN he had
found on his return from Germany.

"About this flying," said Bertie. "I'll take you on. I'll
have a word with my father."

"No need for that," Greig retorted briskly. "I've spoken
to him and he's all in favour."

Two weeks later Lieutenant Coryton took off from Waddon
Lane Aerodrome, Croydon, in a Mono Avro with Bertie in
the open cockpit in front of him and gave him his first lesson,
called simply "air experience." Bertie took the joystick for a
minute or two and gently banked the machine to port and starboard above the green countryside of Surrey. He thought he
liked it better than last time. After half an hour, Bill Coryton
landed and Greig took Bertie's place. Later, they exchanged
notes and decided that they were going to enjoy themselves.

Bertie had been flying for almost a month when Hansel

paid a visit to Waddon Lane. With George now completing his naval training at Dartmouth, the Royal Tutor had retired but was still a part of the Royal Household, with its accompanying privileges. His interest in his charges, now that they were out in the world, remained as intense as ever, and Bertie welcomed Mider's suggestion of a visit. Afterwards Hansell wrote to his sister, whose own children were out in the world, too, although she had lost one of her sons in France.

> Buckingham Palace
> London S.W.
>
> 3 March 1919
>
> My dear Gladys,
>
> You will be interested to hear that I visited Prince Albert at his aerodrome. He & his equerry are taking flying lessons together. HRH. was in wonderful health & v cheerful. I naturally wanted to compare notes with his instructor, a Lieutenant Coryton, who flew in France in the war.
>
> I managed to take this airman aside for a moment. He said he was a very adept pupil, learning fast & quite fearless. He asked me about HRH. as a pupil when he was a boy. As you can imagine I turned the conversation back to flying—&, would you believe it, he asked me if I would like "a flip"! I declined, using my venerable age as an excuse!
>
> Next week I hope to visit Prince Henry at Sandhurst. He has had 'flu but is better, I learn.
>
> > Your loving brother,
> > (signed) Henry

Stick back, nose up, left rudder, left aileron, *keep the stick well forward* now or the nose will fall. Now he was upside down, shoulders tight against the straps, horizon inverted but straight and level. Pull her round gently, don't rush it . . .

Bertie completed a very clean slow roll, and felt pleased with himself. Now all he had to do was to make a gliding, dead-engine landing, right on that mark within the square on the grass field 1,500 feet below. Bertie banked, came in on the final approach, misjudged the strength of the wind, lost height with a brief side-slip, straightened up, held off. His wheels touched in a slightly bumpy but not bad three-pointer, and he taxied in.

Bill Coryton said, "Well done, Sir. I never touched the controls. As you saw, I had my hands on the struts the whole time. And I never felt a flicker of anxiety."

It was 31 July 1919, and Bertie was now a fully-fledged pilot. The head of the newly-formed Royal Air Force, Sir Hugh Trenchard, had done a "Kitchener" on Bertie by refusing to allow him to fly solo, but that took only a little of the edge off Bertie's satisfaction. Later that same day he was given his signed certificate, and the Station Commander, in a brief ceremony, presented him with his wings.

Louis Greig had earned his wings on the same day, so Prince and equerry stood at attention side by side while the Wing Commander pinned on the coveted gold eagles with central crown, and then joined the other officers of the station to celebrate the occasion with a glass of sherry.

Almost as soon as Bertie, age 23, had gained his wings and his new rank of squadron leader, the King proved that he still listened to Hansell's advice by sending him to Trinity College, Cambridge, together with his brother Harry, who had now completed his military training at Sandhurst.

Perversely, however, George brushed aside the advice of the two dons who were to teach them, J.R.M. (Jim) Butler and Dennis Robertson. These two young but experienced and wise men wrote that "The Princes would gain educationally if it were possible for them to live in College. They would certainly see more of men of their own age and so would get more of that mixing with other minds with similar interests which is a very important part of the university system of education . . ."

George, as always, knew best. Lacking all knowledge

and experience of the difference between living in and out of college, he caused Lord Stamfordham to retort that "both Princes, having already passed through the disciplinary period *in statu pupillari* [an expression not of George's choice!], it would be hardly fair to ask them again to give up just that little extra freedom which is enjoyed by living outside walls and gates!"

The King therefore caused a small house off the Trumpington Road, a mile from Trinity, to be rented for his two sons, with Louis and Phyllis Greig as surrogate mother and father. The two young men bicycled to and fro, morning and evening, and had little contact with any other students, either those of their own age who had fought in the war, or younger undergraduates. "It is significant," wrote Bertie's official biographer, "that few, if any, of Prince Albert's friendships in after-life dated from his days at Cambridge." The same applied to the other boys.

Having decided that further education at a distinguished college was just what his sons needed, George decreed that he could spare Bertie for only two terms, though Harry would be allowed to remain for a full year. "One year, and still more a fraction of a year, seems a very short time to get the full advantage of the place," Jim Butler wrote to the Palace. George eventually relented to the extent of allowing Bertie to remain for a full year, and then began, and continued, to demand his presence as his own representative at various functions and ceremonies—the Worshipful Company of Drapers within a few days of the start of his first term, then the Freedom of the City of London, a week later to greet the Shah of Persia and then to remain more or less at his side for the whole of his state visit.

Trinity College
Cambridge

3 November 1919

Dear Mary,

As you see, I am back at Cambridge, but not for long as Papa insists that I greet on his behalf M. &

Mme. Poincaré, the French President & his wife,
next week when they make a state visit to London.
So I am not going to get an honours degree *this*
year!!

I am glad you were not with me at Lord
Curzon's house in Carlton House Terrace the other
night when he & I were joint hosts to the Persian
hierarchy. We should both have had a giggling fit
just like the old days. At the height of the reception
the Padishah, who would break the back of your
strongest horse & is almost completely circular,
tripped at the top of the great staircase. Before
anyone could get to him, he tripped again, & fell
roly-poly right down to the bottom!

> Your loving brother,
> (signed) Bertie

Between lectures on economics and civics and constitutional
history, which he enjoyed most, and frequent duty visits to
London and elsewhere, Bertie endured continuing speech
therapy. In spite of a visit to France the previous year to
receive treatment from a renowned specialist, Bertie's stutter
was still almost uncontrollable under certain conditions. And
the ever-increasing frequency of functions called for speeches,
which caused him (and his audience) agony. Only when he
was allowed to ad-lib could he sometimes express himself
clearly and without hesitation.

Now he had an Italian speech specialist, who brought
about some improvement, but his stutter remained a disability which gave Bertie much misery.

Living away from Trinity offered one benefit to him: he
was in the company of Louis and Phyllis Greig much more
than if he had been in college, and this couple became an
increasingly strong influence for good in his life with their
discreet, tactful guidance and advice. Childhood faults and
weaknesses, which might well have been dealt with at school,
still lingered. Bertie still occasionally fell into rages over
petty setbacks, and in mostly small matters was easily dis-

couraged and angered by failures and defeats at, say, golf or
tennis.

Because Bertie loved and admired Greig so much, he
not only tolerated but acted on the advice which was freely
given to him. His biographer writes of Greig's "sometimes
brutal frankness." Sir Charles Baring recalls a game of tennis*
singles at his parents' house in the Isle of Wight. Bertie was
losing, and was hitting the court with his racket and using
foul language, which, like his father, he had learned in the
Royal Navy. "Behave yourself, Sir!" Greig called out for all to
hear; and Bertie did as he was told.

"My principal contribution," Greig once said, "was to
put steel into him." But it was much more than that. He,
more than anyone else, manipulated away, like an accomplished masseur, the strains and stresses of a difficult and
misunderstood childhood, and helped Bertie to develop a
more trim and balanced mind and body. "Under Louis, his
judgement matured," a friend of the Greigs commented.
"Louis, and Jutland made a man of him."

Deserved promotion came to both Prince and equerry.
Greig was made Comptroller of Bertie's household, while in
the Birthday Honours List of 3 June 1920 there appeared:

> The KING had been pleased to direct Letters Pa-
> tent to be passed under the Great Seal of the United
> Kingdom of Great Britain and Ireland, to bear this
> day's date, granting unto His Majesty's Son, His
> Royal Highness Prince Albert Frederick Arthur
> George, KG, and the heirs male of his body law-
> fully begotten, the dignities of Baron Killarney,
> Earl of Inverness and Duke of York.

---

*Bertie's best sport. In 1921 he and Greig won the Air Force Cup
for doubles at Wimbledon, and reached the semi-finals in singles,
when he was beaten by Greig, "which I knew he was sure to do," he
wrote to his father.

3

The state of mind, and the state of health, of George V in the years immediately following the Great War were at low ebb. The break-up of the old monarchies and the loss of relatives, even if they had been on the wrong side during the war, left the King like an old-time member who wakes up to find the club room almost empty and learns that most of his friends have resigned or are dead.

As to his own family, only Mary and, sometimes, his youngest son, could do right. Harry was mixing in bad company, he had heard; Bertie's stutter and apologetic manner irritated him beyond bearing; David was proving as idle and feckless as he had feared he would be once the war was over. The previous Christmas at York Cottage the King had stomped out of dinner before the end of the meal after exchanging sharp words with David, and had retired to his Study, refusing to see anyone. Only his ever-growing stamp collection gave him any pleasure, and it was in these leather-bound volumes that he sought comfort.

George viewed his official duties with equal distaste, and his taciturnity was noted with concern by Lord Stamfordham as well as by those who had contact with him at functions. He expressed a particular unwillingness to travel abroad. Stamfordham compared his master's enthusiasm at the idea of visiting India after his coronation with his reluctance to go anywhere ten years later. And so it came about that Bertie, now down from Cambridge, and with the title Duke of York, had more and more duties thrust upon him, and was given the European circuit for official functions.

To carry out these duties, he required a new equerry, a young man of his own age, to replace Greig following his promotion to Comptroller. Accordingly Jamie Stuart entered his life, and his service. Bertie had a need for heroes in his life. Greig had filled that need for years, and would continue to do so, but Jamie Stuart fitted perfectly the role of hero-companion, always at his side on social occasions and friend and guide when alone.

Captain the Hon. James Gray Stuart was the third son of the 17th Earl of Moray. The Earl had married an admiral's daughter in 1890, who had given birth to three sons in a row, of whom Jamie was the third. He was a year older than Bertie. In the war he had been a captain in the 3rd Battalion, Royal Scots, and had earned an MC and Bar. The main Stuart residence in Scotland was Kinfauns Castle, Perthshire, within comfortable distance of Balmoral and Glamis.

Jamie Stuart was still uncertain how best to occupy himself after the war when suddenly, early in 1920, "my whole life changed."

"I was asked by Louis Greig to come to London to see him. Prince Albert had gone to Cambridge after the war and the suggestion was that I should join him there about a month before he came down and started his official career. I was to be his first equerry. Such a thought had never entered my head." The pay was a meagre £450 a year, and as the household "cannot afford more than one equerry," he had to do the work of two, which could mean twenty-four hours a day seven days a week.

Apart from making up fours at tennis with Greig, Bertie and Mary at BP, the first duty Jamie had to carry out was to attend Bertie at several royal weddings between distant and not so distant relatives. One of them was in Belgrade, where Princess Marie of Rumania was married to King Alexander of Yugoslavia. Four months later, Bertie was back in the Balkans again as his father's representative at the coronation of King Ferdinand and Queen Marie of Rumania at Alba Julia.

According to the leading figures in these and other ceremonies and foreign functions, Bertie performed extremely well. "He did his part beautifully & his presence was most popular in Serbia," Queen Marie wrote to King George.

The British minister in Rumania wrote to Stamfordham, praising highly the skill and dignity of Bertie's performance under taxing circumstances. ". . . the Duke was by far the most popular of the Royal Representatives who had come on this occasion . . . I hope you will be good enough to tell His Majesty that in my long experience . . . I have never experienced greater pride in recognizing the suitability, and complete popularity, of my country's Special Representative."

To the concern and chagrin of those in Buckingham Palace closest to the King, George appeared to dismiss this praise of his second son with no more than reluctant acknowledgement. Stamfordham was anxious that at least the Queen was made aware of Bertie's success, even if his father seemed indifferent to it. Concerned that May "did not quite realize what an unqualified success the Duke of York was in Rumania" and that "His Majesty's praise was quite inadequate," one British official in Rumania said "he could not exaggerate how admirably in every way His Royal Highness had done—and that once he got away 'on his own' he was a different being, never failing to 'rise to the occasion,' and proved himself to be far and away the most important of the foreign visitors at the coronation."

Alas, another factor had entered into this father-son relationship. The simple explanation was that George found it even more difficult to accept Bertie as a success than as a failure. When Bertie was always being ill, and sorry for himself, and stuttering his apologies for everything, that had been bad enough. But Bertie as a popular figure, praised by all, almost as good a shot as his father, a masterful horseman,*

*The Serbian royal stables, decimated by the war, had been replenished by fine Irish stock. For his ride in a procession, Bertie was assigned an "excessively restive" horse. To the delight of the large crowds he succeeded in controlling it while simultaneously acknowledging the cheers. No one admired fine horsemanship more than Serbians.

invited to "flash" parties where cocktails were served and
Negro bands played horrible music—Bertie the sought-
after hero was more than his father could stand.

This lack of appreciation at home, and success and popularity elsewhere, made Bertie think about other people's
families. With Phyllis and Louis Greig, with the Montagu-
Douglas-Scotts, with the Sutherlands, with the millionaire
American Vanderbilts, too, and even the distant Rumanians,
Bertie became aware that family life did not have to be like
his own.

The Greigs had given him the first taste of what happiness and fulfilment a family could provide. Now that he was
out in the world and travelling widely, he saw, somewhat to
his surprise, that this contentment was commonplace, and he
wanted, above anything else, to become a part of such a
family.

All this first struck Bertie when he was staying for Cowes
Week with Sir Godfrey and Lady (Eva) Baring and their four
children at Nubia House, their large and hospitable establishment next door to the Royal Yacht Squadron. The Greigs
were there too—this was when Charles Baring heard Louis
suppressing Bertie's bad language on the tennis court—and a
large party of lively people fresh from Goodwood week. Much
social sparkle surrounded the serious business of racing yachts
(including the King's *Britannia*, with HM among the crew—
perhaps, people said, it would cheer him up, "get him out of
the dumps").

There were plenty of pretty young women, and Bertie
enjoyed much attention from them. Particularly assiduous
was the Barings' entertaining and much admired eighteen-
year-old daughter Helen, always known as Poppy. Bertie was
charmed and flattered by her, and it was soon obvious that
they were together on every possible occasion and were
dancing with no one else. Phyllis Greig observed what was
happening with some anxiety; Jamie Stuart (inexperienced in
royal courting protocol as he was) was delighted; and Poppy's
parents watched the developing relationship with considerable interest.

Before the Nubia House party broke up and the guests
dispersed, many to shoot grouse, the news that Bertie had

proposed marriage *and been accepted,* inevitably became widely known. But what was kept secret and was not known until later were the contents of a telegram Bertie had received just as he was departing with the Greigs. If it had come even an hour or two earlier, its effect must have been seen, and the correct interpretation made: "On no account will we permit your proposed marriage. Mama."

4

Bertie's elder brother was as deeply in love as he was, and with as little chance of his affair leading to marriage. During the winter of 1917-18 David had been instructed to come home from the war to carry out a tour of armament factories as a contribution to improving morale and output. To offset the tedium of this daytime work (which, as always, he carried out superbly well), at night he "took to going to all the dances—'unbeknownst' to the King." Moreover, according to Asquith's daughter Cynthia, "no girl is allowed to leave London during the three weeks of [the Prince of Wales's] leave and every mother's heart beats high."

One of David's hostesses before he returned to his staff duties was Maud Kerr-Smiley, the American-born daughter of Ernest L. Simpson of New York. Her thirty-seven-year-old husband, Peter, scion of an Irish baronetcy, was serving in the trenches with the 14th Battalion of the Royal Irish Rifles. In early March Maud gave a ball. It went off well, she thought, and everyone enjoyed themselves. The Prince of Wales was able to come after all, and that set the tongues wagging and the mothers' hearts beating. He danced at first mostly with Rosemary Leveson-Gower. But that was before the air raid.

Just before midnight the warning maroons went up over central London. The band stopped and everyone went down to the cellars. The hostess was in the hall when a pretty woman in evening dress with a rather swarthy escort ran up the front steps and asked if they could shelter in the porch. An aeroplane was audible overhead,* so Maud told them to hurry down to the cellar with the others.

In the dim light the Prince of Wales was soon seen to be in animated conversation with this refugee from the night. She turned out to be Freda Dudley Ward, the daughter of a Nottingham lace millionaire. She was estranged from her husband, it appeared, who was a Liberal Party whip and a Vice-chamberlain of the Royal Household. When they could return upstairs again and dancing was renewed, it was noticed by everyone present that the Prince danced every single dance with Mrs Dudley Ward.

It was abundantly clear to all those at the ball that they were witnessing the birth of a grand passion. Freda Dudley Ward did not at once recognize the short figure who had opened the conversation in the half-light of Mrs Kerr-Smiley's cellar, and she had attempted to leave, with many thanks and apologies, when everyone started to go upstairs again. He had merely said that he lived in London, "and sometimes at Windsor." It was not until Mrs Kerr-Smiley had begged her, "Do please stay. His Royal Highness is so anxious that you should do so," that she realized she had been talking with the Prince of Wales.

Lady Rosemary Leveson-Gower and Freda Dudley Ward's escort were not seen again: it was supposed that both just left, while the new friends danced and chatted and laughed the night away. Eventually, David drove Freda home in his car. The following morning he turned up at her house again and took her out to lunch. Thus began one of the great romances of the 1920s.

---

*It was a Giant Gotha, R. 39, which dropped a single 1,000kg bomb, the first of this size, on to Kilburn, destroying or seriousl damaging twenty-six houses and killing a number of people.

David's 1919 Canadian tour was as rewarding and exhausting as he expected it would be. This slight, handsome, smiling Prince was greeted everywhere from St John's Newfoundland to Vancouver, more as a war hero than as heir to the throne. Veterans from the western front were especially enthusiastic, struggling to get near enough to David to shake his hand.

Half-deafened by cheers and shouting, buffeted about by their weight of numbers, his right hand so bruised and swollen that he had to make do with his left, David took it all in his stride. "You might take things easier during the last month of your visit," was the suggestion of his father in a letter of that time, "& give yourself more spare time & more rest from the everlasting functions & speeches which get on one's nerves."

On the contrary, David began to form plans to visit the United States, too, while he was on that side of the Atlantic. "It seemed absurd," he wrote, "to be so near the United States without extending my trip across the border."

He was already on his way back east across Canada by train when the cables began flying. George gave his reluctant permission; by contrast, the American administration reacted positively and joyously, except for the Irish mayor of New York who foresaw political embarrassment.

David and his entourage arrived in Washington just twelve months after the Armistice, on 11 November 1919. The solemnity of the occasion, and the unconnected facts that the President had been stricken with paralysis and prohibition had been introduced only weeks earlier, took none of the edge off the excitement and happiness of the visit. Or almost none. David did confess that "there were times, especially at official banquets, when something more stimulating than water would have imparted more warmth to my response to the usual toast drunk to my health."

There were formal visits to Mount Vernon and the Walter Reed General Hospital, to the Navy Academy at Annapolis, and even to the White House and the crippled President. "Leaving him, I thought that his was the most disappointed face that I had ever looked upon." And in the evenings, when there were not formal dinners, the great hostesses of the day fought to grab him as a guest.

"I knew I was going to love the US and I certainly did,"

David reported afterwards. "Washington was fine, but New York was magic. I knew Paris well by now and loved its sophistication and appreciation of the best things in life. But New York fizzed! I have been back many times and always I have felt the blood run faster as the excitement and novelty and energy of the place strikes you again."

David entered the city for the first time by admiral's barge at lower Manhattan. "The din was deafening as scores of vessels in the stream blasted a welcome with their whistles. All the way to the Battery the barge was serenaded from an accompanying tug by a brass band . . ."

A ticker-tape reception, a City Hall reception, Grant's tomb, the Met, the top of the Woolworth building . . . spontaneous welcomes everywhere, smiling hospitality, cheering crowds. "This Prince was *made* for New York!" a reporter commented truthfully. But above all it was the music, from that first brass band to the *Ziegfeld Follies*, that left the most indelible mark on David.

"A Pretty Girl is Like a Melody" was all the rage—"a haunting little song," as he described it. For months after his return he was whistling it. "Once my father heard me. 'What's that damn tune you are whistling all the time?' he demanded. Oh, I'm sorry if it bothers you. It's just something I picked up in America."

"David could be heard whistling everywhere after he got back from Canada," one of his friends observed. "Whistling always got on his father's nerves. But it was the reason for it that irritated him a great deal more." For David had a mistress, and, not surprisingly, George did not approve. He already dreaded a reversion in his eldest son to the ways of his own father who, for almost all his married life, had at least one mistress. But Papa had married, and married most suitably, and had plenty of children. David did not show any inclination to marriage, and he was already twenty-five!

George remained in ignorance of his son's first youthful flutter with one of his Norfolk neighbours. Lord Leicester at Holkham, just to the east of Sandringham, had a daughter-in-law, Lady Coke, who was twelve years older than David. She was "small, lively, with an individual humour, above all married." David wrote her love letters from France during the war.

Lady Coke was not at the ball at which David met Freda Dudley Ward. If she had been a guest, things might have turned out differently. "Instead," a friend wrote soon after the ignition, "he was consumed by his passion for Freda, and no more was heard of Miriam Coke."

How David Windsor, Prince of Wales, son of "chilly George and May," could call up such heat can only be explained as being some genetic throw-back, perhaps to his paternal grandfather. Anyway, London society had not seen anything like it for years, and hostesses gazed in wonder and awe at the twenty-five-year-old Prince and his mistress together on the dance floor (both were consummately good dancers), or in animated conversation.

There was certainly something unique about Freda Dudley Ward, especially at a time when top society was conformist in style, manner, speech and attitude. Frances Donaldson writes of "her most individual characteristic," her voice, "which was rather thin and high, but with unusual intonations which made it oddly attractive." Her opinions on pretty well everything were charitable yet shrewd, and almost always different from anyone else's. She was a total, and natural, egalitarian, addressing friends, servants, people in shops, everyone in exactly the same friendly tone.

"Absolutely *everyone*, and I mean everyone, loved Freda—doormen and waiters, children and duchesses," a woman, a little younger than her who knew her well, remarked. "She was so terribly terribly friendly in a completely sincere way." She had two little daughters, Penelope and Angela ("Angie"), who called David "Little Prince" and adored him, as he came to adore them. He used to play with them tirelessly.

David telephoned to Freda several times every day. The first call in the morning was known as "the baker's call," and there were others without special names. His visits when he was in London depended on his daily timetable, but if there was any pattern it began with his calling on her at 5 p.m. for tea, although there might have been a morning drive in

David's motor car. He would return later, dressed for the evening, either to take her out to a night club, where they could make up an informal party—easier than in the more public glare of a restaurant—or to St James's Palace where he lived in York Lodge—or they would stay at her house. If they went out, he would return home alone in the small hours; or she would leave him at a similar time.

At the time of David's tour of Canada, the relationship had not settled into a particular shape, although his passion was as ardent as it was to remain for many years.

On the morning of 1 February 1920 George V made a decision which led to much extra work for many people in the Royal Navy and in the United States. Two weeks earlier May had told him that David was keeping a mistress, a married woman, that the affair had lasted for almost two years, and that all the signs pointed to a prolonged relationship. "I think he is in *love* with this woman, George. Grace [sister of one of her ladies-in-waiting] says he has eyes for no one else, sees her every day, almost every evening and almost every night."

George made a few enquiries of his own through Stamfordham, learned of her age (the same as David's) and that she had two children, and that (as he put it) "her bloody marriage is on the rocks." To his secretary, and to male members of his family, he referred to Freda as "the lacemaker's daughter" or, more violently, "that bloody whore." And of David, he was heard to remark, "I suppose that arrogant little puppy will expect the Church of England to make a special dispensation so that he can marry his bloody whore when she gets her divorce."

David's second tour, of Australia, New Zealand and the West Indies was to take place that year. He was due to leave at the end of April and be back home at the end of August. But on that February morning George said to his secretary, "Arthur, I am going to extend my son's tour from the middle of March to the middle of October. Perhaps that will end the madness. Seven months! And we must make sure he is kept happy with suitable women *en route*!"

The King smiled even more infrequently since the war.

He did so now, though it was more a grimace of malice than an expression of happiness. Stamfordham said, in his special gentle voice of mild objection, "It will cause a good deal of rearrangement, Sir, and time is not on our side."

With the characteristic pouting of his lips George inserted a new cigarette between them, struck a match, lit it, and inhaled deeply. "Not as much as you may suppose, Arthur. I was studying its itinerary last night. If we add a visit to the United States at the beginning and another at the end of the Pacific tour it will mean rearranging only the West Indies tour. And my son appears to enjoy the Americans with their filthy Negro bands and cocktails!" And George almost smiled again.

"Very well, Sir. I will ask the Prince of Wales's office to cancel his March and early April engagements."

The depth of David's misery was witnessed by his cousin Dickie Mountbatten, who had persuaded him that he needed some youthful and high-spirited company on a tour of this length with such a packed programme. The need to console the Prince of Wales in his unhappiness at being away for so long made itself felt before they had even left.

On 15 March there was a farewell dinner at BP, and the next morning Mountbatten, now nineteen and a lieutenant RN, drove to Freda Dudley Ward's house to collect David, wearing the rings of a post-captain, and accompany him to Victoria Station.

After a few minutes David emerged from the front door and half-ran to the car. When Mountbatten turned to greet his cousin, he saw that the tears were pouring down his cheeks.

After a moment, as the car turned into Grosvenor Street, David asked chokingly, "Have you ever seen a post-captain cry?"

"No, I don't think I have," Mountbatten said.

"Well, you'd better get used to it. You may see it again."

But Dickie Mountbatten was spared that embarrassment, thanks largely to his own capacity for bringing cheer and hope when most needed during David's seven-month-long separation from his beloved Freda. In southern California and Honolulu (on the way out and on the way back), from Wanganui to Dunedin, from Geelong to Launceston, and around the West Indies, before the *Renown* brought them back to Portsmouth on 10 September 1920, David's young cousin played his part as court jester. He was a cheerful partner or opponent in hundreds of games, laughing when a thousand Australian farmers and their families all wanted to shake David's hand, and giving his support when moods of black depression threatened to overwhelm David at the end of an exhausting day.

The worst that David had to bear was the letters from his father criticizing him for the informal poses he adopted for newspaper photographs, or the uniform (or suit or hat or even jodhpurs at a rodeo) he was wearing, or the wording of some informal speech made to an over-excited, politically motivated crowd of mainly Irish migrants.

"He could do *nothing* right," Mountbatten reported later. "And it was my business to cheer him on."

For his part, David applauded Dickie's "vigour and high spirits." Their previous opportunities to be with one another had been confined largely to official occasions; now these two young men developed a mutual affection. "You've no idea what a friend David is to me," Mountbatten wrote home to his mother. "He may be six years older, but in some respects he is the same age as me . . . He is such a marvellous person, and I suppose the best friend I have."

5

In the last week of October 1921 David was off on the next round of his imperial tours, this time to India, and then later to Japan. Once again, Dickie Mountbatten was invited to join the party. At Delhi, a surprise visitor turned up. She was Edwina Ashley, the elder daughter of Wilfred Ashley, whose wife had died before the First World War. Maud Ashley was the only daughter of Sir Ernest Cassel, the multi-millionaire international banker, and on Cassel's death Edwina had inherited the bulk of the estate, making her one of the richest women in the world.

Edwina and Dickie had met before David's departure, and in Delhi, shortly after Edwina's arrival, the two became engaged—thus signalling the birth of the Mountbatten dynasty, with all its subsequent royal associations.

But this did not make the headlines in England. On the contrary, "In India," wrote one gossip columnist speculatively, "the talk in the royal party led by the Prince of Wales is all of Princess Mary's marriage to Viscount Lascelles DSO. It is most regrettable that the call of the Empire is preventing His Royal Highness from attending the ceremony."

David was a great admirer of Henry Lascelles.* They
had met many times at Guards HQ when Henry was second
in command of the 3rd Battalion Grenadiers, with a heroic
insouciance that was notable even in a regiment renowned for
bravery. Once, as Lascelles was leaving for the front line
again, David remarked, "My God, Harry, I'd give my right
arm to change places with you." The next time he saw him,
Lascelles had his left arm in a sling as a result of a German
bullet breaking it. "Sorry, Sir," he said, "wrong arm!"

That was at Loos, where Lascelles got his first DSO. He
was wounded twice again, was gassed, and earned another
DSO and a Croix de Guerre before the Armistice.

Already rich in his own right, Lascelles inherited another £2 1/2 million from an eccentric great-uncle, Lord
Clanricarde, in 1916. Born 9 September 1882, the eldest son
of the 5th Earl of Harewood, Henry Lascelles went to Eton
(Rev. S.R. James's house) and Sandhurst just like his name-
sake and future brother-in-law, Prince Henry. He grew into a
tall, imposing, severe figure, almost a caricature of the English aristocrat, complete with top hat and monocle. But he
had unexpected depths, and was a great connoisseur and
acquirer of Italian paintings.

Duff Cooper met him in the front line of the trenches in
an "incredibly deep dug-out," "looking extraordinarily ele-
gant, and beautifully clean." Duff Cooper later discovered
that he was "a far pleasanter companion than anyone else in
the mess . . . cultivated and talking about wine, books, pedi-
grees and old houses."

Lascelles always refused to limit his career to soldiering
and dabbled for a while in diplomacy, as honorary attaché at
the British Embassy in Rome, and politics, which soon of-
fended against his extreme fastidiousness. After the war he
took up the responsibilities of running his estates and property, and was out hunting two or three times a week in the

*Before the war Lascelles had fallen deeply in love with Vita Sackville-
West, and she had seriously considered marrying him before, in
September 1912, she had succumbed to the charms of Harold Nicol-
son and married him.

Mary the wartime nurse

*The first Windsors in 1918. The war which led to the adoption
of this name is almost over. (l to r) Bertie, George, Harry,
Mary with their parents*

*David and Bertie (third from left) on the Western Front with
the generals*

Bertie the wartime naval officer

Bertie the airman

Bertie with fellow varsity pilots, July 1921

First to be married: Mary with Lord Harewood, 1922

Engaged, 1923: Elizabeth and Bertie leave for Sandringham

Elizabeth, just married, with her mother . . .

A popular couple: George and Marina posters go up for their wedding

Harry and Alice engaged: Balmoral, September 1935, with Alice's mother on the left

David and Stanley Baldwin. But this is 1926 and their confrontation is still ten years ahead

Honeymooners in 1928: Ernest and Wallis Simpson

Seven years later, and Wallis is with David at the races

David with his mother, November 11, 1936, on their way to the Armistice Day ceremony at the Cenotaph

season. He was also seen, less successfully, at the races where, it was said, "he was one of the best friends of the bookmakers."

In October 1921 Lascelles met Mary at the Grand National, and at a house party at Chatsworth, where she was the guest of honour. The small, shy Princess was next seen almost continuously in the company of the six-feet-four-inches Viscount at a Buxton house party given by the Duke and Duchess of Devonshire. They were also frequently seen out hunting together. As Mary's biographer wrote:

> At this time, on more than one occasion, Princess Mary was seen hunting with the West Norfolk in the company of Lord Lascelles. Once as they were riding home together she saw a horse cast a shoe, and, mindful of the old superstition, she at once slipped from her mount to pick it up, laughingly preventing Lord Lascelles from getting it for her, since the luck is supposed to fly away unless the shoe is actually picked up by the person who intends to keep it.

Invitations, first to Balmoral and then to Sandringham, confirmed for even the most myopic royal-watcher that matters were coming rapidly to a head. Everyone, especially Mary's mother, approved, with the exception of George. He could not bear to face the loss of his only daughter. So there was an ironic, not to say inaccurate, note in the public announcement:

> It is with the greatest pleasure that the King and Queen announce the betrothal of their beloved daughter Princess Mary to Viscount Lascelles, DSO, eldest son of the Earl of Harewood.
>
> At a Council held at Buckingham Palace this evening His Majesty was pleased to declare his consent to the marriage.
> November 22nd, 1921.

Mary's eldest brother received the news before the formal announcement and soon after he arrived in India. "Well I'm blessed, Dickie," he exclaimed. "I had no idea—good old Mary. She won't be short of a penny, bless her heart, though she won't know what to do with all that money. Not a big spender, our Mary."

A few days later, David and Dickie and the whole royal entourage departed from Delhi for the remainder of their tour, which included Ceylon, Singapore and Japan, while Edwina remained for a while with the Readings and made a tour of Nepal. "This confirmed my lifelong love of India," she said.

Mary's "love match from first to last" attracted the attention of a nation emerging from years of suffering and austerity.

> All who saw Princess Mary during the weeks of her engagement will remember her radiant bearing and the unmistakable air of happiness surrounding her. So much more fortunate than many in her position have been, she was marrying the man of her choice, and the knowledge of this fact, combined with the undoubted similarity of their tastes in many things, opened up before her a prospect of great and lasting happiness.

And so the day arrived, the last day of February 1922, and as *The Times* noted, "Everybody knew beforehand that only one thing could possibly be wanting to make Princess Mary's wedding day a perfect one, and that was sunshine. The sun shone brightly, and so it was perfect." Westminster Abbey was packed, as were the streets thronging the route of the procession. "Little mousy Mary," as the hard "bright young things" called her, had her day of unsurpassed glitter and transparent happiness.

> The Princess's wedding dress is composed of an under-dress of silver lamé, veiled with marquisette exquisitely embroidered in English roses worked in relief with thousands of tiny diamonds and seed

pearls, over a faint lattice work. It was girdled with
a silver cord studded with a triple row of pearls.

No one publicly hazarded a guess at its cost, nor the value of
some of the jewellery she now inherited, including the
Clanricarde diamonds. These had been in the strong room of
a London bank for more than a century. A hundred years
before that "it was prophesied that these wonderful gems
should be worn by a King's daughter, and when, after they
had been re-set according to Princess Mary's taste, she herself wore them, the prophecy was fulfilled."

George was heartbroken. That night he wrote in his
diary:

BUCKINGHAM PALACE. Feb 28th.—Today darling Mary married Harry Lascelles. There were
enormous crowds in the streets from here to the
Abbey. They began taking up their places in the
middle of the night. Mary had breakfast with us as
usual, she was quite calm & not a bit nervous. She
drove with me in my coach to Westminster Abbey
where we arrived at 11.30 & I led her by the hand
from the West door to the altar steps. The Archbishop of Canterbury married them. Victor Mackenzie* was best man. It was a beautiful & most
impressive service & I was proud of my darling
child, but it was terribly sad to think that she was
leaving us . . . We took them out on the balcony &
they got a tremendous ovation from an enormous
crowd. Luncheon at 1.45 . . . I went up to Mary's
room & took leave of her & quite broke down.
They left for Weston** at 3.45 . . . They drove with
four greys in open carriage with travelling escort to
Paddington. Felt very low & depressed now that

*Colonel Sir Victor Audley Falconer Mackenzie DSO of Glen-Muick,
Ballater (near Balmoral), where he owned 42,000 acres. Commanded
1st Battalion, Scots Guards, twice wounded. Unmarried, became
Extra Groom-in-Waiting to the King.
**Weston Park, Shifnal, Shropshire, the seat of the Earl of Bradford.

darling Mary has gone. Worked & read all the
evening.

Next day he wrote in his journal (facing a gummed-in facsim-
ile of the royal letter of thanks to the nation for its sympathy
and good wishes): "I miss darling Mary too awfully."

Lala Bill, who had a seat immediately behind the royal
family in the Abbey, wept copiously, too, remembering the
joy of Mary's birth in the year of the Good Queen's Diamond
Jubilee. But her tears were of pure joy.

"Poor Papa," wrote Bertie in his journal on 1 March
1922. "I have never seen him look so miserable." But the rest
of the family (David sent a telegram from India) were delighted,
and Prince Harry and Prince George got rather drunk on '08
Krug champagne.

One of the Windsor's relations whose presence at Mary's
wedding was not widely publicized was sixteen-year-old Princess Marina of Greece. It had not been an easy war for Prince
Nicholas and his family who had, over the years, been in and
out of exile more times than they cared to remember. However, by 1922 their exile from Greece could be considered
permanent, and they wished to settle in England. George
and May would have loved that but politically their position
was even trickier than that of the late Tsar of Russia. The
Greek royal family not only had German origins, but had
given support to the Germans during the war. The family was
scattered all over the place in 1922, and now Prince Nicholas
was determined to bring it together again, united as it had
been for the three beautiful girls in their childhood.

Prince Nicholas, who left Greece with the King,
cabled to his wife and two elder daughters in Paris
and to Princess Marina in England asking them to
join him at once in Palermo.

There the little family re-united. Once more
their roots had been torn up. Their old home had
gone for good. Their fortune was confiscated. A

Republic ruled in Greece. For the second time they were wanderers on the face of the earth.

Princess Marina, then a tall, delicately formed sixteen-year-old, slender as a fawn, looked at her parents and said, with that sudden touch of mischief which lit her face sometimes in the darkest hours: "We really needn't have unpacked our trunks."

They settled in a modest hotel off the Bois de Boulogne in Paris, with very little money, very little to do, and very few friends. Paris was full of refugees at that time—1922-3—eking out some sort of living. Nicholas painted, not very well. They were comforted, however, by having Prince Andrew of Greece and his wife Alice (Dickie Mountbatten's eldest sister) and their children not far away at St Cloud. Alice opened a shop, which was considered very middle-class by the refugee nobility from Russia. She was becoming rather eccentric, liable to drift off into a mystical dreamland of religio-fantasy, like her late aunt the Tsarina.

But neither Prince Andrew's son Philip at St Cloud, nor Marina in the centre of Paris, remembered this period in their lives as either sad or deprived. "I loved playing with my little cousin," Marina recalled. "The difference of fourteen years then, and later, seemed nothing, and we became the greatest of friends. I can remember him on his fourth birthday, 10 June 1925, a year after I came out. He was an entrancing boy, lively and full of curiosity about everything."

6

Louis and Phyllis Greig, four years earlier, had revealed to Bertie for the first time the reality of a happy and harmonious domestic life. At Nubia House in August 1921, the Barings— *"Probitate et Labore"*—had provided a picture of compatible domesticity, children and parents in harmony: and for Bertie the mighty bonus of love, which had been destroyed as swiftly as by a direct hit at Jutland.

The events that followed Bertie's flight from the Isle of Wight now assume the shape of a Scottish myth. Unlike the Greigs, Jamie Stuart had witnessed Bertie's lightning love affair with Poppy with avuncular indulgence. His position was a curious one, as he had increasingly recognized. While Bertie was now a royal duke and his equerry a mere hon. and son of an earl, Jamie had opened the door for him to a new social scene. Bertie, shy, stuttering, found himself at parties in London, and castles in Scotland, where previously he would have felt uncomfortably lost.

Take the Buccleuchs. Jamie had known them since earliest childhood. They were very close, and he had played endlessly with Sybil and Alice when he was around eight or nine. And the Strathmores. Michael, though four years older, had been a great friend, and Jamie had known Rose and her younger sister Elizabeth since their nursery days.

"Even before I was out of the Army, I began to see more of Elizabeth, who had had a much harder time than me, looking after the wounded," Jamie told a friend who had been in the same battalion, Royal Scots.

Elizabeth Bowes-Lyon amused Jamie Stuart, at first like a younger sister (there were three years between them) and then rather more seriously. She teased him, and responded to his direct and completely open way of thinking and talking. Their mutual affection had developed quite seriously when Jamie was appointed Bertie's equerry: Elizabeth was just twenty then.

They saw one another rather more intermittently from the summer of 1920 owing to Jamie's travels and duties at home. But they met at balls, at Cowes, and at Goodwood for the racing, with Bertie in the same party, talking with people he knew and dancing, always skilfully and enthusiastically, and loving it. The ball at 7 Grosvenor Square, was one such occasion. It was given by Lord and Lady Farquhar, another Ayrshire family, on 20 May 1920. Elizabeth was a guest, too, chaperoned by the Annalys ("*Vi et Virtue*"). Bertie later claimed that "he had fallen in love that evening," with Elizabeth, but he was quite mistaken; he scarcely spoke to her, and never danced with her. Besides, Bertie's courtship of Poppy Baring still lay ahead. But he did note, as he had done before, that Jamie paid Elizabeth an unusual amount of attention.

Bertie visited Glamis for the first time that autumn, travelling by motor from Balmoral where he was staying with his parents and younger brothers and David (just back from Australia with Dickie Mountbatten) and Mary.

On his second visit to Glamis Bertie was with David and Mary shortly after Cowes week in August 1921, *en route* to the Sutherlands at Dunrobin. This time he stayed for five days, one of a large shooting party. Grouse were abundant that year and they were out on the moors every day, with the women at their usual task of supervising the picnic lunch in the early afternoon: veal and ham pie (cook's *tour de force*), cold beef and stone jars of malt whisky.

Social life began seriously in the evening, with dancing after dinner. Jamie was discretion itself, dancing several times, but no more, with Elizabeth. And no more times than Bertie danced with her.

Perhaps it was because she was in her own home that Bertie now took more notice of this attractive, ever-smiling, warm young woman, who was acting as hostess in the absence of her mother. The anguish, and the anger, over Poppy Baring were beginning to subside under the influence of the hospitality of all these Bowes-Lyons.

Cautiously, after the rebuff over Poppy, Bertie wrote to his mother, the letter reaching Balmoral the following afternoon. In it he said: "It is delightful here & Elizabeth is very kind to me. The more I see of her the more I like her."

Elizabeth did not recognize the first signs of special interest in herself from Bertie, so hesitant and modest was he in his approaches. As she lavished her friendliness and hospitality so generously and indiscriminately, she was surprised when any young man showed that he thought he was being singled out for special favour, although a number of them had done so over the past two years. She did not include Jamie Stuart among these. Jamie had been a friend for years and years, and they had corresponded all through the war when he was at the front. Many times she had prayed for his safety, with her mother at her side in the chapel. Cecilia loved the boy, too, and had not discouraged the increasing warmth of the friendship when Jamie came home from France.

In the autumn of 1921 Elizabeth Bowes-Lyon cannot be said to have had a first love; but the nearest to being one was Jamie Stuart—so amusing and kind and concerned for her. As for Bertie, she really felt no more than a desire to be kind, especially as he was so shy and had that awful stammer, although that seemed to disappear when they talked and danced together.

So Elizabeth was quite surprised when she was invited over to Balmoral for a ball and to stay for a few nights in two weeks' time. She consulted her mother who was as surprised as she was and advised her to decline. Bertie was only at Glamis because of Jamie—one could not very well invite one without the other. And David, Prince of Wales, was only here because his sister Mary had asked if he could come as he had been away for so long and would so love to meet them. A ball at Balmoral, well that was just acceptable, Cecilia reasoned. But certainly not to stay.

The Strathmores had not altered their attitude to the royal family. "If there is one thing I have determined for my children," Strathmore once declared, "it is that they shall never have any post about the Court." Elizabeth's friendship with Princess Mary was not discouraged because it was based on their mutual enthusiasm for the Girl Guide movement. And, anyway, she seemed a nice, sensible, unpretentious, down-to-earth girl, even if she had once referred in affectionate terms to that dreadful dissipated grandfather of hers, Edward VII. In London, Elizabeth had been permitted to attend one of Mary's small private parties at Buckingham Palace. But that sort of thing was not encouraged.

As for Jamie Stuart, he told a friend at the time what a delicate position he had found himself in. He was very fond of Elizabeth, and he believed she reciprocated his feelings. He was still far from thinking about marrying anyone, though at the back of his mind he *had* begun to think what a good wife she would make. He was more amused than worried when his "boss" (as he called Bertie privately) gave signs of falling for this attractive girl he had known almost since her birth; but he did admit that he was slightly affronted that "the boss had not even twigged that I was pretty fond of the girl myself" as he put it. For the moment, then, he lay low and bided his time, comforted by the likelihood that the Strathmores would not permit such a match anyway.

Jamie Stuart might not have been so calm and confident about the situation at the end of 1921 if he had known that the King and Queen not only knew of their son's ever stronger feelings for Elizabeth Bowes-Lyon, but thoroughly approved of his courtship. Perhaps before the Great War the second in line to the throne would have been required to find himself someone of royal blood—almost inevitably German—as a wife. But the toppling of thrones and the decimation of dynasties had led to a broader range of choice. The Barings

. . . well no; and the girl was thought to be a bit of a flibbertigibbet, too. But the Bowes-Lyons were very different: "1st Lord Lyon, one of the hostages for the ransom of King James I, delivered up to the English 1424, released 1427. This feudal chief was created a peer of parliament, as *Lord Glamis*, in 1445. His lordship was . . ." and so on. That one had a daughter named Elizabeth, too.

It was, then, the Girl Guides and the Hon. James Stuart (unwittingly) who provided the bridge between the Windsors and the Bowes-Lyons. Mary had told her mother about Elizabeth some time earlier, and in due course there had been a meeting. Now May took steps to see her again, and liked her all the more.

It was Mary who, shortly before her own wedding and at her mother's behest, engineered an invitation for Bertie to the Strathmores' Hertfordshire place, St Paul's Walden Bury. Here, on 2 December, a fine winter's afternoon, Bertie invited Elizabeth for a walk—she in a heavy Harris tweed suit, sensible shoes and a cloche hat. Summoning up all his courage, he proposed to her while they were leaning on a gate studying some fine hunters in a field. "Waiting for her answer was worse than Jutland, waiting for the German shells to arrive," he commented to David later.

She refused him, but he told Louis Greig that she did it so kindly that he was determined to try again. "Quite right," said Greig, and told him that he had proposed three times to Phyllis before she accepted him.

So Bertie was no longer "bowing to the inevitable." Jamie was a fellow guest at St Paul's. Fortunately, he knew nothing of the episode. Bertie returned to Balmoral and reported the rebuff to his mother, who told George that evening. Bertie was summoned to George's Study, just like the old days. "Your mother and I like the girl, and you have our blessing," he said; so it was not like the old days after all.

"But she turned me down flat, Papa."

"Well, what are you going to do about that, Bertie?"

"Try again, I suppose. I shall keep on trying."

"You'll be a lucky fellow if she accepts you," George commented, and went back to his stamps.

By what Bertie judged to be amazing good fortune, he

found himself with Jamie back at St Paul's Walden Bury only
ten days later—and for Christmas. He was overjoyed, and
determined to propose again, what is more, this time in Air
Force uniform, recalling that contemporary popular song,
"No girl says no to an airman."

By now, as Bertie's official biographer was to write:

> The relations of Lord and Lady Strathmore with
> their children and the happy badinage and affection
> of a large and closely knit family were a revela-
> tion to him, providing a climate of ideas to which
> he instantly responded, and in which his own per-
> sonality throve and blossomed. He was deeply in
> love . . .

Elizabeth was wonderful with children, too! That Christmas
the house seemed full of Bowes-Lyon children, who adored
their Auntie Elizabeth, who in turn played endless games
with them and sang popular songs of the day. "Her talent for
mimicry was such that it was once said she could have been a
star of the music-hall. She also loved dressing up for the
glamorous occasion. At the party given for Rose she turned
many a head with her pink brocade gown and pearls shining
in her dark hair."

Bertie proposed again on Boxing Day, in the library.
This time she laughed, though very indulgently, even placing
her hand briefly on his. "You spoil me," she said. "You must
know I love proposals. But I'm afraid not, Bertie. It just
wouldn't do."

Bertie was wise enough not to comment on the last
sentence, and was not in the least discouraged. In his mind
he likened it to working a skiff up the River Dart when he
was a naval cadet. It took time and skill, but you got there in
the end.

On their way back from St Paul's to London on New
Year's Eve, Jamie, who was driving, said, "I'm terribly sorry,
Sir, but I've been told I have to ask you to release me from
my duties."

Bertie was stunned; it was as well that he was not at the

wheel. "What do you mean, Jamie? Who has told you and why? And why hasn't anyone told me?"

"It was Greig who told me. But I think he was only obeying orders, too. I'm dreadfully sorry. I've so much enjoyed being with you."

That evening, Bertie lost his temper with Louis Greig on the telephone. "How dare you treat me like this? Whose orders? Why was I not consulted? Is it Papa up to his old tricks?" At length Greig succeeded in calming him down enough to make himself heard. He said he would come round first thing in the morning to explain, but not too early, he added, "as it is New Year's Day and we'll all have fat heads."

"You speak for yourself," snapped Bertie and slammed the receiver back on its hook. His hand was shaking and he felt sick.

But the next day, Bertie was suitably mollified by Greig's explanation. Apparently, Jamie Stuart had had the unexpected opportunity of making himself a small fortune in oil, out in Oklahoma. So he had been told. He had mentioned this to no one at Court, but Greig had learned about it at his club. Jamie had refused to go, saying that his duty lay at Bertie's side. They got on well and he thought he was doing a good job. Greig spoke to Stamfordham, who spoke to George who said (rather roughly), "Well, order the silly bugger to go. Tell him he's sacked."

All this sounded credible and understandable to Bertie. He never, in all his life, learned the truth, which was that his mother had contrived the whole plot after learning from one of her ladies-in-waiting that Elizabeth Bowes-Lyon was "very much in love with the Duke of York's equerry" and would accept a proposal of marriage.

A lucrative post in America was found for Jamie, who was given an MVO to put after his name. "Early in the New Year of 1922 I set off for the unknown, which turned out to be the oilfields of Oklahoma." Lord Cowdray of Pearsons was the fixer." Jamie returned the following year, much better off, became a surprise member of parliament for Moray and Nairn (there was no trouble with the selection committee) and very soon married Lady Rachel Cavendish, a daughter of the 9th Duke of Devonshire. Later he was made a viscount.

The year 1922 was a bleak one for both Bertie and Elizabeth. Bertie was turned down twice more, once in the hunting field and again after dinner at the home of that establishment hostess Mrs Ronnie Greville. One day he opened his heart to Louis Greig, who urged him on in his usual hearty way. But Greig also had words with the Queen. May agreed that a firm policy must be instituted, and from March of that year, the recalcitrant Elizabeth found herself twice at Sandringham and in the summer twice at Balmoral, like it or not—and on the whole she did. Bertie was not always present, but "the Bowes-Lyon gel" was progressively finding herself woven into the Court fabric.

Using her formidable power to the full, May also contrived meetings, casual or otherwise, at hunts and balls and hunt balls and race meetings and shoots where newspaper cameramen were likely to be present. Willy-nilly, Bertie and Elizabeth began to appear in the same photographs in the *Tatler, Bystander*, the *Daily Sketch* and the *Daily Mirror*.

The gossip columnists—and it was the golden age of their profession—scribbled away about both of them. But paradoxically, and irritatingly, not together; they got everything wrong. "The Duke of York to marry Lady May Cambridge," was followed elsewhere by "Mary Ashley, Lady Louis Mountbatten's younger sister, to marry Duke of York," while Elizabeth was variously married off, finally by the *Daily News* to David: "Scottish Bride for Prince of Wales."

None of this nonsense pleased either of them. That unsurpassed gossip and diarist, Sir Henry "Chips" Channon recorded the reaction to this last story at a house party which included Elizabeth, at Firle Place, Lewes:

> The evening papers have announced her engagement to the Prince of Wales. So we all bowed and bobbed and teased her, calling her "Ma'am": I am not sure that she enjoyed it. It couldn't be true, but how delighted everyone would be! She certainly has something on her mind . . .

For Bertie, the year was all the more poignant for the run of weddings of people he knew, headed by his sister and then Edwina and Dickie. At the Mary-Lascelles wedding in February, Elizabeth was one of the bridesmaids "decked out in silver—silver roses worn at hip-level and tied with lovers' knots, diadems of silver rose leaves." Pictured beside her, for the social history books, was another bridesmaid, and Jamie Stuart's future bride, Lady Rachel Cavendish.

At Christmas 1922 Bertie had never felt so low, and confided to his journal, "I am beginning to believe that Elizabeth will never say 'yes.'" He could not know that the tide had turned in his favour, that the Strathmore parents were now reconciled to the inevitable and even found Bertie "a nice young man really and kind," that the unseen pressures of society, combined with those of the Court, were beginning to take their toll on Elizabeth's defences. People like the Countess of Airlie (except that there was no one quite like this formidable yet lovable lady-in-waiting) were using all their weight and guile to bring about the match.

By the time of the house party at Firle Place, Elizabeth had already made up her mind to accept Bertie's next proposal, which she surmised would be at St Paul's Walden Bury in less than two weeks when he came to stay, invited by Cecilia Strathmore. No wonder, then, that Chips Channon observed that Elizabeth had "something on her mind"; not least the irony that everyone had been told she was going to marry the Prince of Wales when they would very shortly learn, this time for certain, that she was going to marry his brother. She nursed her secret, unable to share her joke but enjoying it all the more for that. "Oh, how marvellous, really really marvellous!"

The pressure that had been on her for so long was a factor in her change of heart. But there were other motives, other changes of feeling. She really did like the young man. She liked and admired his moral courage and his directness; and his evident vulnerability and his deprivation of love, which seemed scarce in his family (as Mary had more than once hinted), aroused her motherly feelings. Perhaps, too, it might not be so awful leading a public life, always in the limelight. Perhaps it would be quite nice, really.

And there was one other factor, which she scarcely acknowledged to herself. The silly gossip columnists might "marry off" David to one unlikely girl after another, including herself most recently, but shrewd members of society, Elizabeth knew full well, were of the opinion that the Prince of Wales would never marry, that he preferred a mistress to a wife, a protective, amusing, lively, clever mistress like Freda Dudley Ward, to whom he was all but wed.

Marriage to Bertie, then, was unlikely to make her, as Duchess of York, number two to a Princess of Wales. It was one thing to make all the sacrifices to be number two; but not such a hard sacrifice to be first lady in the land after the Queen. And what was it Mabell Airlie had confided to Elizabeth? "The King thinks the Prince of Wales will never succeed him—or if he does, not for long." And the King, poor dear, was not very well.

Bertie arrived at St Paul's Walden Bury on the morning of Saturday 13 January 1923. He again wore RAF uniform, this time because he had come straight from an official engagement; and he changed before luncheon into a tweed suit. Elizabeth knew exactly what was going to happen. In the afternoon Bertie suggested a walk. They did not follow the same route as they had all those months ago when he first "popped the question." Appropriately, the background of the setting was again horses, but a different paddock, and a pair of rough ponies, whose noses they stroked.

Bertie asked her to marry him. This time she could laugh, without restraint, and did so. "If you are going to keep this up for ever, I might as well say 'yes' now. And so I do."

On their way back to the house, holding hands for all to see, they discussed plans. Elizabeth always liked to get the practicalities settled at once.

Before they reached the house, Bertie said, "Do you mind if I send a telegram to my mother? She'll be frightfully keen to know." Indeed she will, thought Elizabeth, and I suppose I must speak to Mama.

Within the hour a telegram arrived at Sandringham addressed to the Queen. May knew perfectly well that Bertie was going to propose once again this weekend, and that telegram could only mean good news. It was brief. "All right. Bertie."

On the Monday Bertie drove to Sandringham, picking up Louis Greig on the way. Greig slapped him on the back so hard that he set Bertie coughing. "Bertie with Greig arrived after tea," George wrote in his diary, "and informed us [they already knew] that he was engaged to Elizabeth Bowes-Lyon, to which we gladly gave our consent. I trust they will be very happy."

With filial punctiliousness, Bertie wrote again, "I can never really thank you properly for giving your consent." If only he had known how hard May had worked to bring about the match! "I am very happy," he continued, "and I can only hope that Elizabeth feels the same as I do. I know I am very lucky to have won her over at last."

So the popular song title was right after all, and in the end: "No girl says no to an airman." But at that time, on the other side of the Atlantic in Washington DC, Wallis Spencer had made up her mind to leave her airman, who had, she claimed, treated her shamefully. She had for long been separated from her husband, but "I knew that I could not continue to have it both ways," she wrote. "I must either go through with my divorce or return to Win . . . At the back of my mind was a vague notion, picked up from my newspaper reading, that a Paris divorce would be simple. There was one small difficulty: I had very little money."

7

According to his official biographer, "Prince Henry was a little slow, when told by his brother, Prince Albert, of his engagement to the Lady Elizabeth Bowes-Lyon." And after the wedding in Westminster Abbey on 26 April 1923, he complained of tiredness "through standing about most of the day."

"Harry was not a great one for the ceremonials," commented one of his fellow officers in the 10th Hussars. It was one of the great burdens he carried through his life that he was obliged to take part in so many of them, taking salutes, laying foundation stones and opening buildings, endlessly visiting war graves, reviewing troops and assemblies of Boy Scouts, making speeches to mayors and corporations and presidents and senates.

Harry's nickname in the Household Brigade was "Uncle Pineapple." The reason for this was that his bearskin nodded "like the topknot of that fruit" when he fell asleep without falling off his horse during rehearsals for the trooping of the colour ceremony.

He remained unmarried for as long as he did because he found the decision to select a bride an almost overwhelming effort. The early promise at school heralded a false dawn of academic accomplishment. Eton succeeded in teaching him very little, and at Sandhurst "the less attractive subjects, such as law and administration, were seen to be 'distasteful to him' . . ." Later, his Commandant, in a supreme effort to find a few favourable words for his father, wrote that he "only needs encouragement to overcome a certain diffidence as to his powers in order to develop into a really good officer."

But Harry was much liked wherever he went, as much in the mess as in non-army society, at point-to-points, and on and off the polo and hunting fields. Unlike his father, he was fearless and skilful in the saddle. At his first outing with the Quorn, for ten fields or so he was alone with the hounds, and there were only five other riders at the finish. "You must have felt proud," wrote the King generously.

Harry's polo was erratic in its results but no one put more into the game. As for his shooting, even George, "the best shot in Britain," was moved to sing his third son's praises. Woodcock are notoriously difficult birds to kill, but "I was most lucky on Thursday," he wrote to Papa, "in getting four woodcock, the first two being a right & left." Good going!

In August 1922 Harry was the guest of the Duke of Buccleuch at Langholm. It is hardly possible that he did not meet Alice Scott on this, and later, visits. But all that is on record is shooting with her brothers Walter and William. Meanwhile, through the 1920s and early 1930s Harry increasingly took on the tasks of royal travel representative, sometimes with David, more often alone.

He was given two very diverse coronations as official representative of his father—Emperors Hirohito of Japan, and Haile Selassie of Abyssinia—and an extensive tour of Australia and New Zealand.

Harry, Duke of Gloucester from 1928, made a good impression on these tours even if he resented the effort he had to put into them. Conversation was rarely raised above the formal and banal, and there were always opportunities for doing what he did best, hunting, polo, shooting and any other sport that stretched him physically. He was also by far the most impressive looking of George and May's boys. He was tall and held himself well, and was quite a figure in uniform, with his military stance and tidy little military moustache—a real gruff Hanoverian.

If David had the most charm, and George was the most handsome, Harry, to the outside world at least, best represented royal dignity, from Nairobi to Tokyo, and Cape Town to Wellington. Those whom he was expected to impress, he impressed. The fact that he was enthusiastic, indiscriminate and indiscreet in his liaisons did not matter very much. It was a standing joke in home society. Once, in Nairobi, things did get rather out of hand.

On 6 September 1928 David and Harry left England to shoot game in East Africa, and later to spend Christmas with Uncle Alec—Lord Athlone, Governor-General of South Africa.* A certain number of formal visits and functions were involved, but not many. *En route,* Harry picked up with some soldier cronies sailing through the Mediterranean, and heading for India. In Cairo he had lunch with King Fuad— "excellent food." They eventually reached Nairobi on 12 October, where the brothers' ways parted, Harry remaining in Nairobi where "there are some very nice people & some very much otherwise."

Among the "nice" Harry at first numbered the Markhams. Mansfield Markham was the rich younger son of a coal magnate and Liberal MP, Sir Arthur Markham, who had died in 1916. Mansfield had taken a strong fancy to a young woman who was "tall, blonde and attractive in a tomboyish way," a pilot who later became a famous aviatrix.** They had been married for about eight months when Harry briefly entered Nairobi society, and on his first meeting with Beryl Markham "became besotted by her." The affair between pilot and royal Prince took off for all to see.

Mansfield, "much aggrieved by this romance, threatened to sue, and the matter was only settled when a substantial sum was privately paid over," and continued to be paid until Beryl Markham's death in 1986. Harry departed to shoot

---

*Married Princess Alice, only daughter of Queen Victoria's son Leopold, who died from haemophilia when she was one year old. Alice died in 1981 at the age of 97.

**First woman to cross the Atlantic east-west solo.

lion, leaving behind a mortally wounded marriage, which lasted only another year. It was rather a misfortune that the Duke of Buccleuch's brother and George V's closest friend, Lord Francis Scott, was a leading figure in Nairobi society, but his lips remained sealed.

"If only those boys would find some acceptable women and get married," May would often complain between the years of Bertie's marriage in 1923 and 1934. And George would invariably reply in his deep, grouchy voice. "They'll never find another Elizabeth." The King's love and admiration for Bertie's wife was more widely known than his increasing disillusionment with his other sons. George never indulged in any but the simplest principles and beliefs, and he held the strong opinion, supported by the evidence provided by his second son, that marriage for men was, like Epsom Salts, a cure-all.

The trouble was that the devastation of dynasties as well as lives caused by the First World War had dangerously narrowed the choice, the assassination of the entire Russian royal family (with all those pretty and acceptable Grand-Duchesses) sorely narrowing the field. Additionally, the more relaxed social climate after the war, even for the royal Princes, led to more fun for bachelors, while marriage would lead to more restrictions and certainly more royal responsibilities.

When her youngest son showed signs of interest in Princess Marina of Greece, May wrote to Harry, who was on another long tour abroad and having a lovely time, "I hope you my darling boy will think about marrying on your return." And shortly after and more firmly, "Now you will have to follow suit for marriage is in the air."

By 1935, when Harry was thirty-five and his father and mother were celebrating their twenty-five years on the throne with much public rejoicing, they had more or less given up any hope of David getting married but still believed that Harry could be bullied into it. But David compounded his sin of bachelorhood by encouraging his younger brother not to marry, partly because it was more comfortable for him not to be alone in the family in a state of misogamy. He also encouraged Harry's travels which both served to keep him clear of any lasting relationship and, under David's supervision, diminish his alcohol consumption.

But the first half of the 1930s remained an unsettling and depressing period in Harry's life. He was foiled in his ambition to command the 10th Hussars in India. This appears to have had "a great effect on his character & outlook. He became a very disappointed man."

Then, with almost precipitate suddenness, his bachelor days were over. Unlike Bertie and David, Harry kept no record, either as journal or diary: too much effort, all that writing. It is therefore necessary to rely on his contemporaries. Most of them agree that he had had his eye on the handsome and intelligent Alice Scott for some time, and would have courted her if he could have made up his mind.

In the early 1930s Harry continued to visit the Buccleuchs frequently, and regarded William as his best friend. With David involved in another liaison, even tighter and a great deal more potentially scandalous than the one with Freda Dudley Ward, Harry was vaguely aware of some sort of inadequacy in himself, and at the same time a feeling of loss in family life.

But with the Buccleuchs, Harry felt the same sense of comfort and of belonging within a loving family framework as Bertie had experienced almost fifteen years earlier. Perhaps, as he would no doubt have put it, "I ought to take the plunge."

Shortly after the jubilee celebrations, Harry was staying at Windsor with his mother. Alice Scott also happened to be there. Suddenly we find him writing to his father, ill at Sandringham after all the junketing, "I saw Alice Scott several times & met her out riding each morning. I think Mama liked her."

George replied with almost indecent haste and alacrity for a sick man: "Mama thought Alice Scott very nice, glad you saw something of her at Windsor."

Alice Scott knew Kenya, and Nairobi society, much better than Harry, having first lived there shortly after Harry's eventful visit. She stayed on the farm of her Uncle Francis and his family, and was often invited to Government House, once when the Baron and Baroness Blixen, Lord and Lady Delamere, and the white hunter Denys Finch Hatton, were all fellow guests.

On Jubilee Day (1935) Alice was on her way home again, concerned about her father's health. More than anyone else, the Athlones encouraged the match, knowing as they did that there was mutual affection. The courtship was sealed in Richmond Park while they were both walking Harry's dogs.

> There was no formal declaration on his part [she wrote in her memoirs], I think he just muttered it as an aside . . . nor was there any doubt about my acceptance. I was thirty-four, so I had had a very good innings. Apart from my great happiness in getting married, I felt too that it was time I did something more useful with my life.

George's pleasure at the engagement took a severe knock on the first morning when Alice was at Balmoral. Asked what she was going to do that day, she said, "I'm going stalking." The King was stunned into silence. "We exchanged no further conversation," Alice recalled.

Later, out on the moors, she was told by her fiancé that she could not have made a worse *faux pas*. "Ladies at Balmoral at that time were not even allowed to watch the grouse shooting, so the idea that I was intending to go out stalking was completely beyond the pale."

But George forgave her in his relief that Harry had at last found a possible wife. To Alice's father, he wrote, "I must send you a line to say how delighted the Queen and I are that my son Harry is engaged to be married to your third daughter . . . Our families have known each other for so many generations now, that it gives me great pleasure to think that they will be more closely connected still."

And so on 6 November in the glittering royal year of 1935, Prince Henry and Lady Alice Christabel Montagu-Douglas-Scott married, not in Westminster Abbey as originally arranged, but, in deference to the recent death of Alice's father, in the private chapel of Buckingham Palace.

At the time of the death of "little Johnnie" in 1919, his older brother George, no longer "little," was at Dartmouth Naval College not enjoying himself in the least. Of all the royal sailors, from the 1870s to the 1980s, George was the most reluctant. His father never understood why his boys did not enjoy the service as much as he did, and treated this as further proof of their unfitness to be his sons.

Bertie, as always, "bowing to the inevitable," never went as far as to complain to his father's face about his life in the Navy. George did from time to time, but then of all the children George had (with reason) the smallest inferiority complex, and the least to lose by speaking his mind. Because of this, he was also the least detested by his father as a young unmarried man; but that is not to suggest that he was regarded with much more than contempt.

There is a remarkable parallel between the naval careers of Bertie and his brother George, even to their examination results. George's IQ being much higher than Bertie's, this merely confirms that George hardly tried, thus scoring seventy-sixth out of ninety-two, which is a marginal improvement on sixty-eighth out of sixty-eight. "He has kept up the best traditions of the family!" was his father's sardonic comment.

At sea, George was as sick as his elder brother, worse say some. And he certainly complained more vocally. He also shared to a lesser degree Bertie's constitutional weaknesses, in spite of a healthy diet from birth under the supervision of Lala Bill. Bouts of illness demanded shore leave and medical attention, and again like Bertie and at about the same age, he succumbed to appendicitis. He served not in the *Collingwood* but her sister ship the *Téméraire*. Later, George's "Jutland" was a series of gunboat operations in China, which in the mid-'twenties was in its congenital state of xenophobia and revolution.

For all his charm George did not slip as readily as Bertie into an easy relationship with his fellow officers. He did not much mind being called "Babe" or "PG," but he did not care for the toadying or the contrived cheekiness. "Either they

slap you on the back, or they get you under the table," he
once commented of naval officers.

Taking advantage of his father's weakness after a serious
illness in 1928, George told him that he thought he really
ought to help out his brothers at official functions now that
his own capacity was so restricted. The King reluctantly
agreed, and to his infinite relief George was allowed to end
his active service in early 1929.

During this naval period in George's life, his friendship
with David continued to prosper and they travelled widely
together. When David took up occupation of York Lodge, St
James's Palace, and later Fort Belvedere ("the Fort") in Great
Park, Windsor, he set aside rooms for his youngest brother to
use when on leave, and after he left the service. Of his
favourite brother, and close friend, David once wrote:

> George was sharply different in outlook and tem-
> perament from the rest of us. Possessed of unusual
> charm of manner and a quick sense of humour and
> talented in many directions, he had an undoubted
> flair for the arts. He played the piano well, knew a
> good deal about music, and had a knowledgeable
> eye for antiques. Being somewhat Bohemian by
> inclination, he had undoubtedly found life in the
> Navy a bit confining.

One writer has described George as "tall and slim with a
pleasant voice, large dark blue eyes, charming smile and an
aura of shyness." His aesthetic sense he clearly inherited
from his mother. He was very fond of her. He was the only
one of her children who shared her love for antiques and
beautiful things: and he was the only one who ever paid her
compliments . . . she once told a friend sadly: "He often used
to say I looked nice. Nobody else ever did."

He had little in common with his father, hating not only
the sea and the Navy but also shooting—the shooting of
anything. "Whenever he could instead of going to Sandringham
for holidays he preferred the Riviera where he could sun-
bathe during the day and gamble at the casino or go dancing

at night. He was an expert at the tango and once, under an assumed name, won a dancing contest at Cannes."

George was a real 'twenties playboy. He went to the motor races at Brooklands, shared his generation's admiration for W.O. Bentley and bought one of his massive 6½ litre machines. When David bought a De Havilland Gypsy Moth, George learned to fly in it, and unlike Bertie, went solo, and without asking anyone's permission—except his instructor's. Also, like so many of the "fast set" he experimented with drugs—but not very seriously for he was a keep-fit fanatic who ran for amusement and played a fast game of tennis.

Like his elder brother Harry, George indulged in numerous affairs, the more serious ones raising speculations about marriage. And, like Bertie six years earlier, George fell under the spell of Poppy Baring, still unwed in 1927, and according to Duff Cooper, unforgiving of King George and Queen Mary for prohibiting marriage to Bertie.

Duff Cooper, writing from Cliveden to his wife Diana, who was on one of her theatrical journeys playing in *The Miracle* around America, told her of "Poppy sleeping peacefully in the arms of Prince George." A week later (14 January 1927) the scene shifts to Duff and Diana's house, 30 Gower Street in Bloomsbury, a handsome Georgian terrace house on four floors. It was far distant from society's beating heart, but suited their impecunious condition and they loved it.

Among the guests are George and Poppy. They are "very thick" and "there is talk of marriage," reports Duff; who also asks, "Is this true, Poppy? I very much hope so."

"Well, yes, I suppose it is. But I can't bear the royal family."

"I don't think it's worse than other families, Poppy," said Duff in their defence. "I mean you don't have to be on slap-bottom terms with Queen Mary and King George."

Poppy appeared to be considering this sympathetically. She was twenty-five now and was very fond of George.

Later in the evening Poppy began making jokes about the royal family "which rather shocked my loyal nature," Duff later admits. But George, who "is really very nice," doesn't mind a bit and "rocks with laughter."

George, like Bertie before him, proposed a few days

later. Poppy delightedly accepted. So George went to BP and caught his parents after dinner. To his amazement, they took it "quite wonderfully and raised hardly any objections."

Freda Dudley Ward, almost as fond of George as of David, commented, "If Prince George sticks to it firmly, the King and Queen can't stop it."

Rosemary, Viscountess Ednam, said to Poppy, "Lengthen your skirts and stop making up your lips and you'll win the King." Adding as a realistic afterthought, "And lose Prince George."

But in due course, and after making further enquiries, George and May began to put on pressure against the match, and finally stamped it out of existence.

It was not until six years, and numerous affairs, later that the next positive step towards George's marriage was made.

In September 1933 Princess Marina of Greece arrived in London with her sister Olga and Olga's husband Prince Paul. Claridge's Hotel was the meeting place between George and Marina, both guests of that incorrigible socialite and dedicated hostess, Lady (Emerald) Cunard.

Marina had met George many times before, and thought him a nice and attractive young man. Much more stylish than his brothers, with concern for the arts and not much time for the so-called manly sports—like shooting. But at that luncheon she seemed to recognize him in a different light—or perhaps he paid more attention to her.

George's memory of this lunch party was curiously similar to Marina's. He, too, had known her off and on for years. But this time he suddenly saw how beautiful she was, and how nice it was to talk to her. Urged on by David, he decided there and then to court her seriously. She was a year older than Poppy, and since that unhappy business he had experienced a growing need to marry.

Marina's life, based in Paris, was also a peripatetic one, with long visits to Rome and to Belgrade with her married sister, and to London, where she "came out" in 1924. At that time Lady Cynthia Colville, a lady-in-waiting to Queen Mary (Marina's godmother), was "struck by her charm and good looks," and, like so many others, wondered if the Prince of Wales would court her. He did, in the same year, 1927, as his younger brother George was courting Poppy Baring. The David-Marina affair was, according to the scandal-mongering but devastatingly accurate Chips Channon, a strong one and "might well have led to marriage and was progressing very well but Freda Dudley Ward, at the last moment, interfered and stopped it."

All this was old history when Marina's mother brought over the whole of her family to stay at Claridge's in the summer of 1934 in order (so it was said) to give the opportunity for Marina's relationship with George to develop. George took full advantage, and began to pay serious court, taking Marina for walks with his dogs (just like Harry and Alice), for motor drives into the country (George was a safer driver than Harry), and to the theatre and to dances.

When Marina left with her mother, there was vague talk that George might come and join them in Yugoslavia but nothing was settled. He did turn up, and in the most romantic way, in David's borrowed 'plane.

"I like to pretend that it was done on impulse," George said later. "But really I think I had planned it carefully before Marina even left London. I also pretended to David that I was just going to make sure, but I knew perfectly well that Marina was for me, and that she would make a marvellous wife."

On the evening of 20 August 1934 Marina and her family, and their guest, sat about after dinner in a very domestic manner and began to play backgammon. No one remembered who won. All but Marina and George were concentrating on slipping away to bed without appearing to do so. At last, Marina's uncle, Prince Christopher, slipped out (so he recalled), leaving the couple at opposite ends of the sofa.

I had been in my bedroom for about half an hour when I discovered that I had left my cigarette case on the backgammon table. Putting on my dressing gown I went in search of it. The door of the drawing room was open; George and Marina were still seated on the sofa, though no longer, I observed

with satisfaction, at the opposite ends of it. I stole
back to bed without my case.

Shortly after midnight Marina was heard running upstairs,
heading for her sister's bedroom. "I knew before she opened
the door that everything was all right," Olga said. "She was
laughing and crying at the same time. I had never seen her so
happy."

The official announcement on 28 August 1934 that George
was to marry a Greek Princess at first caused more puzzlement than celebration. Who was this Princess Marina? She
was an almost unknown figure in Britain. But as soon as the
picture editors and the social editors had completed some
hasty investigation, and spread photographs across their front
pages, extolling Marina's beauty and charm ("Fairy Princess
to Wed"), the nation fell into a paroxysm of joy and celebration.

Everybody who knew anything of Marina's past and family was sought out and interviewed. Miss Fox, her nursemaid, was one of the victims—"now white-haired but still
pink-cheeked and fresh-faced"—who was discovered on the
quay at Folkestone awaiting the arrival of her one-time charge.
"I feel that my heart will burst with pride that all this should
be for my little Marina. Isn't she lovely?" And so on.

The Greek family's pro-German activities during the war
were now all forgotten. "A great addition to the family,"
remarked George. "I am sure that we will like Marina and
that she will be a charming addition to the family," echoed
May. More privately she said she hoped Marina would have a
"settling influence" on her youngest son.

The royal wedding on 29 November 1934 was all that the
vast crowds hoped it would be. The brief glimpse they had of
the bride passing in her carriage confirmed all they had been
told of her beauty, and because George had not been seen as
often as David and Bertie, relatively few people had appreciated what a handsome Prince he was.

Westminster Abbey was packed with the royalty of Britain, Denmark, Greece, Yugoslavia, and the one-time royalty
of Russia and Germany and Austria and other lesser dynastie
demoted or removed during or after the Great War, and a
few privileged guests from America. These last included M

and Mrs Ernest Simpson, who had bought their present in a sale at Fortnum and Mason's, and had unashamedly told George so. It was a "pair of globe-shaped crackle vases on carved wood stands, fitted as electric lamps, with panelled octagonal shades painted with Chinese scenes." They cost £10.

Two other people in the Abbey that morning, who were not required to give presents, were Elizabeth ("Lilibet"), who was an eight-year-old bridesmaid and Bertie and Elizabeth's daughter, and in the congregation Alice and Andrew's son Philip. This boy's uncle, Commander Lord Louis Mountbatten RN, would dearly have liked to be in the Abbey, too, for there was no one who loved a royal wedding more than he did. But he was in the Red Sea with his First Destroyer Flotilla, *en route* to China. Shortly before the ceremony was to take place, he and the other captains assembled on board the hove-to flotilla leader, and at the exact moment according to the timetable of the pronouncement of marriage, toasted the bride and groom in champagne.

As for the groom's father, King George wrote, "I shall never forget the beautiful service in the Abbey, so simple and yet so dignified, which greatly impressed the Foreigners and indeed all that were present. Then the enormous crowds in the streets and especially the one outside the Palace, who showed their love and affection for us and our family, by their enthusiasm, impressed us more than I can say . . ."

8

While awaiting her divorce from her airman husband, Wallis
Spencer met an Englishman, Ernest Simpson, who had gone to
college, and later worked in his father's successful shipping
business, in America. He had married an American woman,
but their marriage, according to Wallis, "was really on the
rocks" by the time of their meeting.

She described Ernest as, "Reserved in manner, yet with
a gift of quiet wit, always well dressed, a good dancer, fond of
the theatre, and obviously well read . . . an unusually well-
balanced man." But she added cautiously, "I was not altogether sure that my Southern temperament was exactly
suited to his." In fact, his wit was so quiet it was inaudible to
many, and he had few interests outside his shipping business.
"He did not ride or often play golf," said Wallis. "And he did
not shoot." All in all, he was a thoroughly nice, steady, dull
stick; short in stature, dark hair parted in the centre, moustache, always well dressed. After her drunken, cruel, dashing
aviator, Ernest Simpson was just the man Wallis needed:
money, stability, worldliness, kindness.

With his divorce behind him, Ernest wasted no more
time, proposing to Wallis early in 1928. She said, yes; and he
told her that they would go and live in London because he

was taking over the London offices of his shipping company. They were married on 21 July 1928. Ernest had, somewhat uncharacteristically and perhaps to show what a gay dog he *could* be, bought a new yellow Lagonda car for their honeymoon in France and Spain, with a chauffeur to drive them.

On their return to London, Ernest's sister Maud Kerr-Smiley was extremely helpful, practically and socially. They rented a furnished house from Lady Chesham in Upper Berkeley Street. Wallis was lonely, at first hated London, its sooty drabness and unfriendliness. But Maud by stages brought her into society, and introduced Wallis to the strange ways of the English.

Wallis was particularly intrigued at Maud's advice when engaging a new maid: "You'll find that it'll make quite a difference in her attitude if you carelessly drop a few titles into your conversation." The class system and the goings-on of the royal family especially intrigued Wallis. The Court Circular "instantly absorbed my curiosity . . . It surprised me that an entire nation should follow with such rapt attention the purely formal goings and comings of a single family." Maud also told how, at a ball she gave during the war, "the young Prince of Wales had met a beautiful young woman, who became his first true love."

One cold, rainy, winter afternoon Wallis was being driven to the City down St James's Street to pick up Ernest from his office. They were passing St James's Palace, Wallis recalled, when "I saw the scarlet-coated sentries at the entrance suddenly stiffen to attention and present arms. A black motor emerged. As it passed my car, I caught a fleeting glimpse through the side window of a delicate boyish face staring straight ahead, the whole expression suggesting the gravity of a deep inward concern." (This was because David thought his father was dying and that he would soon be King.)

The Simpsons next bought a modern flat, 5 Bryanston Court, George Street, and Wallis began to enjoy herself more as her engagement book filled. Through Maud, their circle of friends, American and English, widened. Ernest found time to take her about the country, and twelve months after their arrival, Wallis was becoming quite an Anglophile.

Chips Channon later noted in his diary: "Lunched with

Emerald [Cunard] to meet Mrs Simpson . . . She is a nice, quiet, well-bred mouse of a woman with large startled eyes and a huge mole." A little later, this shrewd but sometimes rather heartless observer described her at a luncheon he gave in his constituency as "a jolly, plain, intelligent, quiet, unpretentious and unprepossessing woman."

Cecil Beaton, who later tried to catch her likeness but with little success, was kinder and subtler: "I never saw a portrait that looked like her. She's very difficult to draw and paint . . . None of her features is classically correct—her nose, for instance; and her mouth is downright ugly—but they all fit together. She's attractively ugly, *une belle laide*. She has an amusing face."

Lord Beaverbrook gave a typically telling account of his first meeting with Wallis:

> She appeared to me to be a simple woman. She was plainly dressed and I was not attracted to her style of hairdressing.
>
> Her smile was kindly and pleasing, and her conversation was interspersed with protestations of ignorance of politics and with declarations of simplicity of character and outlook, with a claim to inexperience in worldly affairs. Throughout the evening she only once engaged in political conversation, and then she showed a liberal outlook, well maintained in discussion, and based on a conception which was sound.
>
> I was greatly interested by the way the other women greeted her. There were about six women who were present at the dinner or who came in afterwards. All but one of them greeted Mrs Simpson with a kiss. She received it with appropriate dignity, but in no case did she return it.

Thelma, Lady Furness, one of the Morgan daughters who came to know Wallis and was most helpful socially, recorded that, "She was not beautiful; in fact she was not even pretty. But she had a distinct charm and a sharp sense of humour. Her dark hair was parted in the middle. Her eyes, alert and eloquent, were her best feature . . . Her hands were large; they did not move gracefully, and I thought she used them too much when she attempted to emphasize a point."

Another shrewd observer described Wallis:

> When her face is in repose few people would consider it a particularly beautiful face. But it has character, and its most notable feature is the fine high forehead . . . Her hands are competent and strong, but her fingers are short and usually she wears no rings . . . She is exceedingly tidy, and has probably never been seen by anyone looking otherwise than that . . . Her voice is American with a strong Baltimore accent. It would never pass as an English voice. She is good-tempered and with a sense of justice, but can be determined, not to say pigheaded, on occasions. She has the American woman's tendency to reform men in small ways.

Everyone considered her an excellent raconteur with sharp wit, touched with prurience. She told Chips Channon that she "had not worn black stockings since she gave up the Can-Can." And a popular conundrum of hers: "What is the difference between a night on the beach at Coney Island and a night on the beach at Hollywood? At Coney the girls lie on the beach and look at the stars, and in Hollywood the stars lie on the girls and look at the beach."

9

Especially after the Great War and the damage it had done to him, King George V came to depend more and more upon his wife for reassurance, for guidance, for comfort, for pretty well everything in order to keep going. He was aware of this, and it strengthened his belief that his sons, while they remained unmarried, would be like rudderless ships, at any time liable to succumb on a lee shore. Marriage was the only way of saving them from the wickedness and the incomprehensibility of the modern world, and their own considerable demerits and weaknesses. This belief was confirmed in his eyes by what he regarded as the transformation of Bertie since marriage to Elizabeth, whom he soon regarded as only slightly less wise and beautiful than darling May.

Bertie's official biographer has written of George V, "A martinet by nature, and one who held tenaciously to the standards and conventions of his upbringing, the King found it difficult—well nigh impossible—to adjust himself to that new world, with its strangely altered criteria, which had emerged from the First World War. To a very great degree, the younger generation to which his children belonged remained to the end an insoluble enigma."

In a profession in which the imaginative processes are

not encouraged to develop, George V was anyway singularly short of imagination. Already a simple man, his naval training impressed upon his mind throughout his most important development years, that black is black and white is white. What was right for the Navy, was right for everything and everyone: no grey areas, no discussion, no compromise. Exactly the same applied to his sons, who were really only petty officers in disguise.

The mind of George V was like the Grand Fleet Battle Orders in the First World War, which excluded Nelsonian initiative, or any thought or questioning. Being not particularly bright anyway, like most senior naval officers in that war, George found the simple rule book of monarchy and of the Navy synonymous, guiding lights to dutifulness and success.

David was doomed in the eyes of his father from early years. His handsome looks, his charm, his independence of thought, his attraction for all women, his restlessness, his inability to "stick at the job," were all negative marks in his father's log book. Later, his womanizing (actually Harry and George were much worse), his night-clubbing and late nights, the non-stop photographs of him laughing or "making a bloody fool of himself" in the newspapers, were all violently anathema to him.

It was a curious paradox that George was on the one hand increasingly irritated by the clear evidence that David did not want ever to be King, and the equally clear evidence that he would make a rotten one anyway.

David told Elsa Maxwell (and a good many others, too, no doubt), "I don't want to be King. I wouldn't be a very good one." But whatever doubts George might have that his eldest son would ever ascend the throne, and whatever lack of doubt he might have that he would make a rotten King if he were ever to do so, David remained the heir apparent, and therefore the son who most attracted his father's concern and attention.

The younger sons, who went through the ordeal themselves before they married, all recognized that David got the worst of it. "It was difficult for David," Bertie once said. "My father was so inclined to go for him." Although he qualified this: "It was a pity that David did the things which he knew would annoy my father."

The "going for him" was worse for David when it included public humiliation, especially in front of the household staff, who, to a man and woman, adored David. George's biographer has written that "he did not stop to mince his words even in the presence of the servants, and his loud and trenchant chaff or criticism would ring out, not sparing the object of his wrath, in a publicity which obviously increased the embarrassment of a youthful victim."

As a recipe for bad son-father relations, then, there is not a single missing ingredient, and it is sharpened by jealousy on a wicked scale. Altogether, not a pretty relationship; nor was it a pretty sight to witness the one-sided contests that were so often played out before anyone who happened to be present.

The biographer Kenneth Rose, in an understanding and compassionate study of George V, has written:

> There must be a strong element of spiritual pride in anyone who places exaggerated weight on the rights of parental authority, a feeling of revolt against any assumption of equality on the part of the so-recently dependent child . . . The King loved everything old, the Prince loved everything new (possibly in reaction) and they were separated by a generation gap that had been unnaturally widened by the war. Yet the King seems never to have made any attempt to understand the younger man's point of view or to sympathize with his aspirations.

Rose also rightly draws attention to the disappointment and pain the King must have felt because of his eldest son's "unassuageable devotion to Mrs Dudley Ward." But who can tell to what extent the mother's unbending, cold, shy and seemingly unsympathetic attitude towards David, and his father's evident feelings of distaste and disapproval, and the gratuitous cruelty he showed towards him, drove David into the Lala Bill-like maternal arms of married women. They were, one and all, experienced in life and soothing with their sympathy. In all his relationships, he only once, with Marina, sought out a younger woman, a virgin who would expect a dominance and experience he did not possess.

As a grown-up this Prince of the realm sought the guidance, the understanding leadership and love so conspicuously absent in his parents. It was not just his "delicate boyish face" glimpsed by Wallis Simpson, which lingered into old age, that appealed to women and made them ache to give comfort; that short figure, that round face, lined with anxiety when not wrinkled with a puckish smile, really was the complete Peter Pan figure: the Little Prince who never grew up.

Among those who became friends of the Simpsons after they had settled into London life were the Benjamin Thaws. He worked at the American Embassy; his wife Consuelo, "Connie," was the sister of Thelma, Lady Furness, and Gloria Vanderbilt. Out of the blue, on Monday 5 January 1931, there came an invitation to the Simpsons to spend a hunting week-end at Burrough Court, Melton Mowbray, the Furness's country place. Among their fellow guests would be David, Prince of Wales.

"My first reaction," Wallis wrote, "was a mixture of pleasure and horror . . . Like everybody else, I was dying to meet the Prince of Wales; but my knowledge of royalty, except for what I had read, had until now been limited to glimpses at a distance of King George V in his State Coach on his way to open Parliament."

Ernest was made of stouter stuff. "Of course we must go," he insisted. "It's really a great honour."

Luckily for Wallis, she had recently returned from Paris where she had bought her winter wardrobe, including "an attractive blue-grey tweed dress with a cape of the same material edged with nutria," from Molyneux, who were never shy about the size of their labels. Unluckily, she had an appalling head cold and temperature when they left by the 3.20 p.m. train from St Pancras on Saturday 10 January. *En route*, she practised her curtsies.

Ernest Simpson takes up the story of "*that* week-end," as he referred to it ever after:

There was thick fog when we drew into Melton Mowbray, and Wallis complained about the cold in the car that drove us to Burrough Court. I remember feeling very sorry for her at this point, as any woman would want to make the best impression on such an occasion as this, and her cold really was bad.

Thelma's step-daughter Averill met us at the door. She said, "How nice of you to come all this way on such a terrible day: you must come into the warm quickly."

A man took our bags and a maid led us upstairs to our room, a very nice comfortable one, with a banked-up coal fire burning in the grate. I remember Wallis eyeing the bed longingly and saying, "I would give anything just to lie down and go to sleep with three aspirins." I sympathized with her and she smiled wanly and went to the dressing table, where the maid had already laid out her make-up. She had the aspirins anyway.

Then we went down to tea. Thank goodness there were two more American couples already there at the round table in front of the fire, the Ambrose Clarks of New York and the Robert Strawbridges of Philadelphia. We knew them slightly already and we talked about the hunting, and about the houses they rented nearby, to which we were invited at some unspecified date.

The tea got cold and still there was no sign of the Prince of Wales, or of our hostess for that matter. A maid came in and drew the curtains, and soon after another maid cleared away the tea and told us apologetically that the royal car was delayed by the fog.

In fact it was not until after seven o'clock that we heard the sound of tyres on gravel, and soon after, Thelma appeared at the door with *two* royal Princes—Prince George as well as the Prince of Wales. We all got hastily to our feet, the ladies curtseying and the men giving a slight bow as Thelma introduced us in turn.

I thought the Prince of Wales looked perfectly awful. I just couldn't take my eyes off his violent check tweed suit. He might almost have been that music-hall comedian, Max Miller, "the cheeky chappie"—about the same height too. Prince George was much taller and more discreetly dressed. I glanced sideways at Wallis to see how she was reacting. Her curtsey was quite a professional effort, and in no time at all she was rattling away, seemingly quite un-shy, to the Prince who was talking about Baltimore—obviously briefed beforehand by his equerry, Brigadier-General Gerald Trotter.

It is not true to say that I had any premonition of what was soon to happen between my wife and the Prince. Even if there had been some evidence, the proposition of some sort of liaison would have seemed so ridiculous that I would not have entertained it for one minute.

There was no formal dinner party on the Saturday evening, George disappeared to his hostess nearby, Lady Wodehouse, and most people went to bed early, to the relief of Wallis who was half asleep anyway by then. On Sunday the men and one or two of the women were given horses for the hunt, and Wallis, her Molyneux suit under a long tweed coat, and wearing brogues, went by motor car to the meet with Ernest and their hostess. It was a crisp, clear morning, and it made a fine traditional English scene with the hounds eager to be of and a lot of shouting and banter over the stirrup cup.

Back at Burrough Court there were cocktails before a light lunch, after which Wallis went upstairs for a sleep while Ernest played cards with some of the other non-hunters. That evening Thelma Furness had laid on a dinner party which included Prince George and his hostess.

"It was not a big party," Wallis recalled, "but what it lacked in numbers was more than made up in interest!"

One of the American wives present later recalled, with the help of her diary, the details of that evening:

Thelma was always a brilliant hostess, and that night she was at her best, with the Prince of Wales on her right and Prince George on her left. I only caught snippets of their conversation from half way down the table, but it was very light-hearted with a great deal of laughter from the two Princes, and only once (as far as I could hear) touched on a serious topical event—something about India and Gandhi being let out of prison again, which caused the Prince of Wales to remark, "He should never have been put in."

I cannot remember and made no note of what we ate that evening, but Alfred [her husband] remarked after on the 1906 Krug champagne, which he stuck with through the meal.

What I remember most clearly was Mrs Ernest Simpson sitting opposite me and looking most striking but not at all beautiful in a blue dress and a diamond necklace, her black hair parted in the centre and finger-waved at the temple to frame her face.

I know I am writing six years later [January 1937] but I remember clearly noticing at the time that she frequently cast darting glances past her neighbour on her right to the Prince of Wales at the far end of the table, looking as always like some mischievous boy when he laughed with his hostess. My diary confirms this. "All interested in POW who supposed having affair with Thelma, no one more than Mrs S. Later saw them leaving backgammon table and sitting out with brandies on window seat."

It was interesting being "in at the beginning" as Alfred put it!

In the privacy of their bedroom, it was (according to Wallis) Ernest who was the more impressed by his first meeting with the Prince of Wales, in spite of his violent suit. Wallis quoted him as remarking, "I have come to the conclusion that you Americans lost something that is very good and quite irreplaceable when you decided to dispense with the British Monarchy."—"Ernest's admiration of the royal family had been profoundly enhanced."

A few weeks later Wallis wrote to her beloved Aunt Bessie, who had taken the place of Wallis's mother since her death, "I do hope Thelma Furness will ask us again with the Prince." But it was not until the middle of May 1931, after David's return from a visit to South America with George, that the two met again.

PART FIVE

"MAKING US ONE"

"Fitted for a Great Task"
Headline in *The Times*, 21 January 1936

1

In Grosvenor Square there stands a handsome terrace house on five floors, built of Portland stone and with deep Georgian-style windows. In 1931 it required twelve servants, and in addition accommodated a chauffeur and his assistant who were responsible for running and maintaining the big Daimler limousine and the smaller Rolls-Royce 20/25.

Number 21 Grosvenor Square was the London home of the forty-eight-year-old shipping magnate Lord Furness and his wife Thelma, who for the last three years had been the favourite mistress of David, Prince of Wales. David had left for South America a few days after the week-end party at Melton where he had first met Wallis. He had got back to Paris on 29 April, and Thelma had at once left to greet him there, and to travel back to England with him.

On 15 May Thelma arranged a large afternoon reception in Grosvenor Square to celebrate his return. It was a beautiful day and the afternoon sun shone brightly through the drawing-room windows as she escorted David among her guests, introducing him or reintroducing him where required. He wore a doublebreasted light brown suit, brown ankle boots and a Guards tie, while Thelma was in a calf-length woollen navy blue top with a folded girdle and pleated skirt.

"As he passed by his glance happened to fall on me," Wallis wrote of this reception. "He then nudged Thelma and seemed to be asking her in a whisper, 'Haven't I met that lady before?' In any event he presently came over to where Ernest and I were standing to say, 'How nice to see you again. I remember our meeting at Melton . . .' It was a mark of attention that was flattering."

Later during that summer of 1931 a friend suggested that Wallis should be presented at Court. After the ceremony at Buckingham Palace—a deep curtsey to George and May— Wallis and Ernest were invited back to Grosvenor Square to celebrate the occasion. Once again the Prince of Wales arrived in Thelma's company, and again paused briefly by Wallis, this time to say, "I do admire your dress, Mrs Simpson."

David left with his equerry after a few minutes, and the Simpsons left soon after and were surprised to see the Prince still standing beside his car, almost as if he had delayed his departure in order to see her again.

David stepped forward and asked if he could give them a lift. The Simpsons had their own car but this was not an offer to refuse.

"Thank you so much, Your Royal Highness," Wallis replied, and stepped in through the wide door of the Daimler which he held open for her. Wallis sat between the Prince and his groom-in-waiting,* with Ernest on the jump-seat facing them.

" 'G' and I are on the way to the Fort, which the King was kind enough to let me have last year as a sort of country hide-away," David said with a light laugh. "It's grand to have an escape like this near Windsor. I spent most of my time in South America dreaming about it and what I was going to do with the garden."

He chatted away as the car crossed Oxford Street, heading for Marylebone, with Wallis saying, "How lovely for you, Sir . . . How interesting!"

"Yes, it's in a terrible state, but I plan to . . ." And speaking rapidly in a voice with more than a hint of an

---

*Brigadier-General G.F. ("G") Trotter, a vivid, amusing character who had lost his right arm in the Boer War.

American accent, as if accommodating himself to his audience, he outlined some of his plans. "If I get up early tomorrow, I can get in two or three hours' work outside before I have to leave for London."

At Bryanston Court, David jumped out of the car before his driver had pulled on the hand-brake, offering his arm to help Wallis step down to the pavement in George Street.

"Would you and General Trotter care to come up for a moment and have a drink in our flat?" Wallis asked.

"I'd like very much to see your flat one day," David replied with a smile that confirmed that he really meant it. "I'm told it's charming, and seeing it might give me some ideas for brightening up the Fort. But I have to be up so early. Still, if you would be so kind as to invite me again, I'd like to do so."

Wallis dropped a slight curtsey, Ernest Simpson gave a bow that was no more than a nod of the head, the Prince leapt back into the car, gave a brief wave and a smile, and the Daimler purred away into the rush-hour traffic.

"He really is most charming," Ernest conceded. "I think we should invite him, don't you?"

Wallis said nothing except "Good evening" to the commissionaire, and then they were in the lift. She was conscious of the honour of recognition by such an exalted figure as the heir to the throne. But for someone brought up in a democratic republic, it was more difficult for her than for her husband to appreciate the near inviolability of rank separating commoner from royalty in the reign of George V, thirty years before the King's granddaughter and her consort invented the "walk-about." Any American found it difficult to distinguish the difference in status between, say, film star and common citizen in the United States and a member of the royal family and the man in the street in Britain.

That summer was a very social one for Wallis by contrast wih her early and sometimes lonely months in London. With time on her hands and few of the money constraints that were to bedevil her later, when the financial slump hit Ernest's shipping business so seriously, she enjoyed herself with dinner and luncheon parties, week-end parties, and all the fun of the English season. She was often to be seen with Gloria Vanderbilt and her sister "Tamar," and Edwina Mountbatten and Edwina's sister-in-law Nada Milford Haven.

Countess Nada de Torby, a daughter of Grand-Duke Michael of Russia, had married Dickie Mountbatten's elder brother George, and they were not a happy couple. Nada was a notorious lesbian, but Wallis in her innocence did not realize this until she went on an "all girls" holiday to a hotel in Cannes in August. Among others in the party were Tamar and Gloria. What happened in the South of France Wallis never recounted. She wrote to her Aunt Bessie that men seemed to be very scarce but that none of them seemed to care about that. She also tried to make out that she had a lovely time. But she returned home abruptly, and early. And from that time, the names of Nada and Gloria Vanderbilt were hardly ever again mentioned by Wallis. Although, according to Lord Mountbatten, her looks and manner held a strong appeal for lesbians, she did not care at all for that sort of thing.

By the end of 1931 Wallis had given up all hope of seeing the Prince of Wales again. She could reconcile herself to this as her expectations had been low from the beginning. "Why should he bother with me?" she asked herself time and again. But all the same, she had sensitive antennae for men's responses and thought that she had awoken something in him, however slightly, and she still held a sliver of hope that they might meet again.

Then, at a small party before Christmas, she caught sight of David again, their eyes met, and he came straight over to her, enquiring how she was and reminding her of her invitation to visit their flat. Ever the opportunist, Wallis replied, "Well, Sir, would you consider doing us the honour of coming to dinner?"

David's bright blue eyes, their "crows' feet" lines etched by his famous smile, peered straight at Wallis so that speech was scarcely necessary. But she heard him say, "That really would be a pleasure—thank you so much. Will you telephone my secretary?"

There were eight other guests, including Thelma. Later

Wallis wrote, "I decided to give him a typical American dinner: black bean soup, grilled lobster, fried chicken Maryland, for the sweet a cold raspberry *soufflé* . . . Everything, I am happy to say, went very well. The Prince seemed to enjoy his American dinner and paid me the compliment of asking for my recipe for the raspberry *soufflé*."

A few days later Wallis received an invitation to spend the week-end at the Fort with the Prince of Wales. The Fort, "that half-enchanted castle," as Wallis described it, "the most romantic house I have ever known," was a grace-and-favour building that had fallen vacant in 1929.

"When I went to my father to ask him if I might live there," wrote David, "he was surprised. 'What could you possibly want that queer old place for? Those damn week-ends, I suppose . . . Well, if you want it, you can have it.' "

The origins of Fort Belvedere went back to the early eighteenth century, but in Queen Victoria's reign the place fell into partial ruin. "By the time I came upon it, it had become a pseudo-Gothic hodge-podge," David wrote of it, "overrun with weeds and shrubs. Northwards the land descends in a gentle slope towards Virginia Water, where as a child I had paddled in row-boats with Mary and my brothers. The Fort laid hold of me in many ways. Soon I came to love it as I loved no other material thing—perhaps because it was so much of my own creation. More and more it became for me a peaceful, almost enchanted anchorage, where I found refuge from the cares and turmoil of my life."

Some of the guests at the Fort might have disputed the Prince's claim that it was his "own creation," including Ernest Simpson, because David was quite ruthless in pressing his week-end guests to roll up their sleeves, seize a saw, and set about the undergrowth. Acording to Wallis, "exercise was a pursuit that Ernest only favoured in the role of a spectator," but he was soon recruited to join the Prince of Wales—who looked, according to Wallis, "an incongruous figure in baggy plus-fours, a thick sweater, hair tousled, and carrying in one hand a billhook . . ."

2

"Looking back on this period in the whole Wallis Simpson-David Windsor affair," wrote one of their friends later, "it assumes the shape of some classic fairy tale—the castle, the lonely Prince, the romantic maiden whom he woos so ardently." And as a correcting afterthought: "Perhaps hardly a maiden, this twice-married woman of the world, and the outcome might have provided the happy ending of a fairy tale if she *had* been a simple maiden."

David himself was to write, quite unselfconsciously in this same fairy-tale vein, "In ancient times the love of a Prince would have been lauded by the poets. The modern folk-tale, however, has taken a more rigid form; a Prince's heart, like his politics, must remain within the constitutional pale. But my heart refused to be so confined . . ."

When did David's love for Wallis "burst into flames" as someone described it at the time? There have been many guesses, but neither Wallis nor David gave more than a hint. David himself wrote, "And then one day Wallis began to mean more to me in a way that she did not quite comprehend."

Wallis remembered one occasion during that first magical week-end at the Fort. He and "G" were playing a card game called "Red Dog" with Thelma and Wallis. After several hands David said to Wallis with a smile, "I don't think you need any more instruction from me. I'd better look after myself."—"It was," wrote Wallis, "the first notice that he had taken of me that could be described as other than formality." Then Thelma put on a record and suggested a dance. "I found David a good dancer," says Wallis, "deft, light on his feet, and with a true sense of rhythm . . ."

Or was it this moment? "Ernest went upstairs for a sweater. While he was gone, the Prince took me out on the terrace to show me the grounds . . . He tried to sound casually matter-of-fact as he described what he had done; but his inner pleasure burst through the guise of nonchalance."

More invitations to the Fort followed and Wallis, who was wonderful with other people's servants (though terrible with her own), became a firm favourite of Frederick Finch, who, now sixty-eight years old and grey-haired, remained as David's butler. But these visits were well spread out because both David and the Simpsons had duties abroad. But it was evident that his interest in her had by no means waned. When Ernest and Wallis sailed for New York in March 1934, a *bon voyage* cablegram followed them, signed "Edward P."—which incidentally ensured their special treatment by the ship's company and officers. On their return invitations came in thick and fast from the Prince, including a dinner party at Quaglino's for Wallis's birthday. But it was never less than a foursome together, always Ernest and nearly always Thelma. Then, while skating at Virginia Water in January 1933, Wallis met for the first time the Duke and Duchess of York, Bertie and Elizabeth.

It was clearly inappropriate, and almost impossible anyway, to curtsey wearing skates, so Wallis made do with a slight nod of her head as she was introduced, and dropped in several "Sirs" and "Ma'ams" to confirm her deference.

"Is that David's new friend?" Bertie asked Elizabeth when they were out of earshot. "American, isn't she?"

Elizabeth, looking very fetching in a white fox fur hat and matching fur wrapped twice round her neck, confirmed Bertie's conjectures. "And a very common-looking woman too. Give me Lady Furness any time. She at least was pretty and had some style."

"Won't last. They never do with David," Bertie said emphatically as they drew alongside the wooden jetty where a mixed party of cold non-skaters awaited them.

But if Bertie had known of the presents David had begun to lavish on Wallis, he might not have been so positive in his prediction: first a signed photograph of himself in a leather frame, then jewellery and more jewellery of rapidly increasing value.

The next, and decisive, stage in the Wallis-David relationship is recounted by, of all people, Thelma Furness, who was obliged to leave the country on a visit to America at the end of January 1934.

> Three or four days before I was to sail, I had lunch with Wallis at the Ritz. I told her of my plans, and in my exuberance I offered myself for all the usual yeoman's services. Was there anything I could do for her in America? Were there any messages I could deliver? Did she want me to bring anything back for her? She thanked me and said suddenly: "Oh, Thelma, the little man is going to be so lonely."
>
> "Well, dear," I answered, "you look after him for me while I'm away."

And so she did. The degree of dependence on a woman in his life which the Prince had developed—as he had depended on Freda Dudley Ward earlier—was revealed within a few days, with invitations arriving at Bryanston Court for Wallis and Ernest almost with every post. The first week-end after Thelma's departure, they were at the Fort, dinners followed, then David asked if he could drop in at their flat for cocktails from time to time and did so, with increasing frequency.

Wallis called in her friends to help amuse David, and they rallied round gladly, cutting other engagements to do so.

> He seemed to find stimulation in the changing company in front of my little cocktail table. In the beginning he stayed briefly. Then one evening he stayed on and on. The other guests, one by one, had to excuse themselves. Finally, only the three of

us were left— Ernest, the Prince and I. By now it
was long after dinner time, and finally in despera-
tion I suggested, "Sir, would you like to take pot-
luck with us?" The upshot was that in a few minutes
the Prince was seated at the table between Ernest
and me. This was the beginning of many such pot-
luck dinners.

Ernest Simpson's position in what was rapidly developing
into a *ménage à trois* was a curious and increasingly embarrassing one. At first he had been flattered by the attention of
a figure as exalted as the Prince of Wales. Ernest was a
decent, patriotic Englishman, much in love with Wallis whose
exuberance, wit and winning ways had intrigued him since
their first meeting, and had led to his proposing to her. He
could sometimes show exasperation at Wallis's extravagance
(a fifteen-shilling massage when their finances were at their
lowest, for example), but soon forgave her—as well he might
as they were dependent from time to time on generous
cheques from Wallis's Aunt Bessie in America.

One of Ernest and Wallis's friends from the American
Embassy, George Kilensky, who was often at their flat in the
evenings, recalls his meetings with the Prince:

He was always courteous and his manners were
impeccable [he writes]. In the early days, he paid
equal attention to Ernest as to Wallis, and the rest
of us for that matter. All that you saw if you watched
closely—and that was not easy—was that his blue
eyes lingered on her face for a moment after she
had finished talking and someone else had taken up
the general conversation.

But Kilensky was not the only one of their friends who
observed a subtle difference, dating from Thelma Furness'
departure for America.

One evening towards the end of January 1934 I
dropped in for cocktails with the Simpsons at about
6.30 [Mrs James Montgomery reported]. I remem-

ber it was a filthy foggy evening, and Wallis greeted me with the words, "Don't you just get too sick with this weather? It's the one thing about London I really hate." The Prince of Wales was already there and he stood up when I came into the room, as he invariably did for everyone. There were half a dozen other people there, all friends, and Ernest mixed more martinis for them and a sidecar for me. As the evening wore on, everyone left except the Prince and me. Ernest was looking tired and at around 8.30 he made some excuse and left the room. The Prince was in an especially lively mood, alternately teasing Wallis and telling her and me about some social services scheme he was launching: he could even make that sound interesting. When I left I experienced a feeling of unease, as if trouble lay ahead for Ernest and Wallis, two of my dearest friends. It was the new sense of intimacy in the conversation and exchanged looks between the Prince and Wallis.

Of this critical period in her life, Wallis herself wrote:

Ernest developed the art of tactfully excusing himself and retiring to his room with his papers. The Prince seemed to have a new enthusiasm every visit, whether it was a new housing project that he was sponsoring or a design for a new planting at the Fort or . . . even the latest American jazz record.

Wallis's letters to her beloved Aunt Bessie became few and far between at this period as David's toll on her time became even heavier. "Forgive me for not writing," she wrote on 12 February, "but this man is exhausting."

Thelma Furness returned from New York on 22 March 1934. David was her first visitor at her own smaller house in Regent's Park. It was not a happy reunion. David had already

heard that his lover had been seen frequently in the company
of the dashing young multi-millionaire Prince Aly Khan.

There was a perfunctory kiss for Thelma in the hall of the
Regency house, then Thelma led David into the drawing
room and offered him a cocktail. "He seemed a little distrait,"
Thelma wrote of this moment, "as if something was bothering
him. I made his martini a strong one to try to cheer him up,
but the Prince was never a great drinker and alcohol had no
more effect on him this time than it ever did."

They talked desultorily, she about New York and parties
and people, and the return voyage and the charm of the
ship's captain.

"There was someone else on board who was quite charming, wasn't there?" David suddenly asked, with a faint hint of
accusation.

"What do you mean, darling?"

"I hear Aly Khan has been very attentive to you."

Thelma thought he was joking and quipped, "Are you
jealous, darling?"

David stood up without replying and made his way towards
the door, leaving his glass half-full. He muttered a few
banalities, took his coat from the butler and walked out
through the door.

Still unsuspecting, Thelma tried to telephone Wallis but
all she got was the maidservant at Bryanston Square who said
only that Mrs Simpson could not be disturbed. She tried
again after dinner, and at last got through at 10.30 p.m. She
heard the voice at the other end saying, "Thelma darling,
how lovely that you are back! Did you have a good crossing?"

Thelma said, "Yes, yes, Wallis. But what is the matter
with the Prince? He came round tonight and could hardly
bear to talk to me. He left all in a huff, grumbling away about
the Aly Khan. He had heard that I had been seen with him.
Well, my dear, one is seen with all sorts of people in New
York—and in an ocean liner for that matter."

Wallis sounded puzzled, too, and then Thelma said, "I'll
be at the Fort this week-end, of course. Do you think you
and Ernest could come, too? It might help things along—you
always cheer him up."

Wallis, forbearing to say that she had already been invited, told Thelma that of course she would be there. "We'll cheer up the little man," she said with a laugh, and rang off.

Saturday night at the Fort. It is 10.30 p.m., David's usual hour for dinner. The guests are the Metcalfes,* Dickie Mountbatten (briefly back from the Mediterranean Fleet) and Edwina, two members of the Swedish royal family and the Simpsons. They have all been drinking cocktails for two hours but no one seems the worse for drink.

They dine in the small dining room at the oval table, sparkling with silver and glass and with an enormous vase of daffodils in the centre. They sit down, David with Wallis on his right, Edwina on his left, Thelma (who has a wretched cold) distantly opposite. On the way in, the Crown Prince of Sweden has been recounting some story ("as long as a Scandinavian winter's night" as Edwina quipped later) in a monotone. On sitting down everyone starts talking at once, silencing Gustav in mid-sentence. He has to be dealt with in this ruthless manner.

Edwina dropped a bombshell, a silencer of all other conversation, by announcing that she was demolishing Brook House, the gigantic Park Lane "marble mausoleum" (as it was nicknamed) she had inherited from her grandfather in 1921. "Darlings, it's ridiculous. You could run the Navy on what it costs me to run that place."

"But where are you going to *live?*" David asks.

Course follows course, David thanks Fruity for his help in felling a larch that afternoon, Dickie discourses on his new destroyer, the *Daring,* and the luxury bathroom he is having fitted in her. Thelma, already feeling miserable with her cold, notices with growing comprehension and alarm the private jokes David and Wallis are exchanging at the other end of the table.

Before the cheese, a bowl of salad is offered to each

* Major Edward Dudley ("Fruity") Metcalfe, an old friend of David's for long on his staff. In 1925 he married Lady Alexandra, a daughter of Lord Curzon of Kedleston.

guest, in the French manner. Thelma notices that, absent-mindedly, David picks at his with his fingers. Wallis notices, too, and at once reaches across and slaps the back of his hand, rebuking him with a mock frown.

"Wallis looked straight at me," Thelma wrote in her memoirs, "and then and there I knew the 'reason' was Wallis . . . I knew then that she had looked after him exceedingly well. That one cold, defiant glance had told me the entire story."

Thelma slipped away from the after-dinner coffee and li-queurs without saying good-night to anyone, and took herself miserably, heavy with tears and her cold, to the bed she had shared so many times with David.

Two, or perhaps three, hours later, while she still lay awake, there was a knock on the door. She feigned sleep, but with her half-closed eyes saw the door open, a widening strip of light revealing the silhouette of her Prince.

David walked quietly to her bedside. "Is there anything I can have sent up for your cold?" he asked.

There was a moment of silence, then Thelma turned over and looked up, her dark eyes wide. "Darling, is it Wallis?" she asked.

Thelma wrote later: "The Prince's features froze. 'Don't be silly,' he said crisply. Then he walked out of the room, closing the door quietly behind him."

No more than thirty minutes later David was awaiting Wallis as he lay in bed, wearing the white pyjamas with scarlet piping she had given him for Christmas.

Wallis came in quietly, closing the door with scarcely a click. For a moment she sat on the edge of his bed, holding his hand. "Did you go to Thelma?" she asked.

There was the slightest trace of hysteria in David's voice as he replied, "Yes, my darling, I went and asked her if there was anything I could do for her cold."

Wallis giggled just as if she were back at Oldfields school with "lights out" at 10 p.m. She lifted up his hand and kissed it. "What did she say?"

David linked his hands round Wallis's neck and pulled

her down towards him. "She said, 'Will you give me an aspirin, darling?'"

It was not until some years later that Ernest Simpson understood Wallis's special appeal to the Prince of Wales. David was, he realized, firstly, a very lonely man with no inner resources whatever. Ernest never saw him with a book in his hands and observed that he couldn't even read a newspaper for more than a few minutes without getting up and pacing about the room, fiddling with objects, taking a cigarette, tapping the end of it on his case before lighting it. Also, the virtual absence of a mother in his infancy and boyhood had left him dreadfully deprived and stunted in his emotional development.

It did not require a psychologist to see that he was in need of a mother figure upon whom he could lean, a woman with experience of life. That was why his mistresses were always married women. Ernest knew Wallis well enough to see that she filled his need for someone who would gently penetrate his loneliness, provide sympathy and keep him amused.

Ernest realized that he should have recognized this much earlier than he did; not that he could have prevented the inevitable. As everyone saw later, no power on earth could have kept him from her, and no sacrifice was too great to keep her. To suggest that duty could be an impediment to his relationship was to suggest a fallen rivet could halt the launch of a ship.

Wallis herself explained it more matter-of-factly:

The only reason to which I could ascribe his [David's] interest in me, such as it was, was perhaps my American independence of spirit, my directness, what I would like to think is a sense of humour and of fun, and, well, my breezy curiosity about him and everything concerning him.

The year 1934 was an eventful one for all the Windsors with the preparations for the Silver Jubilee the next year, and the

most glamorous and popular of all the royal weddings, that of
George (now Duke of Kent) with Princess Marina. This event
also led to a growing friendship between Wallis and David's
youngest brother, who came to live at the Fort for the weeks
leading up to the wedding in November. When David was
absent on duty, Wallis was often alone with George, who was
attracted to her for the same reasons as his brother, enjoying
her liveliness and wit. On 6 November he escorted Wallis to
the theatre, and a few nights earlier Wallis dined at the
Embassy Club—David's favourite night club—with George
and David, Edwina and another couple. "I do well with the
Windsor lads," she claimed lightheartedly in a letter to Aunt
Bessie.

By the end of 1934 Wallis was strongly established in the
top echelon of the London social scene, and was enjoying
herself as never before. Winston Churchill was only one of
many who met Wallis and David together, and commented
on their relationship. "He delighted in her company, and
found in her qualities as necessary to his happiness as the air
he breathed," Churchill wrote. "Those who knew him well
and watched him closely noticed that many little tricks and
fidgetings of nervousness fell away from him. He was a completed being instead of a sick and harassed soul."

Then at the state reception at Buckingham Palace to
celebrate the royal wedding, Wallis at last met George V and
Queen Mary. The guests formed into two lines along the
sides of the reception rooms, Wallis in a simple dress of violet
lamé with a vivid green sash—"the most striking gown in the
room," as Prince Paul of Yugoslavia described it.

After the royal party had proceeded down the full length
of guests, pausing here and there for a word, David took
Wallis over to his parents. "It was the briefest of encounters—a
few words of perfunctory greeting, an exchange of meaning-
less pleasantries, and we moved away," Wallis wrote. "But I
was impressed by Their Majesties' great gift for making everyone they met, however casually, feel at ease in their
presence."

That evening the innermost circle of the royal family
were at last alone with the departure of the last banquet
guest—George and May and the Harewoods, Henry and

Mary. Mother and daughter were talking together, both exclaiming at their weariness, but going over the events of the day, noting several of the dresses and commenting, on the whole favourably, about the people they had spoken to.

George, like Henry with a last whisky and soda in his hand, was taking a more jaundiced view of the events and the people. The King was feeling ill. Every bone in his body was aching from the strain of standing for so long, and the hip which had been so gravely damaged in the fall in France all those years ago was agony.

"Met that bitch today," George said, spitting out the words.

His son-in-law, accustomed to George's expletives, merely asked, "Which one, Sir?"

"That Simpson woman. Looked like a whore, all make-up and a flashy dress."

"Is that the American woman David's runnin' around with?"

George nodded and took a long sip, then put down his glass to take out another cigarette, extending his lips to receive it in his characteristic manner. "That Furness woman was bad enough. He's chucked her, I'm told. And now he's got this American whore. Married, of course. And divorced before that."

"That doesn't sound too good. Why can't the boy just marry a decent Englishwoman, like Bertie. Doesn't have to be royal nowadays." Henry laughed like the beginning of a donkey's bray. "Look at me."

But George was in no mood to listen to jokes. "Harry, I'm not going to last long. Feel pretty rotten most of the time. And I'll tell you one thing. When David succeeds me, he won't last a year. Just as well for the country and the Empire, too. Bertie and Elizabeth will do well, you mark my words. I told Bertie the other day when he was here. 'Your bloody brother's not going to last a year after I'm gone, Bertie,' I said. He pretended not to believe me, but he knows I'm right really. So does Elizabeth. She'll make a grand Queen."

King George pulled himself slowly and painfully from the depths of his chair. "It's long past my bedtime," May turned in her chair and got up as her husband said, "Come along, May, it's been a long day."

The Harewoods followed them from the room, Mary kissing her mother and father good-night. "You did wonderfully, Papa," she said, kissing him a second time.

3

By January 1936 the love between Wallis and David was as strong as George V's hold on life was frail and slipping. At Sandringham, where David had known such carefree days with Mary and Bertie in the secure warmth provided by Edward VII and Grandmama Alix, Finch and Lala Bill, his father lay in bed, eyes closed, breathing stertorously. He had not smoked a cigarette for three days, nor taken more than a sip or two of liquid for two days.

On Saturday morning, 18 January, David went up to see his father with May and Lord Dawson, who had been at Sandringham all week. He watched the doctor take his father's pulse. He wanted to hold his mother's hand but feared that he might be repulsed. May stood beside the bed, straight and tall, grey-faced and looking ten years older than her sixty-eight years.

When Dawson unbuttoned George's pyjamas in order to listen to his chest, the patient stirred and half-opened his eyes. Some spittle fell on to his beard, and the nurse who had stood almost unseen behind the bed-head leant forward and wiped his mouth with some cotton waste.

"It's all right, Sir," Dawson said quietly. "The Queen is here, and the Prince of Wales."

George moved his head perceptibly on the pillow and tried to focus his eyes on his wife, but gave up and closed them again.

Dawson left the nurse to button up the pyjamas, and the three withdrew silently, David closing the door behind him.

"How long, Lord Dawson?" May asked in an even voice.

"It is impossible to say, Ma'am. Perhaps one or two days." And he bowed as May turned and walked away down the wide corridor. The sleet was slashing against the windows and outside the bare trees were being thrashed by the wind.

David followed behind his mother, neither expecting nor receiving a word. He made for his own room, where a fire burned brightly in the grate, sat at his desk and wrote:

My own Sweetheart

Just a line to say I love you more and more and need you so to be with me at this difficult time. There is no hope whatsoever for the King it's only a matter of how long . . . You are all and everything I have in life and WE* must hold each other so tight. It will work out right for us. God bless WE. Your

David

The King survived that week-end. David came up to London to report on his condition to the Prime Minister, Stanley Baldwin, but to his chagrin could only speak to Wallis on the telephone before returning to Sandringham.

Wallis sat out the week-end in London, calling on friends and having others in for cocktails on Saturday. On Monday she went with some more friends, including Nada and Edwina's sister Mary, to a charity première, in aid of the League of Mercy, of the new film *The Amateur Gentleman*. It starred Douglas Fairbanks Jnr, Elissa Landi and Gordon Harker. Half-way through the screen went blank, the lights were turned up, and the manager came on to the stage holding a piece of paper. "Ladies and gentlemen, I have a grave announcement

*Wallis-Edward, a compound form of endearment.

to make." He held up the paper and read: "The King's life is moving peacefully to its close. Signed Lord Dawson of Penn."

After a decent interval the film resumed. At the end there was a poignant silence as the packed audience rose from their seats to listen to "God Save the King."

Wallis was invited back to their home by her friends for some supper. Just before she was going to leave, the maid came in and said to her mistress in an awed voice, "Madam, the Prince of Wales is on the telephone for Mrs Simpson."

Wallis was given the privacy of her host's study, and listened to David say, "It's all over."

"I'm so very sorry."

David's anguish was clear from his voice. "Darling, I can't tell you what my own plans are, everything here is so upset. But I shall fly to London with Bertie in the morning and will telephone you when I can."

It was only after she had replaced the receiver on its cradle that Wallis realized that the maid had been misled into a major inaccuracy. Wallis had been talking to King Edward VIII, not the Prince of Wales.

For almost two years David had determined to marry Wallis Simpson, and had first spoken to her of his intention at the beginning of 1935. Wallis had treated these suggestions lightly and laughed off the idea. As she wrote to Aunt Bessie, when she expressed concern at the development of her relationship with David, "I am still very fond of Ernest and think I can keep the two of them." Knowing the Prince's record with Freda Dudley Ward and Thelma Furness (among others), she could not believe that this would be a permanent arrangement—and meanwhile, why not enjoy herself to the full?

But by the summer of 1935 Wallis began to realize that, for reasons she did not fully understand, she had become indispensable to him. He told her so over and over again, and when they were separated, however briefly, he would write obsessive notes to her—like this one, written on board a warship at 1 a.m. during a review of the fleet: "Wallis—a boy is holding a girl so very tight in his arms tonight . . . A girl knows that not anybody or anything can separate WE—not even the stars—and that WE belong to each other for ever . . ."

Then, three weeks before George V's death, when David and Wallis were again house guests at Melton Mowbray, David slipped a note to her. It was the first morning of 1936, and he wrote of the year "making us *one*."

Step by inevitable step, events in 1936 marched towards their cataclysmic conclusion.

Even before the Prince of Wales had become King, Ernest Simpson had had enough. Every time he showed his face in public, he sensed that people were regarding him as a cuckold. He took the decision to have it out with the King on 12 February, when he knew that he was at York House. Then, by an extraordinary coincidence, his telephone rang, and it was the King, inviting him round right away for a talk. So he phoned Bernard Rickatson-Hatt, editor-in-chief of Reuters and an old wartime friend, and asked him if he would come with him. They had a light supper in the King's small dining room, and immediately it was over got down to the miserable business. At one point Ernest said, "If I let Wallis go, will you promise to marry her?" At this point Rickatson-Hatt tried to leave, but Ernest said, "Please stay a moment. I want you to listen to the answer." It was, Ernest realized, a strange way to talk in front of your sovereign, but the man had, after all, shamelessly stolen his wife, whom he had loved. At this point the King rose from his chair, as if to emphasize what he was about to say. "Do you really think I would be crowned without Wallis by my side?"

That was all Ernest needed. "I will promise not to contest a divorce if you promise to marry Wallis." Nor did he say "Sir" or "Your Majesty."

The King merely said, "Of course." And that was that.

A few days after this incident at York House, another conversation took place at 10 Downing Street, this time between the Prime Minister, Stanley Baldwin, and Lord Wigram.

"It is kind of you to spare me the time, Prime Minister," the King's private secretary opened the proceedings formally.

"You appear to be troubled, Lord Wigram." Stanley Baldwin had been Prime Minister (for the second time) since June 1935. He gave the impression of being a lethargic man, but he knew a great deal more than most people realized about what was going on, and he handled the House of Commons with considerable skill. "Are you having trouble with our new sovereign?"

Lord Wigram coughed deferentially and said in a low voice, "I'm getting on in years, Prime Minister, and I think perhaps my useful working days are almost over. Would you consider allowing me to offer my resignation to His Majesty?"

Baldwin tapped out his pipe into a glass ashtray and at once started filling it again, a function that often accompanied what he wished to be interpreted as deep thought. In fact he knew precisely what he was going to say long before the bowl of his pipe was full and the tobacco rammed by his first finger.

"Well, Lord Wigram, you know that you do not require my permission. It is something between you and the King, but I appreciate your letting me know in good time. I also suspect that you are not quite as happy with your new lord and master as your last one?"

"We are facing some problems, as one would expect. We are all set in our ways and to believe that things would go on just as before would be a mistake."

Baldwin had his pipe going satisfactorily, blue smoke rising towards the chandelier. "Let me speak bluntly, Lord Wigram. I have heard that the King's lady is causing some trouble, distracting His Majesty from some of his duties, like reading and signing his boxes, and persuading His Majesty to sack some of his staff, some of whom worked with the late King for all his reign."

"I think, sir, that there has been unhappiness, some of it caused by economics, some by rather abrupt dismissal, including at the top General Trotter, who came to see me last week in somewhat low spirits."

Baldwin's wife Lucy used to say that her husband let his pipe go out deliberately, such was the pleasure he derived from re-lighting it. "He has shares in Bryant and May," she would quip to friends. He did this now, with a considerable flourish of flame and extinguishing.

"Mr Eden, I can tell you in utmost confidence, is worried about the boxes on several counts. The first is the delay, sometimes of weeks, in dealing with them. Secondly, there is virtually no security at Fort Belvedere, unlike BP and York House, and Mrs Simpson is a notorious gossip. And Anthony is also concerned about the King's connections with Germany, which are believed to be very close. And, as you know, Prussian sabre-rattling is getting louder every day."

"What is to be done about all this, Sir?"

"Well, for the first time in this country's history, the Foreign Office is screening the boxes that go to the Fort. Those that are urgent or highly confidential are now being withheld."

"It is as serious as that, Sir?"

"It is, Lord Wigram. And I am deeply grieved that you wish to resign, but quite understand your reasons."

4

David's loss of popularity as soon as he became King began in the innermost circles, and steadily worked outwards during 1936. As Prince of Wales he had been immensely popular with the world at large; with the working classes whose deprivations and unemployment were the object of his sympathy; with the middle classes because of his courage and cheerfulness, his "good" war and lack of "side"; with his household, which he treated with kindness and consideration. He had often shown impatience in the past, and had never suffered fools gladly, but the arrogance and selfishness and ruthlessness he displayed as soon as he succeeded to the throne dismayed and disappointed many more people than the Prime Minister and Lord Wigram. They also dismayed his younger brother.

Bertie was not so much treated thoughtlessly: he was virtually ignored, as if he were now no more than some plebeian instead of the next in line of succession. David knew that his brother, and especially his wife, disapproved of his affair with Wallis. So did Wallis, whose venomous feelings towards Elizabeth knew no bounds. That was quite sufficient to exclude Bertie from all consultations, let alone decision-making.

Of the radical changes David made at Balmoral, for example, Bertie was told nothing except as a *fait accompli*. As Bertie wrote sorrowfully to his mother, "David only told me what he had done after it was over, which I might say made me rather sad."

Another episode concerning Balmoral saddened a much greater number of the King's subjects. Soon after he succeeded to the throne, his office received an invitation to open a new extension to the hospital in the nearby Scottish town of Aberdeen some time in September. It would have taken an hour. He mentioned the subject casually to Wallis, who commented, "Darling, you know how precious your time is at Balmoral. Why not get Bertie to do it? He's got nothing else to do."

The excuse was made that the King would still be in mourning so please address your invitation to the Duke of York. Meanwhile, throughout the summer, and very publicly, the King and his lady were seen laughing and chatting, and with no sign of mourning. On the day Bertie was doing his duty nearby, a short distance away the King was seen driving his own car to the railway station for Balmoral in order to pick up Wallis.

That evening at Birkhall, on Deeside, while Bertie was changing for dinner, Elizabeth entered his dressing room and exclaimed, "Do you know what I have just heard from Flora?"

Bertie paused to ask his valet to leave. "What is it, dear?"

And Elizabeth told him about Wallis's arrival that day. "Those terrible Herman Rogers were in the back of the car, and Mrs Simpson sat in front with David."

"I can only think that he's going loopy. Really, after the *Nahlin* business . . ."

The cruise of the motor yacht *Nahlin*, which displayed publicly both the intimacy of relationship between the new King and Wallis Simpson and the new style of informality which was to govern the British monarchy, in sharp contrast to George V's reign, was first discussed between David and Wallis (in bed as it happens) at the Fort towards the end o

July 1936. They were discussing their plans for August, when traditionally the King went north for Balmoral and the shooting. "WE" had other plans, which most irritatingly were being disrupted politically.

"Cannes is off, Wallis," David announced. "The Foreign Office have advised against, very strongly. And as they said our lives would be at risk, I guess we'd better do as we're told."

"You mean the French can't guarantee the English King's safety in their own country? That's disgraceful."

"Apparently it will stir up a lot of trouble among the local communists. The red flag's flying all over the place—even in Cannes. And then there's the war in Spain which is also upsetting things in the south. And on top of it all—Italy."

A full-scale European crisis had arisen over Mussolini's invasion of Abyssinia, and relations between Italy and Britain had been dangerously bitter for months. "So what are we going to do?" Wallis asked. Once she had been able to take rebuffs stoically, but no longer.

"I thought you might enjoy a cruise, darling?"

"But you know how I hate the sea. Really, David . . ."

"This won't be the proper sea. Just drifting along the coast, calling on friends and having a good time. Annie Yule has offered her yacht. We could start at Sibenik, a lovely place in Yugoslavia. Paul and Olga are very keen for us to call on them and later we could see the Greeks. I thought we could take along the Rogers and the Duff Coopers, Hugh Sefton's always fun and 'Poots' Butler and anyone else you'd like."

Wallis considered this entirely new prospect in silence. Then she lifted her head from the pillow and kissed David. "Yes, that'll be grand, darling."

On 8 August the party boarded a private carriage on the Orient Express and headed across Europe to the warm waters of the Adriatic. The King had originally intended to travel as the "Duke of Lancaster," but American and French newsmen, especially, rumbled that before the journey began, and the massed crowds of photographers and journalists were exceeded only by the local peasantry, who turned out in thousands, giving as much attention to Wallis ("*Zivila L j-ubav!*"— "Long live love!" they cried) as to David.

At port after port, in blazing weather, David and Wallis strode ashore, followed by their bemused and amused guests, waving and smiling for the locals and the photographers, dressed in the beach clothes of the period. Pictures appeared of the King and his mistress sunbathing on the sand of some obscure cove, swimming from a dinghy, playing beach games with their guests.

It was all a revelation of informality, a public snub against protocol, a flaunting of the new style of "modern" monarchy the King was determined to pursue. His staff* were beside themselves with anxiety and tried without the slightest effect to clear away the men with their Leicas and long lenses. One photograph, reproduced internationally at the time, and thousands of times since, showed Wallis with her hand on his arm, while he looks at her with transparent adoration and trust.

Later, as the *Nahlin* proceeded through the Corinth canal *en route* to Athens, David appeared on the bridge wearing nothing but shorts, binoculars about his neck, smiling at the crowds lining the bank only a few yards distant. It all appeared, to guests and crowds alike, to be a carefree and utterly happy holiday party. But it was in Greek waters that the spell was broken.

It has been related that one evening at dinner on board the *Nahlin*, always an informal occasion dominated by laughter and the consumption of much champagne, the subject of their imminent host, the King of the Hellenes, was raised. The conversation went like this.

Kate Rogers: "Wallis, darling, you will love him. So kind and brave."

Wallis: "And his family?"

Kate Rogers: "Well, you've met some of them, haven' you, darling." Laughter. " I mean Marina, and Olga the othe day . . ."

Wallis (always concerned about this): "And is he happy do you think?"

*They included Sir Godfrey Thomas, Bt and Sir John Aird, Bt.

Kate Rogers: "Happy? Yes, I think so, though frustrated, of course."

Wallis: "Frustrated? What do you mean?"

Kate Rogers: "Well, you know, he has this gorgeous mistress. Has had for years."

Wallis: "Why doesn't he marry her?"

Silence all round the table. David, head down, concerns himself with groping for a cigarette.

Kate Rogers: "Well, darling. First she's married already. And second, she's a commoner. So that puts the kibosh on that!"

From that moment the life went out of the holiday. The host sank into a deep depression from which it proved impossible to arouse him. Even Wallis's efforts were to no avail. During the day the party broke up into little groups, and any laughter was suppressed. "Did he," asks his biographer, "in his disturbed state feel the irrational anger which can be provoked in an undisciplined mind by a messenger with bad news?"

No one will ever know. But Dickie Mountbatten, who was not there but knew David as well as anyone and had witnessed his black moods of frustration as long ago as India 1921, once explained that his friend had almost certainly been in a "state of almost religious exaltation of love" which blinded him to the unreality of his plan to marry Wallis.

Another friend, "Fruity" Metcalfe, used to speak of David's powers of self-delusion "which combined dangerously with his arrogance." He was King, he was omnipotent, he would, as always, have his way—somehow.

Those few words, spoken in the dining saloon of the *Nahlin,* had broken through his defences—or as someone present remarked, "The blindfold was lifted for a moment, and he was stunned and horrified at what he saw."

5

The ripples of disquiet deepened soon after the return, separately, of David and Wallis from their holiday. The reason was that it became known that a divorce suit between Wallis and Ernest had been put down for hearing at, of all places, the east-coast seaside resort of Felixstowe,* and this could only strengthen the belief that the King was planning to marry his mistress.

On 13 November 1936 David returned to the Fort from a hugely successful visit to the fleet at Portsmouth, and, as always, was met on the doorstep by Finch, who had been privy for years to every stage and every change in his master's relationship with his women. David was perfectly well aware of this, Finch knew that he knew; and not one word had ever been spoken by either of them on the subject, although David spoke freely about his relations with all members of his family—his special affection for George, the agony of his relationship with his father, right to the end, the

The suggestion that this obscure and inconveniently placed town had been selected to conceal the case from the public for as long as possible is quite incorrect. The reason was the need for speed, and London and many other courts were full for more than a year.

unbroken boundary of frozen misunderstanding separating him from his mother, and so on.

Finch was also, at this time, well aware of the rapidly developing crisis that was building up about his master, and his master's apparent indifference to it. On this evening Finch had resolutely risked stepping a fraction out of line with a word or two of warning, just as, thirty years earlier, he might have given notice in a grave voice that David's father wished to see him and that the news was not good.

The reason for this was that, earlier in the day, Major Alexander Hardinge, the King's private secretary, had called unannounced at the Fort with a letter addressed "The King, Fort Belvedere, Sunningdale, Ascot," and marked in the left-hand top corner "Urgent & Confidential." "Finch," Hardinge said in a tone that matched the message, "this letter is of the utmost urgency and importance. Please see that His Majesty opens it as soon as he arrives."

No good news could possibly be contained in a letter delivered in this manner, and Finch also knew from the ever-efficient "downstairs" grapevine that senior members of Stanley Baldwin's government had met that day to discuss a single subject. Finch had also seen (he could not avoid doing so) some of the American press cuttings concerning the *Nahlin* cruise, which the British press had discreetly refrained from printing.* His master had dropped most of them unread into the waste paper basket, while one or two were left lying on his desk to show to Wallis.

"Major Hardinge, Sir, called a short while ago and left a letter," Finch began as he helped David out of his coat. "He instructed me to ask you to open it as soon as you arrived. It is on the boxes beside your desk."

---

*In the context of the 1980s it is hard to understand how the press was effectively "gagged" in connection with the indiscretions of the monarch. The answer lies in the fear (unknown today) of being socially ostracized and thus losing your influence if you did not "toe the line." The great press barons like Beaverbrook and Rothermere had achieved their power and their honours by conforming to the code of the establishment as well as by their skill at running newspapers.

"I am extremely tired and cold, Finch, and have been hard at it all day. Major Hardinge no doubt has done no more than play two rounds of golf. It will have to wait."

"I think I should warn you, Sir, that I have every reason to believe that it does not contain good news."

"Oh well, perhaps you would have it sent up to my bathroom."

When David eventually opened the letter while in his dressing gown, all thoughts of the comfort of a bath disappeared. Anger and outrage took their place. Never since Mider's day had he been so outspokenly warned and implicitly rebuked; and then he had been a boy, while now he was King-Emperor of the greatest nation and greatest Empire on earth.

The first warning contained in the letter was that there was a limit to the self-imposed silence of the British press on the subject of his relations with Mrs Simpson. It could not be maintained for longer than a day or two. "The effect," wrote Hardinge, "will be calamitous." Then, the resignation of the government over the matter "can by no means be excluded" —which of course meant it would resign unless there was a resolution of the business. No other leader in the House of Commons would be able to form a new government. There would then have to be a dissolution and a general election, "in which Your Majesty's personal affairs would be the chief issue."

And the solution? David could only scarcely believe his eyes as he read on. Mrs Simpson must go abroad "*without further delay,* and I would *beg* Your Majesty to give this proposal your earnest consideration before the position has become irretrievable."

David wrote, "I was shocked and angry—shocked by the suddenness of the blow, angry because of the way it was launched, with the startling suggestion that I should send from my land, my realm, the woman I intended to marry."

Later, David asked Wallis to come with him to his study. He was white-faced and Wallis noticed the tic in his right cheek, always the signal of acute tenseness. "What is it, darling?" she asked.

David drew his key ring from his pocket and opened one

of the red boxes on his desk, drawing out the letter which
had been returned to its envelope. "Wallis, I want you to
read this alone. After you've read it, I think you'll agree that
there is only one thing for me to do—send for Mr Baldwin."
He turned and left the room.

Wallis began reading the letter, at first very slowly and
then more rapidly, turned it over in her hand as if there
might be more on the reverse of the heavy Buckingham
Palace paper, and then began reading it again. She had not
finished when David returned quietly to the room. "Well,
what do you think?"

"I don't know what to think—I'm simply stunned," Wallis replied. "All I know is that I must leave immediately."

"Leave?"

"Yes, go to France—anywhere."

"You'll do no such thing. I won't have it. This letter is an
impertinence." His voice was shaking.

Wallis was swallowing hard in her effort to control her
feelings and her voice. This is what she had been secretly
dreading for weeks: she had tried hard to pretend to herself
that everything would continue smoothly, but in her heart
she also knew that affairs had been heading for a crisis. "I
think Alex is being sincere in this letter. He's only trying to
warn you that the government will insist that you give me
up."

David, beside himself with frustration and anger, half-
shouted, "They can't stop me. On the throne or off, I'm going
to marry you." He came towards her, arms outstretched, an
expression of agony on his face. "You're not to go, Wallis. I'm
nothing without you—just a husk. King or not, I can't live
alone. I must have you."

She fell into his arms, sobbing on his shoulder. "It's
madness to think of giving up the throne. Your people love
you," she said through her tears. "Look how they cheer you
wherever you go. Those sailors, the out-of-work miners you
went to see. They won't let you go . . ."

After a few moments they broke apart. "I'm finished
with Alex," David said, the tic working faster than ever, face
as white as the paper on which the letter had been written.
"Walter's going to act for me from now on. And the Prime

Minister must come to see me. I'm going to fight this through
to the end."

Walter Monckton had been at Oxford with David, where
they became friends. Since then he had built up a considerable practice as a barrister. His insignificant appearance—
short in stature, sloping shoulders, horn-rim spectacles, black
hair parted in the centre—belied his astuteness, knowledge
and wit.

David had already confided in Monckton his determination to marry and had been advised to keep his intentions
quiet for the time being because, in any case, he could not
marry Wallis until a decree nisi was declared six months after
the divorce case.

Now David made a rendezvous with his old friend at
Windsor Castle. When they met he showed Monckton
Hardinge's letter. After reading it without comment, Monckton
asked David, "What do you intend to do now, Sir?"

"Walter, I've lost all trust in Alex after this. Will you act
as a go-between with Baldwin? I must have someone I can
trust."

"Yes, I see that, and I'm very honoured—and of course
pleased to do whatever I can. What do you plan to say to the
Prime Minister?"

"I propose to tell him that if the government insists that
I cannot marry the woman I love as King, then I'll marry her
as an ex-King."

Walter considered this in silence for a moment, as if he
were in court preparing his words in a difficult case. "He will
not like to hear that," he said.

"And I shall not find it easy."

6

"Elizabeth, David is meeting the Prime Minister at BP this evening. I fear the worst."

"The children will be down in a minute, so tell me quickly."

Bertie leaned back in his chair, placing the tips of his fingers together. "I think he's going to t-t-tell him that he's going to marry that Simpson woman—and to hang with anything else."

"Anything else being the government. Oh, my darling, what a mess! What will Baldwin say?"

"I c-c-can only sur-surmise, my dear. But I suppose Baldwin'll say he'll have to r-r-resign and that there'll have to be a general el-el-election." He took another cigarette from the box beside him and was lighting it as the two girls ran into the room, their arrival lifting the air of gloom and foreboding.

Two hours later Baldwin was driven from 10 Downing Street along Birdcage Walk to the back entrance of the Palace. Alex Hardinge met him in the hall as the footman was taking Baldwin's coat.

"Good evening, Prime Minister," he said. They walked down the wide corridor towards the King's study. "I think perhaps I should warn you that you should expect a somewhat dramatic announcement from His Majesty."

Baldwin thanked him, and passed through the open door, bowing to his sovereign. David had an air of more-than-usual briskness about him, passing his Prime Minister a stiff whisky and soda without ice, as he knew he liked it, without asking him.

The King went straight to the heart of the matter, speaking swiftly and walking up and down, smoking but without a drink.

"I understand that you and several members of the Cabinet have some fear of a constitutional crisis developing over my friendship with Mrs Simpson."

"That's true, Sir."

"You do understand that I intend to marry her?"

Baldwin did some pipe relighting, his every movement emphasizing that this was no ritual to be hastened. He puffed smoke vertically into the air, shook out the flame from the match and placed it in the ashtray.

"I think it is my duty, Sir, to point out that the position of the King's wife is different from the position of any other citizen in the country."

David listened impatiently as if he knew every word the Prime Minister was going to say.

"This is part of the price which the King has to pay. His wife becomes Queen, the Queen becomes the Queen of the country, and therefore, in the choice of a Queen, the voice of the people must be heard."

David almost clipped off Baldwin's last word in his eagerness to make the announcement of which Hardinge had warned. "I want you to be the first to know that I have made up my mind and nothing will alter it. I have looked at it from all sides. I mean to abdicate to marry Mrs Simpson."

"Sir, this is a very grave decision," Baldwin said in a shocked voice. "I am deeply grieved."

Having delivered himself of his announcement, David appeared quite light-headed with relief and happiness. "I shall marry as soon as Mrs Simpson is free. If I could marry her and remain King, well and good. I would be happiest at that, and would probably be a better King for it. But if the government opposes the marriage, then as I say, I shall go."

The repetition of the statement seemed to shock Baldwin more than the first announcement, and his pipe went out for once spontaneously. The seconds passed, recorded by the grandfather clock in the corner of the study. Then the Prime Minister dragged himself to his feet, peering at the King intently.

"This is most grievous news, Sir. I feel unable to say more just now, if you'll forgive me."

Later, Baldwin was to comment on this momentous incident: "The King's face wore such a look of beauty as might have lighted the face of a young knight who had caught a glimpse of the Holy Grail."

But Baldwin also noticed that there were tears in David's eyes as he held Baldwin's hand for a long time while saying goodbye. "Well, Your Majesty, Esmond* and I have held back Fleet Street for about as long as we can, but I guess by tomorrow or the day after the pack'll be loose."

It was not the first warning the King had received from another of his friends, Lord Beaverbrook, proprietor of the *Daily Express,* the *Sunday Express* and the *Evening Standard.* "Since the Bishop spilt the beans, there'll be no holding them back. Geoffrey Dawson will be after you and Mrs Simpson in *The Times* and that'll be extremely damaging."

David did not at once reply and for a few seconds there was silence on the line between Beaverbrook's home, Stornoway House, and the Fort. Then the drawling Canadian voice continued, "Sir, I beg you to allow your friends like Esmond and myself, and many others who can see nothing wrong in your marrying Mrs Simpson, to speak up for you."

"No, Max," David said decisively. "I will not have Wallis dragged through the mire."

"With due respect, Sir, I think you may change your mind tomorrow. Please allow your friends to come to your aid."

*Esmond Harmsworth, son of the newspaper baron, Lord Rothermere, and close friend of the King.

" No, I will not have it . . ." It might have been Prince David, age eight, arguing with Lala Bill.

The Bishop who had "spilt the beans" was Dr A.W.F. Blunt, Bishop of Bradford. On 1 December in a speech to his Diocesan Conference, he had made a reference to the new King's need for self-dedication. "We hope," said the Doctor, "that he is aware of this need. Some of us wish that he gave more positive signs of such awareness."

This was picked up, first by several provincial newspapers, and then by the nationals, which interpreted this slight on the King in different ways. David did his best to keep the newspapers away from Wallis but she managed to get hold of them, and in the early morning of 3 December, still in her nightgown, she ran into David's dressing room, clutching a dozen newspapers, all of which headlined, in various degrees of shrillness, the King's crisis and the American divorcée, Mrs Ernest Simpson.

Wallis threw them on to the floor, the tears streaming down her cheeks. "David, I can't stand it. You *must* do something—and I must go."

David looked at her, then cast his eyes over the black headlines. So this is what his people had done to the most precious thing in his life—this woman he loved beyond everything—throne, country, wealth, privilege. He reached out and drew her to him. "Oh my love—what shall we do? What shall we do?"

"You must not abdicate, darling. You mustn't let them beat you. You must stay and fight—and I must go away. I should have gone long ago."

David walked over the scattered newspapers, kicking at them viciously as he made for the telephone. "William,* will you get Mr Rogers at his villa?"

The Herman Rogers at their Cannes villa, "Lou Viei," said that of course they would accommodate Wallis and her party for as long as was necessary, and Wallis at once summoned her maid to start packing.

"Darling, you must broadcast to your people," she begged

*William Bateman, the King's ever-faithful private telephone operator, privy to his most private conversations.

David later in the morning. "Tell Baldwin that you must do that tomorrow at the latest. Say that I have gone away, don't say for how long. In a few weeks it will all have blown over, and perhaps some time, somewhere, we'll be able to meet again. But not for a long time."

"What are you saying, Wallis?" David replied indignantly. "You know that I would kill myself rather than give you up. You are MINE!"

"No, darling, it is best—truly, David, it is best. Your duty is here. You are King." She reached down to the floor. "Look what this newspaper says, 'The private and public life of our King-Emperor are indivisible, and steadfast duty demands . . .'"

"Duty? Duty is nothing, a speck of dust, compared with you. What I shall do is to follow you abroad in a few days after my broadcast. A Council of State will take over my work. Then, according to how my people feel, I will either abdicate or come back for the coronation. After that no one can stop me marrying you . . ."

The argument went on for most of the morning, interrupted by telephone calls and outbursts of tears that added yet more poignancy to this moment of ultimate human drama. Late in the afternoon, Ladbrook brought Wallis's Buick to the Fort with Perry Brownlow* and Inspector Evans of Scotland Yard, the King's private detective, who were to accompany Wallis on the long drive through France.

The final parting was less of an agony than both had feared. The hall was crowded, Brownlow was worried about the time, David had convinced himself (if not Wallis) that they would be together in a few days, and Wallis was crying over the parting with her beloved little dog, Slipper.

At the end, they gave each other no more than a social kiss, and Wallis handed the dog into his arms. Perry Brownlow was calling, "Please hurry, please hurry." The stench of the exhaust fumes from the Buick filtering through the open front door added to the sense of urgency.

*Peregrine Cust, 6th Lord Brownlow, Lord-in-Waiting to the King. He had served with him in the Grenadier Guards and later served in the RAF: a man of scrupulous loyalty and honour.

The last word of their argument was Wallis's. She had scribbled a brief note which she thrust into Finch's safe hand as he closed the door of the car. She said only "Goodbye, dear Finch." He would know. Later, David read, "Be calm with B but tell the country tomorrow I am lost to you . . ."

To be calm with Baldwin was not difficult, but for the King to persuade him that he must broadcast to the nation in order to put his case to his people was another thing altogether. Within four hours of Wallis's departure, and back at Buckingham Palace, David began to realize the strength and implacability of the forces closing about him.

"No, Sir," Stanley Baldwin had replied to David's request, "I am afraid that will not be possible. Constitutionally, I can only give my assent with the support of my ministers. And this, I regret to say, is not forthcoming."

Barely able to contain his anger, David said, "You want me to go, don't you?"

Baldwin, not in the least rattled, solemnly filled his pipe without replying. When he did so, he spoke slowly, choosing his words with care:

"What I want, Sir, is what you told me you wanted: to go with dignity, not dividing the country, and making things as smooth as possible for your successor. To broadcast now would be to go over the heads of your ministers and speak to the people. You will be telling millions throughout the world— among them a vast number of women—that you are determined to marry one who has a husband living. They will want to know all about her, and the press will ring with gossip . . . No, Sir, I am sorry."

7

Two days earlier that massive edifice, that wonderful example of Victorian strength and endurance, the Crystal Palace, had burst into flames that were seen from distant parts of London and the south-east of England. People asked how could a building believed to have been built of iron and glass be consumed so swiftly and spectacularly. Now, on the evening of 3 December, there remained only the glow of embers. The parallel with the reign of King Edward VIII was almost too close for comfort. Already people were talking about the reign of King Edward VIII in the past tense, and those newspapers that were not highly critical of his defection were sorrowfully mourning his imminent departure.

At 10 p.m. on that cataclysmic and exhausting day, David drove to Marlborough House to see his mother, and inform her that his decision was now final. Bertie was already there, and had been discussing the crisis with May and complaining at the King's failure to inform his family of what was going on. Just before David was announced, Bertie was remarking, "He doesn't seem to realize, Mama, that if he abdicates I'll be King. He has told me nothing. N-n-nothing."

"Your father always said that David is a very passionate

boy. He also told me more than once that he did not think he
would last a year on the throne."

At that moment David was shown into the room, still in
the tweed country suit which he had worn all day. He looked
very sporty by contrast with Bertie in his dinner jacket, but
Bertie bowed his head briefly to him, as he always had on the
few occasions when they had met since their father had died.

David advanced across the room and kissed his mother's
hand. "I am sorry to be so late, Mama. I know how you like
to get to bed early, but I have something important to say."

"Well, tell us. We have been wondering when we might
hear from you."

David helped himself to a whisky and soda and stood
with his back to the coal fire. "Mama, I find I cannot live
alone as King and I must marry Mrs Simpson."

Considering the massive implications of her son's statement, May took the news calmly, and as always with complete dignity. "So what will you do, David?"

"I shall abdicate. I have tried to persuade Mr Baldwin,
but he won't even allow me to broadcast to my own people.
Mrs Simpson is everything in my life, and all that matters is
our happiness."

"No, you are mistaken, David. All that matters is your
duty. Consider the millions of young men who sacrificed
their *lives* for their country in the Great War. And you will
not give up for your country a twice-married woman who is
not even yet free to marry you!"

"No, Mama, all that matters is our happiness. That is
all."

Bertie now broke in, white with passion, and David
turned as if surprised to find him still in the room. "And what
of Elizabeth and me, and our children? Have you considered
them, and the sacrifices you are demanding of us—all the
t-t-terrible pub-publicity. I am not fit to be King, David. You
have prepared for it all your life."

As if this was of equally trivial importance with the
nation and Empire, David merely said in an off-hand voice,
"You'll make a very good King. Will you ring me at the Fort
tomorrow morning and we'll talk more about it."

He kissed May's hand again and paced swiftly from the

room, just as if, in his bright herringbone tweed, he were walking to tee-off for the first hole.

"Do you think he'll change his mind?" Bertie asked his mother.

"No, dear, I do not. I think he is not well—not well—" and she tapped her head "—if you know what I mean. He has always been an over-excitable boy, like poor little Johnnie. He is wrong in almost everything he is doing, and only right in one thing."

"What is that, Mama?"

"In his belief that you'll make a very good King. And as Papa always said, Elizabeth will make a wonderful Queen."

All through the following day, a Friday, and all over the week-end, Bertie tried to pin his brother down to a meeting, while Bertie and Elizabeth fretted over the uncertainty. Not until Monday did Bertie manage to get through to him.

> My brother rang me up at 10 minutes to 7.0 p.m. [Bertie wrote in his journal] to say "Come and see me after dinner." I said "No, I will come and see you at once." I was with him at 7.0 p.m. The awful & ghastly suspense of waiting was over. I found him pacing up & down the room & he told me his decision that he would go.

For the King, the sudden turning of his people against him as soon as it was known that he was abdicating was truly terrible. One minute, or so it seemed, he was being almost deafeningly cheered in an aircraft-carrier's hangar at Portsmouth and by Welsh miners, and the next he was reading that Churchill had been howled down in the Commons for being his defender. It was like Michelangelo suddenly being told that he was no good, with his paintings being burned publicly.

One of many diarists of these epochal events, Blanche Dugdale, wrote, "He is very upset by the newspapers, never having seen anything but fulsome adulation for all his forty years!"

The only consolations for David in London and Wallis in the South of France during these last days of his reign, were the telephone calls they made whenever they could. But even these were unsatisfactory. The line was never clear, partly because it was being tapped by reporters, and much of the time was taken up with pleading by Wallis for David to change his mind and not abdicate, and by him for Wallis not to leave him.

By now there was no one left, not even Wallis, who believed that the King would stay on. Baldwin made a simple, moving speech in the House, and it was announced that the ex-King would leave the country immediately after he had spoken to the nation, which he was now permitted to do in order to bid farewell to his people. Only those who understood the laws of divorce realized that he would not be allowed to see Wallis until her "nisi" was granted six months after the divorce hearing at Felixstowe.

8

Nine in the morning 9 December 1936. At 145 Picadilly Elizabeth, normally an early riser, lay in bed with a temperature of 101° and a headache. "What a time to have flu!" she greeted Bertie. "Just when I might be of some use to you." She smiled and indicated that he should sit on the bed, but at the far end. "And we certainly don't want *you* to catch it."

Bertie was dressed in a black morning coat, ready to leave on a gruelling round of visits. "I'll manage, dear, don't worry. Are the girls all right?"

"Yes, they're fine. Lilibet understands perfectly what is happening and is being very grown up about it. I only wish *I* could understand. It seems unbelievable and yet we knew it was inevitable. You knew, too, really. But just as David deluded himself that he could remain King when it was obviously impossible, you managed to delude yourself when you knew it was inevitable."

"Dear Elizabeth, you're so sensible. I really don't think I could have faced all this without you."

"Of course you could. But one thing is worrying me, Bertie. It has kept me awake half the night. What title are you going to give David? He can't be Mr Edward Windsor as he was born the son of a duke, and so he is Lord Edward

Windsor anyway. But if he keeps that title he can stand and be elected to the House of Commons, and that woman might easily persuade him to do that."

Elizabeth, Duchess of York, once Elizabeth Bowes-Lyon, soon to be Queen Elizabeth, fixed her shrewd blue eyes on her husband. "Yes, I've been thinking hard about this and no one seems to have discussed the matter. I think you'll have to make him a royal duke. Then he can't even sit and vote in the House of Lords. So why not make him HRH The Duke of Windsor—but no HRH for her," Elizabeth added decisively. "As she's already left two husbands she might easily chuck David in a year or two. Then we'd have a three-times divorced American royal duchess let loose on society—just imagine that!"

Bertie considered this, and nodded and smiled. "Not only could I not face this without you—*none* of us could." He blew her a kiss and told her to go back to sleep before the doctor came.

Bertie saw his mother twice that day, once at Marlborough House after he left Elizabeth, and again after seeing his lawyer and Baldwin, and then David at the Fort. "But I could see," Bertie wrote of this last meeting, "that nothing I said would alter his decision." Then of the second visit to his mother:

> I went to see Queen Mary & when I told her what had happened I broke down & sobbed like a child. A few minutes later I was told from No 10 that I was wanted to witness together with my two younger brothers D's instrument of abdication at 10 a.m. on Thursday Dec 10th.

Later, Bertie wrote of "the fateful moment which made me D's successor to the Throne."

> Perfectly calm D signed five or six copies of the instrument & then five copies of his message to Parliament, one for each Dominions Parliament. It was a dreadful moment & one never to be forgotten by those present . . . I later went to London where

I found a large crowd outside my house cheering madly. I was overwhelmed.

"You can hear them, Elizabeth. They're cheering you, too. They said so, and one old lady asked how you were."

Elizabeth propped herself up on her pillows, smiling as she watched the tears pouring down Bertie's cheeks. "I told you they would love you, dear. It's not going to be all nightmare. Now go and see Lilibet—she has waited up specially to see you. She's so proud . . ."

All those who saw David during his last hours in England remarked on his cheerfulness. One even said, "He was positively jaunty, as if he didn't have a care in the world."

Certainly none of his servants at the Fort who had assembled in the hall and watched their master coming down the stairs two at a time, as he usually did, observed any sign of solemnity. He moved among them smiling: "Goodbye, Elsie, I'll miss you. And you, Arnold, too. Who's going to empty my ashtrays now?" And a laugh. Addressing them all, he said, "I'll miss you all and thank you for everything. I have seen that you'll be properly looked after."

Finch was at the door, holding David's hat and coat. He had already been told that he could retire on a pension, and a furnished cottage awaited him if he so wished. "Goodbye old friend," David said to him in a low voice. "Life without you is going to be very difficult."

As I drove off down the hill towards Virginia Water [David wrote], I turned for a last look at the place I loved so much. The Fort was in sight for only a few seconds before the motor turned out of the gates and it disappeared. In that moment I realized how heavy was the price I had paid . . .

None of those present at the farewell dinner for the ex-King at Royal Lodge, Windsor, could ever forget it, its uniqueness and solemnity, the extraordinary reason for the occasion, nor the absence of the woman who had brought about the downfall of a monarch and—but for the wisdom and firmness of bishops, politicians and the family alike—might have destroyed the Royal House of Windsor.

There were present Bertie, of course, and Mary, both with memories of racing downhill on their bicycles at Sandringham thirty-five years ago; Harry and George, newly wed to beautiful young women (who were not present); their mother, the very essence of royalty, strong and dignified, straight of back and solemn of expression; Aunt Alice of Athlone, one of Queen Victoria's favourite grand-daughters, and her tall husband, Uncle Algy, Queen Mary's brother. That was all.

However deeply David had failed all these people assembled for "the last supper," he did not fail them that evening, smiling and talking to right and left, rescuing what might have been a sombre and embarrassing occasion. Even under these circumstances he was the perfect guest. All David wrote of it was, "Dinner passed pleasantly enough under the circumstances."

At one point Mary, on David's right, said—as if it had only just occurred to her—"We don't even know where you're going tonight."

David laughed. "It's all right, the Navy's looking after me." Then he added, "I've found somewhere to rest my head in Austria. The Rothschilds have very kindly offered to look after me at their *schloss* until the divorce is through."

A moment later the butler whispered in David's ear, "Mr Walter Monckton is here, Sir."

David excused himself. "I have to talk on the wireless now, but I'll be back as soon as I can."

Monckton was in the corridor, and escorted David to the waiting car. "How is it all going, Sir?" he asked.

"I'm trying not to be the spectre at the feast," David quipped. "I only wish we had my brothers' wives there."

Arrangements had been made for the broadcast to be made from Windsor Castle itself: and what more fitting venue for the first King to accede as a Windsor to give up the throne? Sir John Reith, Director-General of the BBC, towering above both David and Monckton, greeted them at the top of the Gothic staircase in Augusta Tower like some giant mythology. The microphone had been rigged on David's old desk, with wires trailing in all directions. David sat down, businesslike and efficient.

"Would you mind doing a test reading?" Reith asked, handing him a copy of the day's *Times*.

David remembered later, "The paragraph I picked at random had an unexpected relevance. It was the report of a speech by Sam Hoare at a tennis gathering, to whose attention he hopefully commended the fact that the new King was an ardent tennis player."

This struck one more bizarre note in an evening strongly touched with unreality.

Then Reith announced solemnly, "This is Windsor Castle. His Royal Highness . . ."

At long last I am able to say a few words of my own. I have never wanted to withhold anything, but until now it has been not constitutionally possible for me to speak.

A few hours ago I discharged my last duty as King and Emperor, and now that I have been succeeded by my brother, the Duke of York, my first words must be to declare my allegiance to him. This I do with all my heart.

You all know the reasons which have impelled me to renounce the throne. But I want you to understand that in making up my mind I did not forget the country or the Empire which as Prince of Wales, and lately as King, I have for twenty-five years tried to serve. But you must believe me when I tell you that I have found it impossible to carry the heavy burden of responsibility and to discharge my duties as King as I would wish to do without the help and support of the woman I love.

And I want you to know that the decision I have made has been mine and mine alone. This was a thing I had to judge entirely for myself. The other person most nearly concerned has tried up to the last to persuade me to take a different course. I have made this, the most serious decision of my

life, upon a single thought of what would in the end
be best for all.

This decision has been made less difficult to
me by the sure knowledge that my brother, with
his long training in the public affairs of this country
and with his fine qualities, will be able to take my
place forthwith, without interruption or injury to
the life and progress of the Empire. And he has one
matchless blessing, enjoyed by so many of you and
not bestowed on me—a happy home with his wife
and children.

During these hard days I have been comforted
by my mother and by my family. The ministers of
the crown, and in particular Mr Baldwin, the Prime
Minister, have always treated me with full consideration. There has never been any constitutional
difference between me and them and between me
and Parliament. Bred in the constitutional tradition
by my father, I should never have allowed any such
issue to arise.

Ever since I was Prince of Wales, and later on
when I occupied the throne, I have been treated
with the greatest kindness by all classes, wherever I
have lived or journeyed throughout the Empire.
For that I am very grateful.

I now quit altogether public affairs, and I lay
down my burden. It may be some time before I
return to my native land, but I shall always follow
the fortunes of the British race and Empire with
profound interest, and if at any time in the future I
can be found of service to His Majesty in a private
station I shall not fail.

And now we all have a new King. I wish him,
and you, his people, happiness and prosperity with
all my heart. God bless you all. God save the King.

Far away in her villa, Wallis, along with millions of other
awaited the voice of the ex-King:

As the moment approached [she wrote] everyone in
Lou Viei, including the domestic staff, gathered
round the radio in the sitting room. David's voice
came out of the loudspeaker calmly, movingly. I
was lying on the sofa with my hands over my eyes,
trying to hide my tears. After he finished, the others quietly went away and left me alone. I lay there
a long time before I could control myself enough to
walk through the house and go upstairs to my room.

The next day on the telephone, David was to tell of the scene
at Royal Lodge when he returned from the Castle. There
were murmurs of approval and the tension seemed to have
eased. "Mama and Mary were the first to leave, then Aunt
Alice and Uncle Algy, leaving us brothers alone. A footman
brought in a tray of whisky and soda, glasses were raised,
Harry grunted something about a 'smooth crossing.' Then I
shook them by the hand, bowing to Bertie first, and then we
embraced. George was shaking his head as I turned to go,
and he suddenly cried out, 'It isn't possible! It isn't happening!' "

But, as David wrote in his memoirs, "It had happened.
It was all over."

9

With David's departure from his country, a mere duke and an exile, the romance ended in the eyes of the world. Worse still, the knives came out and the fairy tale became a horror story.

"So much scandal has been whispered about me, even that I am a spy," Wallis complained to David less than a week after he had left England, "that I am shunned by people." And to David's hostess, Kitty, Baroness Eugène de Rothschild, "The newspaper notoriety is appalling and disgusting and nothing but lies . . ."

The Home Office announced that, under the circumstances, the two detectives guarding Wallis were to be withdrawn—although an outraged David succeeded in reversing his decision. But even the pending divorce was questioned. Baldwin had earlier warned David that there might have been irregularities, and now Wallis's solicitor told her that someone had entered an intervention to give evidence that would lead to the divorce not being made absolute. This was later withdrawn but not before it had driven Wallis almost to despair—"the last straw."

But it was not the last straw. Misfortunes piled up like rocks from an avalanche, culminating (or so it seemed at the time) in the death of her little dog Slipper, sent out later, who had been such a comfort in her isolation. He was bitten by a viper and died soon after—a pet who "had been so faithful through our many trials."

At the same time in Austria, David was suffering his own trials and humiliations. His private financial means were comparatively modest. Even before leaving England, he had considered that he was being treated harshly over money, and his state of (very relative) penury was to haunt him for the rest of his life. There were also signs of brusqueness in Bertie's behaviour, though, like Wallis, he blamed this on Elizabeth: even so Bertie was referred to by Wallis as "your wretched brother."

Then David could reasonably expect to have been made a personal ADC to the new sovereign, but his name was prominently absent from the honours list. "Fruity" Metcalfe David's guest at the time, was witness to an interesting little sign of the new order, as he wrote to his wife:

> Tonight he was told at dinner that HM wanted to talk on the telephone to him. He said he couldn't but asked for it to be put through at 10 p.m. The answer to this was that HM said *he would talk at 6.45 p.m. tomorrow* as he was *too busy to talk any other time*. It was pathetic to see HRH's face. He couldn't believe it! He's been so used to having everything done as he wishes. I'm afraid he's going to have many shocks like this.

And so the dreary, miserable, lonely weeks for Wallis and David dragged by. Then at last, on 3 May 1937, Wallis solicitor telephoned to say that the decree had become absolute and she was free to marry.

It was decided that a wedding on the French Riviera might have raffish connotations. By good fortune, an immensely rich French-born naturalized American, Charles Bedaux, had earlier offered his home, Château de Candé, a refuge for Wallis, who now enquired whether it could both her meeting place with David and the scene of the wedding. Bedaux and his wife were delighted, and it was

Candé on 4 May that the couple fell into one another's arms, David saying, "Darling, it's been so long. I can hardly believe that it's you, and I am here."

Wallis remembered, "Later, we took a walk. It was wonderful to be together again. Before, we had been alone in the face of overwhelming trouble. Now we could meet side by side."

Arrangements for the wedding at once went ahead, some of them, but not all, satisfactorily accomplished. Dickie Mountbatten claimed he had offered his services as best man, as David had been at his wedding, in the course of a brief visit to David in his Austrian retreat. David had thanked him, according to his cousin, and had explained, "This will be a royal wedding, and my two youngest brothers will come over as supporters in the usual way."

Now, he learned, Harry and George had been informed (by whom?) that they were not permitted to act as supporters, nor even to attend the wedding. So "Fruity" Metcalfe was conscripted at the last moment. Others in David's circle somehow dissolved away in the last days, including most of his staff, as if retreating from some plague. Only Hugh Thomas and Randolph Churchill and one or two others braved the threatened disgrace, though a publicity-seeking clergyman risked (and later lost) his reputation by volunteering to conduct a religious ceremony.

The Reverend R.A. Jardine was warmly welcomed, as was Walter Monckton, though not the letter he brought from Bertie. This told David that his younger brother had been pleased "to declare that the Duke of Windsor shall, notwithstanding his act of Abdication . . . be entitled to hold and enjoy for himself only the title, style or attribute of Royal Highness." Then to rub in the salt: "So however that his wife and descendants, if any, shall not hold the said title or attribute."

Angry and outraged, Wallis declared, "David, you're already a royal duke, so the only purpose of this rotten message from your wretched brother is to make clear that I'm not to be a Royal Highness."

"This is a nice wedding present," was all that David said at first to his friend, who said he sympathized and apologized

for being the bearer of bad news. But after a few minutes,
when the news had sunk in, he exploded with wrath. "I know
Bertie," he declared. "I know he couldn't have written this
letter on his own. Why in God's name would they do this to
me at this time!" Later, Monckton wrote to the Home Secretary to warn him not to underestimate the bitterness this act
would arouse.

Frances Donaldson correctly described the effect of this
letter on David:

> The Duke of Windsor received the news as he
> would have a wound in battle. It struck at his
> deepest emotions and it altered him as gunshot
> might have altered him. From now on he would
> live with this fact and never forget it, any more
> than a man who lives in pain can forget it . . .

But in spite of the recently inflicted pain, David appeared
transparently happy on the day of the wedding, 3 June 1937
a brilliant early summer day. A temporary altar was rigged
up, and an organ played in the next room. The tiny congregation sat in two rows on priceless Louis XIV chairs, Jardine
came in, then David and "Fruity" Metcalfe together. Wallis
came in through the other door on the arm of Herman
Rogers. She wore a long blue dress, a short tight-fitting coat
and a blue straw hat with feathers and tulle. On her wrist was
a diamond and sapphire bracelet, David's wedding present.

Throughout the ceremony Metcalfe held the prayer book
for David. It had been given to David on his tenth birthday
by May and was inscribed "To darling David from his loving
Mother."

The ceremony went smoothly, Wallis's voice sounding
shade lower than David's. Metcalfe's wife later wrote in her
diary, "It could be nothing but pitiable & tragic to see a King
of England of only six months ago, an idolized King, married
under those circumstances, & yet pathetic as it was, his
manner was so simple & dignified & he was so sure of himself
in his happiness that it gave something to the sad little
service which it is hard to describe. He had tears running

down his face when he came into the salon after the ceremony. She also could not have done it better."

Three weeks earlier Wallis with David at her side had
listened to the magnificent coronation ceremony in London
on the wireless. "The words of the service rolled over me like
an engulfing wave," Wallis wrote. "I fought to suppress every
thought, but all the while the mental image of what might
have been and should have been kept forming, disintegrat-
ing, and reforming in my mind . . ."

The same poignant words, "what might have been," had
passed through Bertie's mind time and again back in December 1936 when he had first had to come to terms with the
truth that duty had called him to the highest office, The
Sovereign, His Majesty King George VI. But for the abdication of his brother, but for the obsession of his brother with a
divorced American woman, he and Elizabeth might have
continued to live the relatively obscure family life with their
two daughters, as Duke and Duchess of York, carrying out
their royal duties as before, watching over the progress of
Lilibet and Margaret-Rose, holidaying in Scotland where he
could enjoy the shooting and Elizabeth her fishing . . .

"What might have been." In the hall of Fort Belvedere
where they had stood on that terrible December night while
David prepared for his departure, Bertie had opened his
heart in appeal to his cousin, Lord Louis Mountbatten.

"Dickie, this is absolutely terrible," Bertie had exclaimed
out of hearing of the rest of them. "I never wanted this to
happen; I'm quite unprepared for it. David has been trained
for this all his life. I've never even seen a state paper. I'm
only a naval officer, it's the only thing I know about."

Always ready with the apt response, Mountbatten harked
back to an earlier hurried and unexpected promotion to standing in direct line to the throne.

"This is a very curious coincidence," he said reassuringly.
"My father once told me that, when the Duke of Clarence
died, your father came to him and said almost the same
things that you have said to me now, and my father answered

'George, you're wrong. There is no more fitting preparation for a King than to have been trained in the Navy.' "

Back at 145 Piccadilly, still for the present their London home, Elizabeth from her sick bed added further strength to Bertie's resolve—a strength that was to sustain him all through his difficult and eventful reign. Bertie gave expression to this in his first wireless broadcast to the nation. Even the making of it, with his old stutter still evident, required great will-power. In it Bertie said, "I realize to the full the responsibilities of my noble heritage. I shoulder them with all the more confidence in the knowledge that the Queen and my mother Queen Mary are at my side . . ."

Stanley Baldwin, the Prime Minister, added his own measure of encouragement to the man he, more than anyone else, had placed upon the throne. "Sir, if I may say so, you need have no fear for the future so far as you are concerned. The whole country is behind you with a deep and under-standing sympathy."

But these were the anodyne words of a politician. The whole country was not behind Bertie. The crowds outside Buckingham Palace during the height of the abdication crisis were crying "Down with Baldwin, we want the King."

"These were very difficult times for the new King," said Mountbatten, who had done his best to give him strength and resolution. "There was a new republican feeling in the country, and you must remember, even at his best my cousin never looked very robust."

The millions who had heard the hesitancy in their new King's speech were easy prey to the rumours of his ill-health. These rumours were granted added veracity by Bertie's deci-sion not to face a formal visit to India. David had agreed to be "Durbared," like his father in 1911, and all preparations were in hand. But Elizabeth, ever conscious of the limited capacity of Bertie to withstand the strains and stresses of these distant formal ceremonials, put her foot down, determined that her husband should conserve all his strength for the forthcoming coronation.

As for the republicanism, this was exposed most clearly to the world by the Independent Labour Party member of parliament, James Maxton, who moved an amendment to the

Abdication Bill when it came up for debate: "This House declines to give a second reading to a Bill which has been necessitated by circumstances which show clearly the danger to this country and to the British Commonwealth of Nations inherent in an hereditary monarchy . . ."

"We are doing a wrong and foolish thing," Maxton declared, "if, as a House, we do not seize the opportunity with which circumstances have presented us of establishing in our land a completely democratic form of government which does away with old monarchical institutions and the hereditary principle."

Bertie prayed fervently that there would be an improvement in his public image. Elizabeth set about ensuring that there was, knowing full well that her husband could never aspire to the charisma of the wretched David, but that, deep in their hearts, what the British people really admired was a happy unified family, with father doing his work and duty and mother being loyal and loving and caring for the children. They would win, even if it took time.

And it would take time. An American reporter, for example, wrote (though the British did not read it) for the *New York Herald-Tribune* of the family's departure for Christmas at Sandringham.

> King George VI, hat in hand, bowed right and left automatically as he drove up [to the station]. Scarcely a hat was raised in reply . . . [The King] and his family walked bowing across the platform.
> Perhaps half the men in the little throng raised their hats. There was a subdued murmur which might have been a suppressed cheer—or might not. In short, on his first public appearance after his succession to his brother, King George VI was given an extremely cold shoulder.

It may have been that only a small proportion of the British public learned about the Palace's rough treatment of David and Wallis, but they were an influential minority. Chips Channon, at the beating heart of society, wrote that May "and the Court group hate Wallis Simpson to the point of hysteria, and are taking up the wrong attitude: why persecute her now that all is over? Why not let the Duke of Windsor, who has given up so much, be happy? They would be better advised to be civil if it is beyond their courage to be cordial."

The "punishment" of poor Perry Brownlow was an example of this gratuitous lack of charity. In his capacity as Lord-in-Waiting to David he was *ordered* by his master to accompany him to France after the abdication. He returned, expecting to continue his duties. Instead he was brushed aside without a word, only learning by telephone that "his resignation had been accepted."

These indignities, perpetrated by the Palace hierarchy but with the full knowledge of Bertie and Elizabeth, did not do their reputation among those who knew what was going on any good at all.

But with the arrival of spring 1937 and the imminent prospect of the coronation, everyone cheered up and past indignities and resentments were pushed aside; or as Bertie's official biographer put it: "The gloomy memories of the abdication crisis were crowded from the public mind by the approach of spring, and with it the glories of the Coronation Day."

"This coronation," a world-weary sophisticate was heard to exclaim, "is the first in our island history when the previous incumbent is not only alive but happier than he's ever been in his life."

But such levity was uncharacteristic. It is difficult for a nation as sentimental as the British not to enjoy "a jolly good coronation." The people poured into London as never before, hundreds of thousands of them setting up camp overnight along the route of their new King and Queen between Buckingham Palace and Westminster Abbey. Flags and bunting fluttered, every size of union flag was on display, from hand-held for toddlers to massive flags from the public buildings and stores. Every lamp-post was decorated, and as dusk fell on the evening before, two hundred buildings burst into floodlight.

The composer Vaughan Williams's "Flourish for a Coro-

nation" was played repeatedly on the wireless. The poet
Brendon Moore created a piece of doggerel to celebrate the
occasion, and it was very popular. Part of it ran:

A King is crowned in Westminster, where on another day
        His father knelt and took the vows, lived them,
                and went his way;
And all about him breathes the past, and in the future lies
    This moment, making history for other unborn eyes.
A man is crowned in Westminster, and on this twelfth of May
The cheering of a multitude shall greet him on his way;
But not the splendour and the pomp nor all the pageantry
        Shall be as glorious a thing as each man's loyalty;
For he who passes to be crowned is, to all those who wait,
        The symbol of their heritage, their dreams,
                their hopes, their fate . . .

Osbert Sitwell composed a somewhat more intellectual "Ode
for the Coronation," which was found among Bertie's papers
after his death and preserved among the Royal Archives.

Bertie's own account of that day makes the best reading
of all, dominated as it is by human, mostly mundane, detail.
"We were woken up very early," he confides, "about 3.0
a.m. by the testing of the loud speakers which had been
placed in Constitution Hill; one of them might have been in
our room."

We also learn that he could eat no breakfast, in spite of
the prolonged ordeal he faced because he "had a sinking
feeling inside." There were "hours of waiting" before leaving
for the Abbey at 10.30 a.m. "At last the time came & we
drove in the State Coach in our robes."

Then everything was held up by the fainting of one of
the chaplains. "There was no place to which he could be
taken," Bertie lamented. But this was only the begining of a
chapter of accidents, of which the public knew nothing. The
Dean of Westminster insisted he should put on his surplice
inside out "had not my Groom of the Robes come to the
rescue."

The Order of the Service was almost interminable, seventeen items in all, from The Recognition to The Anointing, The Golden Spurs, The Sword and The Orb, to The Benediction, The Inthronization and The Homage. "I had two Bishops," Bertie recalled, "Durham and Bath & Wells, one on either side to support me & to hold the form of Service for me to follow. When this great moment came neither Bishop could find the words so the Archbishop held his book down for me to read, but horror of horrors his thumb covered the words of the Oath."

And so it went on. "My Lord Great Chamberlain was supposed to dress me but I found his hands fumbled & shook so I had to fix the belt of the sword myself. As it was he nearly put the hilt of the sword under my chin trying to attach it to the belt." So Dickie Mountbatten had been right. There *was* no better training for a King than that of a naval officer.

At last the moment came to place the crown on Bertie's head—all seven pounds of it. But neither the Dean nor the Archbishop could decide which way round it went. "They juggled with it so much I never did know whether it was right or not.

"Then I rose to my feet & walked to the throne in the centre of the amphitheatre. As I turned after leaving the Coronation Chair I was brought up all standing, owing to one of the Bishops treading on my robe. I had to tell him to get off pretty sharply."

Another diarist, Chips Channon, saw and recorded only the almost overwhelming grandeur of the scene and the ceremonials. "I tried to remember the great moments of the ceremony: I think the shaft of sunlight, catching the King's golden tunic as he sat for the crowning; the kneeling Bishops drawn up like a flight of geese in deploy position; and then the loveliest moment of all, the swirl when the Peeresses put on their coronets: a thousand white gloved arms, sparkling with jewels, lifting their tiny coronets . . ."

And if Samuel Pepys had been in the Abbey that day in May 1937, he could only have repeated what he wrote in April 1661 on the occasion of another coronation: "Thus did the day end with joy everywhere . . . Now, after all this, I can say, that, besides the pleasure of the sight of these glorious things, I may now shut my eyes against any other objects, nor for the future trouble myself to see things of state and show, as being sure never to see the like again in this world."

ACKNOWLEDGEMENTS

I wish to express my gratitude to Mr Hugo Vickers for his critically constructive and extremely helpful reading of the manuscript. I also wish to thank Mr Michael Bloch and Maître Suzanne Blum for their kind permission to allow me to quote from the late Duke of Windsor's *A King's Story*, and the late Duchess of Windsor's *The Heart Has Its Reasons*, and from the volume, edited by Michael Bloch, *Wallis and Edward: Letters 1931-1937*. Dr Noble Frankland generously allowed me to quote from his official life of the late Duke of Gloucester, *Prince Henry Duke of Gloucester*. My thanks are also due to Collins Publishers for permission to quote from *The Memoirs of Princess Alice, Duchess of Gloucester*, and to Macmillan for permission to quote from J. Wheeler-Bennett's *King George VI: His Life and Reign*.

Hugo Vickers, whose knowledge of the exalted people who appear in this book is unsurpassed, kindly corrected me on a number of facts, and solecisms, for which I am most grateful to him.

The Illustrations

All the illustrations are copyright © the BBC Hulton Library, with the exception of one which is reproduced by courtesy of the Estate of the Duchess of Windsor. This illustration shows Ernest and Wallis Simpson on their honeymoon.

ATTRIBUTABLE SOURCE REFERENCES

The approximate position on the page of the quotation's opening line is indicated by a decimal figure, reading from the top.

Part 1

5.6   *A King's Story: the Memoirs of H.R.H. The Duke of Windsor* (1951), p 7

6.9   Queen Victoria's Diary, Royal Archives

8.8   *A King's Story*, p 17

9.4   H. Nicolson, *King George V: His Life and Reign* (1952), p 51

10.2   Sydney Lee, *King Edward VII* (2 vols 1925, 1927), 1 p 605

11.3   Queen Victoria's diary

12.1   M.C. Carey, *Princess Mary* (1922), p 37

15.1   *A King's Story* pp 9, 13

23.3   Broadlands archives, Victoria Milford Haven Recollections (1942, unpublished)

25.9   E. Longford, *Victoria R.I.* (1964), p 558

26.3   ibid, p 559

29.9   *A King's Story*, p 13

30.6   R. Hough, *Louis & Victoria, the First Mountbattens* (1974), p 203

36.9   *A King's Story*, p 15

39.3   ibid, p 18

40.6   ibid, p 19

42.3   ibid, p 20

42.8   J. Pope-Hennessy, *Queen Mary* (1959), p 373

43.7   *A King's Story*, p 36

43.9   ibid, p 37

46.3   J. Wheeler-Bennett, *King George VI: his Life & Reign* (1958), p 28

46.5   ibid, p 29 fn

46.9   ibid, p 28

51.8   H. Nicolson, p 258

52.2   F. Donaldson, *Edward VIII* (1974), p 8

52.5   *A King's Story*, p 45

55.3   ibid, p 55

59.1   N. Frankland, *Prince Henry Duke of Gloucester* (1980), p 4

59.5   ibid, p 10

60.2   ibid, p 11

64.7   *A King's Story*, p 82

65.2   *A King's Story*, p 42

65.6   *Daily Express* 2 March 1958

65.7   quoted G. Wakeford, *The Princess Royal* (1973), p 208

65.9   *The Times* 29 March 1965

66.6   G. Wakeford, p 208

66.9   *A King's Story*, p 55

67.4   ibid, p 57

67.7   J. Gore, *King George V: a personal memoir* (1941), pp 247–8

68.2   *A King's Story*, p 57

68.7   ibid, p 59

69.5   ibid, p 60

69.9   ibid, p 61

74.2   ibid, p 63

74.7   ibid

75.9   J. Wheeler-Bennett, p 32

76.8   ibid

78.3   ibid, p 33

78.7   ibid

Part 2

83.2   *A King's Story*, pp 69–70
84.3   C. Hibbert, *Edward VII* (1976) p 290
84.9   H. Nicolson, *King George V*, p 105
86.1   *A King's Story*, p 72
86.9   ibid, p 76
87.6   ibid, p 79
87.8   Speeches by H.R.H. The Prince of Wales 1912–1927 (1927), p 1
89.2   J. Wheeler-Bennett, *King George VI*, p 43
90.6   ibid, p 45
91.4   ibid, p 47
93.5   N. Frankland, *Prince Henry Duke of Gloucester*, pp 26–7
93.6   ibid
93.9   ibid, p 30
94.3   ibid, p 33
94.8   ibid, p 32
95.4   *A King's Story*, p 75
96.1   ibid, p 79
96.4   ibid, p 80
97.6   M.C. Carey *Princess Mary*, p 62
99.9   G. Battiscombe, *Queen Alexandra* (1969), pp 21–2
107.4 H. Cathcart, *The Queen Mother Herself* (1979), p 24
108.7 ibid
112.4 Duchess of Windsor, *The Heart Has Its Reasons* (1951), p 44
113.1 ibid
114.4 ibid, p 47

Part 3

123.3 *A King's Story*, p 108
123.8 K. Rose, *Kings, Queens and Courtiers*, p 193

124.2 H. Nicolson, *King George V*, p 247
126.5 J. Wheeler-Bennett, *King George VI*, p 73
127.6 ibid, p 74
127.9 ibid, pp 74–5
129.2 ibid, p 76
135.4 H. Bolitho, *King Edward VIII: his Life & Reign* (1937), p 53
140.2 *A King's Story*, p 114
142.4 ibid, p 115
143.7 ibid
143.8 ibid, pp 116–7
146.7 W. & L. Townsend, *The Biography of H.R.H. The Prince of Wales* (1929), p 124
147.3 *A King's Story*, p 117
148.3 ibid, pp 117–8
150.2 ibid, p 119
150.6 H. Nicolson, p 267
151.2 F. Watson, *Dawson of Penn* (1950), p 138
151.4 H. Nicolson, p 268
151.9 ibid, p 262
160.2 ibid, p 64
162.9 E. Graham, *Princess Mary, Viscountess Lascelles* (1930), p 82
164.4 M.C. Carey *Princess Mary*, p 77
165.7 *The Times* 12 July 1917
169.5 J. Wheeler-Bennett, p 76
170.6 ibid, p 77
172.4 ibid, p 82
172.8 ibid
173.8 ibid
174.3 ibid, p 84
174.5 ibid
178.8 ibid, p 89
179.8 ibid, p 95
180.2 ibid
181.7 ibid, p 93
182.3 ibid, p 94
182.7 ibid

183.7   ibid
184.3   ibid, pp 96–7
184.7   ibid, p 96
184.8   ibid, p 97
184.9   ibid, p 100
185.7   ibid
188.7   C. Asquith, *The Duchess of York* (1928), p 96
189.3   *ibid*, p 97
190.2   *ibid*
190.9   *ibid*
192.4   H. Cathcart *The Queen Mother Herself*, pp 32–3
193.8   C. Asquith, pp 122–3
194.6   ibid, pp 115–6
195.3   ibid, p 119
197.4   *The Memoirs of Princess Alice, Duchess of Gloucester*, p 41
197.7   ibid, p 45
198.2   *The Heart Has Its Reasons*, p 50
198.3   ibid, p 50
198.8   ibid, p 53
199.3   ibid, p 58
199.7   ibid, p 60
203.1   H. Nicolson, p 308
203.4   Royal Archives O 1106. 65
204.1   E. Longford, *The Royal House of Windsor* (1974), p 22
204.5   Conversation with H.M. Queen Elizabeth the Queen Mother
204.8   R. Hough, *Louis & Victoria*, pp 319–320

Part 4

209.9   K. Rose, *Kings, Queens and Courtiers*, p 210
212.3   *A King's Story*, p 120
212.4   R. Hough, *Louis & Victoria*, p 328
212.8   *A King's Story*, p 128

213.4   J. Gore *King George V*, p 159
213.6   *A King's Story*, p 129
214.2   J. Pope-Hennessy, *Queen Mary*, p 511
214.3   ibid
215.8   *A King's Story*, p 133
217.2   J. Wheeler-Bennett, *King George VI*, p 104
218.7   ibid, p 103
218.8   ibid
219.8   ibid, p 108
220.1   ibid, p 109
221.3   ibid
221.4   ibid
225.1   ibid, pp 129–130
225.3   ibid, p 130
227.2   Conversation with Sir Charles Baring
230.6   J. Stewart, *Within the Fringe* (1967), p 42
231.2   J. Wheeler-Bennett, p 146
231.3   ibid, p 147
233.8   Sir Charles Baring
235.4   Cynthia Asquith, *Diaries 1915–1918* (1968), pp 416–7
237.4   *A King's Story*, p 144
237.9   ibid
238.1   ibid, p 145
238.3   ibid
238.4   ibid, p 148
238.5   ibid, p 151
239.1   F. Donaldson, *Edward VIII*, p 57
239.5   ibid, p 59
241.8   R. Hough, *Mountbatten: Hero of Our Time* (1980), p 46
242.7   *A King's Story*, p 152
242.8   R. Hough, *Mountbatten*, p 47
244.7   Duff Cooper, *Old Men Forget* (1953), p 76
245.3   E. Graham *Princess Mary, Viscount Lascelles*, p 154

245.7   ibid, p 151
246.4   ibid, p 155
246.8   *Illustrated London News*,
        25 November 1922
248.2   J. Gore, p 535
248.7   J. Wentworth Day,
        *H.R.H. Princess Ma-
        rina Duchess of Kent*,
        p 66
253.3   J. Wheeler-Bennett, p 148
254.2   R. Sencourt, *The Reign of
        Edward VIII* (1962),
        p 18
255.1   Debrett 1912, p 1,856
255.8   J. Wheeler-Bennett, p 150
256.4   D. Sinclair, *Queen &
        Country* (1979), p 47
257.8   J. Stewart, p 1 and p 57
258.8   K. Rose, pp 311–2
        (*quoted*)
259.2   P. Mortimer, *Queen
        Elizabeth* (1986), p 58
261.1   J. Wheeler-Bennett, p 150
261.3   ibid, 150–1
261.8   *The Heart has its Reasons*,
        p 98
263.1   N. Frankland, *Prince
        Henry Duke of Glouces-
        ter*, p 63
263.2   ibid, p 66
264.2   ibid, p 47
264.4   ibid, p 61
265.5   ibid, p 82
265.7   *The Times*, 5 August 1986
265.9   ibid
266.7   N. Frankland, p 117
267.2   Brigadier C.B. Harvey to
        Frankland, 28 Decem-
        ber 1976
268.3   *The Memoirs of Princess
        Alice, Duchess of
        Gloucester*, p 104
268.5   ibid, p 106
268.6   ibid, p 105
269.9   F. Donaldson, p 112
270.5   *A King's Story*, p 239

270.7   S. King, *Princess Marina*
        (1969), p 111
271.7   A. Cooper (ed), *A Durable
        Fire: the Letters of
        Duff and Diana Cooper
        1913–1950* (1983), pp 246–9
273.2   Channon, *Diaries*, 8 May
        1934
274.2   S. King, p 117
274.5   ibid, p 119
275.7   A. Whiting, *The Kents*, p 79
277.7   *The Heart has its Reasons*,
        p 125
278.4   ibid, p 142
278.5   ibid, p 143
278.6   ibid, pp 145–6
278.9   Channon, *Diaries*, 23
        January 1935
279.2   ibid, 5 April 1935
279.3   J. Bryan III & C.J.V.
        Murphy, *The Windsor
        Story* (1979), p 9
279.4   Lord Beaverbrook, *The
        Abdication of Edward
        VIII* (1966), pp 34–5
279.9   G. Vanderbilt & T.
        Furness, *Double Exposure*
        (1956), p 274
280.1   Bryan, Murphy, p 26
280.3   C.A. Lyon, Daily Express
281.7   J. Wheeler-Bennett, p 140
282.7   Bryan, Murphy, p 113
282.9   ibid, p 115
283.2   J. Gore, p 368
283.5   K. Rose, 60–1
284.5   *The Heart has its Reasons*,
        pp 166–67
288.7   ibid, p 170

Part V

292.1   *The Heart has its Reasons*
        p 174
295.1   Michael Blòch (Ed),
        *Wallis & Edward,
        Letters 1931–37* (1986)

295.3   ibid, p 49
295.4   *A King's Story*, p 256–7
297.7   ibid, p 256
297.9   *The Heart has its Reasons*, pp 183–4
298.2   *Letters*, p 55
299.4   ibid, pp 83–4 (*quoted*)
299.8   *The Heart has its Reasons*, p 86
301.6   *Letters*, p 86
304.2   ibid, p 91 (*quoted*)
304.5   ibid (*quoted*)
305.7   ibid, p 99
306.4   ibid, p 102
306.5   M. Gilbert, *Winston Churchill* vol V, p 810
306.8   *Letters*, p 103
310.4   ibid, p 148
311.4   *The Heart has its Reasons*, 219
311.9   *Letters*, p 128
311.9   ibid, p 145
312.2   J. Wheeler-Bennett *King George VI*, p 273

319.4   F. Donaldson, *Edward VIII*, p 214
329.4   ibid, p 248
335.4   J. Pope-Hennessy, *Queen Mary*, p 578
335.8   Baffy Dugdale, *The Diaries of Blanche Dugdale 1936–47*, p 34
338.6   J. Wheeler-Bennett, p 286
338.8   ibid
339.7   *A King's Story*, p 411
343.6   *Letters*, p 223
343.9   ibid, p 233
345.2   ibid, p 235
346.2   ibid, p 281
346.4   ibid, p 279
346.5   F. Donaldson, pp 310–11
347.2   *Letters*, p 286
348.2   ibid, p 288
348.3   F. Donaldson, p 223
349.2   *Letters*, p 287
353.6   J. Wheeler-Bennett, p 312
354.6   ibid

A SELECTION OF
PUBLISHED BOOKS

Cynthia Asquith, *The Duchess of York* (Hutchinson 1928)

Georgina Battiscombe, *Queen Alexandra* (Constable 1969)

Michael Bloch (editor), *Wallis & Edward: Letters 1931-1937* (Weidenfeld 1986)

Hector Bolitho, *King Edward VIII: His Life & Reign* (Eyre and Spottiswoode 1937)

Basil Boothroyd, *Philip: An Informal Biography* (Longman 1971)

J. Bryan III & C.J.V. Murphy, *The Windsor Story* (Granada 1979)

J. Wentworth Day, *HRH Princess Marina, Duchess of Kent* (Hale 1962)

Frances Donaldson, *Edward VIII* (Weidenfeld 1974)

David Duff, *George & Elizabeth: a Royal Marriage* (Collins 1983)

Noble Frankland, *Prince Henry Duke of Gloucester* (Weidenfeld 1980)

The Memoirs of Princess Alice, Duchess of Gloucester (Collins 1983)

John Gore, *King George V: a Personal Memoir* (Murray 1941)

E. Graham, *Edward, Prince of Wales* (Ward Lock 1929)

Richard Hough, *Edwina, Countess Mountbatten of Burma* (Weidenfeld 1983)

Richard Hough, *Louis & Victoria, the First Mountbattens* (Hutchinson 1974)

Richard Hough, *Mountbatten: Hero of Our Time* (Weidenfeld 198_)

Stella King, *Princess Marina, Her Life & Times* (Cassell 1969)

Penelope Mortimer, *Queen Elizabeth: a Life of the Queen Mother* (Viking 1985)

Harold Nicolson, *King George V: His Life and Reign* (Constable 195_)

James Pope-Hennessy, *Queen Mary* (Allen & Unwin 1959)

Kenneth Rose, *King George V* (Weidenfeld 1983)

Kenneth Rose, *Kings, Queens & Courtiers* (Weidenfeld 1985)

G, Wakeford, *The Princess Royal* (Hale 1973)

Speeches by HRH The Prince of Wales 1912-1926 (Hodder 1927)

John Wheeler-Bennett, *King George VI: His Life and Reign* (Macmillan 1958)

The Heart Has Its Reasons: The Memoirs of the Duchess of Windsor (Michael Joseph 1956)

A King's Story: The Memoirs of HRH the Duke of Windsor (Cassell 1951)

K. Woodward, *Queen Mary: a Life and Intimate Study* (Hutchinson 1927)

INDEX

ABOUT THE AUTHOR

RICHARD HOUGH began his career as a naval historian and biographer in 1958 and has written many well-received biographies including *Louis and Victoria: The First Mountbattens, Mountbatten: Hero of Our Time* and *Edwina: Countess Mountbatten of Burma*. He lives in London.